Design Patterns
Explained

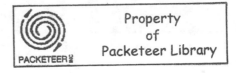

Property
of
Packeteer Library

PACKETEER INC

W9-BTL-929

The Software Patterns Series

Series Editor: John M. Vlissides

The Software Patterns Series (SPS) comprises pattern literature of lasting significance to software developers. Software patterns document general solutions to recurring problems in all software-related spheres, from the technology itself, to the organizations that develop and distribute it, to the people who use it. Books in the series distill experience from one or more of these areas into a form that software professionals can apply immediately.

Relevance and *impact* are the tenets of the SPS. Relevance means each book presents patterns that solve real problems. Patterns worthy of the name are intrinsically relevant; they are borne of practitioners' experiences, not theory or speculation. Patterns have impact when they change how people work for the better. A book becomes a part of the series not just because it embraces these tenets, but because it has demonstrated it fulfills them for its audience.

Titles in the series:

Design Patterns Explained: A New Perspective on Object-Oriented Design, Alan Shalloway/
    James R. Trott

Design Patterns Java™ Workbook, Steven John Metsker

The Design Patterns Smalltalk Companion, Sherman Alpert/Kyle Brown/Bobby Woolf

The Joy of Patterns: Using Patterns for Enterprise Development, Brandon Goldfedder

The Manager Pool: Patterns for Radical Leadership, Don Olson/Carol Stimmel

.NET Patterns and Practices, Christian Thilmany

Pattern Hatching: Design Patterns Applied, John Vlissides

Pattern Languages of Program Design, edited by James O. Coplien/Douglas C. Schmidt

Pattern Languages of Program Design 2, edited by John M. Vlissides/James O. Coplien/
    Norman L. Kerth

Pattern Languages of Program Design 3, edited by Robert Martin/Dirk Riehle/
    Frank Buschmann

Small Memory Software, James Noble/Charles Weir

Software Configuration Management Patterns, Stephen P. Berczuk/Brad Appleton

Design Patterns Explained

A New Perspective on Object-Oriented Design

Alan Shalloway

James R. Trott

 ADDISON–WESLEY

Boston, San Francisco, New York, Toronto, Montreal
London, Munich, Paris, Madrid
Capetown, Sydney, Tokyo, Singapore, Mexico City

Many of the designations used by manufacturers and sellers to distinguish their products are claimed as trademarks. Where those designations appear in this book, and Addison Wesley Longman Inc., was aware of a trademark claim, the designations have been printed with initial capital letters or in all capitals.

The authors and publisher have taken care in the preparation of this book, but make no expressed or implied warranty of any kind and assume no responsibility for errors or omissions. No liability is assumed for incidental or consequential damages in connection with or arising out of the use of the information or programs contained herein.

The publisher offers discounts on this book when ordered in quantity for special sales. For more information, please contact:

Pearson Education Corporate Sales Division
201 W. 103rd Street
Indianapolis, IN 46290
(800) 428-5331
coprsales@pearsoned.com

Visit AW on the Web: www.awprofessional.com

Library of Congress Cataloging-in-Publication Data
Shalloway, Alan.
    Design patterns explained : a new perspective on object-oriented design / Alan
    Shalloway, James Trott.
        p. cm.
    Includes bibliographical references and index.
    ISBN 0-201-71594-5
        1. Object-oriented methods (Computer science)   2. Computer software—Development.
    I. Trott, James   II. Title.

QA76.9.O35 S52 2001
005.I'17--dc21

                                                                        2001031645

Copyright © 2002 by Addison-Wesley

All rights reserved. No part of this publication may be reproduced, stored in a retrieval system, or transmitted, in any form, or by any means, electronic, mechanical, photocopying, recording, or otherwise, without the prior consent of the publisher. Printed in the United States of America. Published simultaneously in Canada.

Text printed on recycled and acid-free paper.
ISBN 0201715945
6 7 8 9 1011 MA   06 05 04 03
6th Printing   July 2003

To Leigh, Bryan, Lisa, Michael, and Steven
for their love, support,
encouragement, and sacrifice.

—Alan Shalloway

To Jill, Erika, Lorien, Mikaela, and Geneva,
the roses in the garden of my life.
sola gloria Dei

—James R. Trott

Contents

Chapter 13
The Principles and Strategies
of Design Patterns _____ 217

PART V
Handling Variations with Design Patterns_____ 227

Chapter 14
The Strategy Pattern _____ 229

Chapter 15
The Decorator Pattern _____ 241

Preface

Design patterns and object-oriented programming. They hold such promise to make your life as a software designer and developer easier. Their terminology is bandied about every day in the technical and even the popular press. But it can be hard to learn them, to become proficient with them, to understand what is really going on.

Perhaps you have been using an object-oriented or object-based language for years. Have you learned that the true power of objects is not inheritance but is in "encapsulating behaviors"? Perhaps you are curious about design patterns and have found the literature a bit too esoteric and high-falutin. If so, this book is for you.

It is based on years of teaching this material to software developers, both experienced and new to object orientation. It is based upon the belief—and our experience—that once you understand the basic principles and motivations that underlie these concepts, why they are doing what they do, your learning curve will be incredibly shorter. And in our discussion of design patterns, you will understand the true mindset of object orientation, which is a necessity before you can become proficient.

As you read this book, you will gain a solid understanding of the ten most essential design patterns. You will learn that design patterns do not exist on their own, but are supposed to work in concert with other design patterns to help you create more robust applications. You will gain enough of a foundation that you will be able to read the design pattern literature, if you want to, and possibly discover patterns on your own.

Most importantly, you will be better equipped to create flexible and complete software that is easier to maintain.

From Object Orientation to Patterns to True Object Orientation

In many ways, this book is a retelling of my personal experience learning design patterns. Prior to studying design patterns, I considered myself to be reasonably expert in object-oriented analysis and design. My track record had included several fairly impressive designs and implementations in many industries. I knew C++ and was beginning to learn Java. The objects in my code were well-formed and tightly encapsulated. I could design excellent data abstractions for inheritance hierarchies. I thought I knew object-orientation.

Now, looking back, I see that I really did not understand the full capabilities of object-oriented design, even though I was doing things the way the experts advised. It wasn't until I began to learn design patterns that my object-oriented design abilities expanded and deepened. Knowing design patterns has made me a better designer, even when I don't use these patterns directly.

I began studying design patterns in 1996. I was a C++/object-oriented design mentor at a large aerospace company in the north-west. Several people asked me to lead a design pattern study group. That's where I met my co-author, Jim Trott. In the study group, several interesting things happened. First, I grew fascinated with design patterns. I loved being able to compare my designs with the designs of others who had more experience than I had. I discovered that I was not taking full advantage of designing to interfaces and that I didn't always concern myself with seeing if I could have an object use another object without knowing the used object's type. I noticed that beginners to object-oriented design—those who would normally be deemed as learning design patterns too early—were benefiting as much from the study group as the experts were. The patterns presented examples of excellent object-oriented designs and illustrated basic object-oriented principles, which helped to mature their designs more quickly. By the end of the study sessions,

I was convinced that design patterns were the greatest thing to happen to software design since the invention of object-oriented design.

However, when I looked at my work at the time, I saw that I was not incorporating *any* design patterns into my code.

I just figured I didn't know enough design patterns yet and needed to learn more. At the time, I only knew about six of them. Then I had what could be called an epiphany. I was working on a project as a mentor in object-oriented design and was asked to create a high-level design for the project. The leader of the project was extremely sharp, but was fairly new to object-oriented design.

The problem itself wasn't that difficult, but it required a great deal of attention to make sure the code was going to be easy to maintain. Literally, after about two minutes of looking at the problem, I had developed a design based on my normal approach of data abstraction. Unfortunately, it was very clear this was not going to be a good design. Data abstraction alone had failed me. I had to find something better.

Two hours later, after applying every design technique I knew, I was no better off. My design was essentially the same. What was most frustrating was that I knew there was a better design. I just couldn't see it. Ironically, I also knew of four design patterns that "lived" in my problem but I couldn't see how to use them. Here I was—a supposed expert in object-oriented design—baffled by a simple problem!

Feeling very frustrated, I took a break and started walking down the hall to clear my head, telling myself I would not think of the problem for at least 10 minutes. Well, 30 seconds later, I was thinking about it again! But I had gotten an insight that changed my view of design patterns: rather than using patterns as individual items, I should use the design patterns together.

Patterns are supposed to be sewn together to solve a problem.

I had heard this before, but hadn't really understood it. Because patterns in software have been introduced as *design* patterns, I had always labored under the assumption that they had mostly to do with design. My thoughts were that in the design world, the patterns came as pretty much well-formed relationships between classes. Then, I read Christopher Alexander's amazing book, *The Timeless Way of Building*. I learned that patterns existed at all levels—analysis, design, and implementation. Alexander discusses using patterns to help in the understanding of the problem domain (even in describing it), not just using them to create the design after the problem domain is understood.

My mistake had been in trying to create the classes in my problem domain and then stitch them together to make a final system, a process which Alexander calls a particularly bad idea. I had never asked if I had the right classes because they just seemed so right, so obvious; they were the classes that immediately came to mind as I started my analysis, the "nouns" in the description of the system that we had been taught to look for. But I had struggled trying to piece them together.

When I stepped back and used design patterns and Alexander's approach to guide me in the creation of my classes, a far superior solution unfolded in only a matter of minutes. It was a good design and we put it into production. I was excited—excited to have designed a good solution and excited about the power of design patterns. It was then that I started incorporating design patterns into my development work and my teaching.

I began to discover that programmers who were new to object-oriented design could learn design patterns, and in doing so, develop a basic set of object-oriented design skills. It was true for me and it was true for the students that I was teaching.

Imagine my surprise! The design pattern books I had been reading and the design pattern experts I had been talking to were saying that you really needed to have a good grounding in object-oriented design before embarking on a study of design patterns. Nevertheless, I saw, with my own eyes, that students who learned object-oriented design concurrently with design patterns learned object-oriented design faster than those just studying object-oriented design. They even seemed to learn design patterns at almost the same rate as experienced object-oriented practitioners.

I began to use design patterns as a basis for my teaching. I began to call my classes *Pattern Oriented Design: Design Patterns from Analysis to Implementation*.

I wanted my students to understand these patterns and began to discover that using an exploratory approach was the best way to foster this understanding. For instance, I found that it was better to present the Bridge pattern by presenting a problem and then have my students try to design a solution to the problem using a few guiding principles and strategies that I had found were present in most of the patterns. In their exploration, the students discovered the solution—called the Bridge pattern—and remembered it.

In any event, I found that these guiding principles and strategies could be used to "derive" several of the design patterns. By "derive a design pattern," I mean that if I looked at a problem that I knew could be solved by a design pattern, I could use the guiding principles and strategies to come up with the solution that is expressed in the pattern. I made it clear to my students that we weren't really coming up with design patterns this way. Instead, I was just illustrating one possible thought process that the people who came up with the original solutions, those that were eventually classified as design patterns, might have used.

A slight digression.

The guiding principles and strategies seem very clear to me now. Certainly, they are stated in the "Gang of Four's" design patterns book. But it took me a long time to understand them because of limitations in my own understanding of the object-oriented paradigm. It was only after integrating in my own mind the work of the Gang of Four with Alexander's work, Jim Coplien's work on commonality and variability analysis, and Martin Fowler's work in methodologies and analysis patterns that these principles became clear enough to me to that I was able to talk about them to others. It helped that I was making my livelihood explaining things to others so I couldn't get away with making assumptions as easily as I could when I was just doing things for myself.

My abilities to explain these few, but powerful, principles and strategies improved. As they did, I found that it became more useful to explain an increasing number of the Gang of Four patterns. In fact, I use these principles and strategies to explain 12 of the 14 patterns I discuss in my design patterns course.

I found that I was using these principles in my own designs both with and without patterns. This didn't surprise me. If using these strategies resulted in a design equivalent to a design pattern when I knew the pattern was present, that meant they were giving me a way to derive excellent designs (since patterns are excellent designs by definition). Why would I get any poorer designs from these techniques just because I didn't know the name of the pattern that might or might not be present anyway?

These insights helped hone my training process (and now my writing process). I had already been teaching my courses on several levels. I was teaching the fundamentals of object-oriented analysis and design. I did that by teaching design patterns and using them to illustrate good examples of object-oriented analysis and design. In addition, by using the patterns to teach the concepts of object orientation, my students were also better able to understand the principles of object orientation. And by teaching the guiding principles and strategies, my students were able to create designs of comparable quality to the patterns themselves.

I relate this story because this book follows much the same pattern as my course (pun intended). In fact, from Chapter 3 on, this book is very much the first day of my two-day course: *Pattern Oriented Design: Design Patterns from Analysis to Implementation.*

As you read this book, you will learn the patterns. But even more importantly, you will learn why they work and how they can work together, and the principles and strategies upon which they rely. It will be useful to draw on your own experiences. When I present a problem in the text, it is helpful if you imagine a similar problem that you have come across. This book isn't about new bits of information or new patterns to apply, but rather a new way of looking at object-oriented software development. I hope that your own experiences, connected with the principles of design patterns, will prove to be a powerful ally in your learning.

Alan Shalloway
December, 2000

From Artificial Intelligence to Patterns to True Object Orientation

My journey into design patterns had a different starting point than Alan's but we have reached the same conclusions:

- Pattern-based analyses make you a more effective and efficient analyst because they let you deal with your models more abstractly and because they represent the collected experiences of many other analysts.

- Patterns help people to learn principles of object orientation. The patterns help to explain why we do what we do with objects.

I started my career in artificial intelligence (AI) creating rule-based expert systems. This involves listening to experts and creating models of their decision-making processes and then coding these models into rules in a knowledge-based system. As I built these systems, I began to see repeating themes: in common types of problems, experts tended to work in similar ways. For example, experts who diagnose problems with equipment tend to look for simple, quick fixes first, then they get more systematic, breaking the problem into component parts; but in their systematic diagnosis, they tend to try first inexpensive tests or tests that will eliminate broad classes of problems before other kinds of tests. This was true whether we were diagnosing problems in a computer or a piece of oil field equipment.

Today, I would call these recurring themes patterns. Intuitively, I began to look for these recurring themes as I was designing new expert systems. My mind was open and friendly to the idea of patterns, even though I did not know what they were.

Then, in 1994, I discovered that researchers in Europe had codified these patterns of expert behavior and put them into a package that they called Knowledge Analysis and Design Support, or KADS. Dr. Karen Gardner, a most gifted analyst, modeler, mentor, and human being, began to apply KADS to her work in the United States. She extended the European's work to apply KADS to object-oriented systems. She opened my eyes to an entire world of pattern-based analysis and design that was forming in the software world, in large part due to Christopher Alexander's work. Her book, *Cognitive Patterns* (Cambridge University Press, 1998) describes this work.

Suddenly, I had a structure for modeling expert behaviors without getting trapped by the complexities and exceptions too early. I was able to complete my next three projects in less time, with less rework, and with greater satisfaction by end-users, because:

- I could design models more quickly because the patterns predicted for me what ought to be there. They told me what the essential objects were and what to pay special attention to.

- I was able to communicate much more effectively with experts because we had a more structured way to deal with the details and exceptions.

- The patterns allowed me to develop better end-user training for my system because the patterns predicted the most important features of the system.

This last point is significant. Patterns help end-users understand systems because they provide the context for the system, why we are doing things in a certain way. We can use patterns to describe the guiding principles and strategies of the system. And we can use patterns to develop the best examples to help end-users understand the system.

I was hooked.

So, when a design patterns study group started at my place of employment, I was eager to go. This is where I met Alan who had reached a similar point in his work as an object-oriented designer and mentor. The result is this book.

I hope that the principles in this book help you in your own journey to become a more effective and efficient analyst.

James R. Trott
December, 2000

A Note About Conventions Used in This Book

In the writing of this book, we had to make several choices about style and convention. Some of our choices have surprised our readers. So, it is worth a few comments about why we have chosen to do what we have done.

Approach	Rationale
First person voice	This book is a collaborative effort between two authors. We debated and refined our ideas to find the best ways to explain these concepts. Alan tried them out in his courses and we refined some more. We chose to use the first person singular in the body of this book because it allows us to tell the story in what we hope is a more engaging and natural style.
Scanning text	We have tried to make this book easy to scan so that you can get the main points even if you do not read the body, or so that you can quickly find the information you need. We make significant use of tables and bulleted lists. We provide text in the outside margin that summarizes paragraphs. With the discussion of each pattern, we provide a summary table of the key features of the pattern. Our hope is that these will make the book that much more accessible.
Code fragments	This book is about analysis and design more than implementation. Our intent is to help you think about crafting good designs based on the insights and best practices of the object-oriented community, as expressed in design patterns. One of the challenges for all of us programmers is to avoid going to the implementation too early, doing before thinking. Knowing this, we have purposefully tried to stay away from too much discussion on implementation. Our code examples may seem a bit lightweight and fragmentary. Specifically, we never provide error checking in the code. This is because we are trying to use the code to illustrate concepts.
Strategies and principles	Ours is an introductory book. It will help you be able to get up to speed quickly with design patterns. You will understand the principles and strategies that motivate design patterns. After reading this book, you can go on to a more scholarly or reference book. The last chapter will point you to many of the references that we have found useful.

Show breadth and give a taste	We are trying give you a taste for design patterns, to expose you to the breadth of the pattern world but not go into depth in any of them (see the previous point).
	Our thought was this: If you brought someone to the USA for a two week visit, what would you show them? Maybe a few sites to help them get familiar with architectures, communities, the feel of cities and the vast spaces that separate them, freeways, and coffee shops. But you would not be able to show them everything. To fill in their knowledge, you might choose to show them slide shows of many other sites and cities to give them a taste of the country. Then, they could make plans for future visits. We are showing you the major sites in design patterns and then giving you tastes of other areas so that you can plan your own journey into patterns.

Feedback

Design patterns are a work in progress, a conversation amongst practitioners who discover best practices, who discover fundamental principles in object orientation.

We covet your feedback on this book:

- What did we do well or poorly?
- Are there errors that need to be corrected?
- Was there something that was confusingly written?

Please visit us at the Web site for this book. The URL is *http://www.netobjectives.com/dpexplained*. At this site, you will find a form that you can use to send us your comments and questions. You will also find our latest research.

Acknowledgments

Almost every preface ends with a list of acknowledgments of those who helped in the development of the book. We never fully appreciated how true this was until doing a book of our own. Such an effort is truly a work of a community. The list of people to whom we are in debt is long. The following people are especially significant to us:

- Debbie Lafferty from Addison-Wesley, who never grew tired of encouraging us and keeping us on track.

- Scott Bain, our colleague who patiently reviewed this work and gave us insights.

- And especially Leigh and Jill, our patient wives, who put up with us and encouraged us in our dream of this book.

Special thanks from Alan:

- Several of my students early on had an impact they probably never knew. Many times during my courses I hesitated to project new ideas, feeling I should stick with the tried and true. However, their enthusiasm in my new concepts when I first started my courses encouraged me to project more and more of my own ideas into the curriculum I was putting together. Thanks to Lance Young, Peter Shirley, John Terrell, and Karen Allen. They serve as a constant reminder to me how encouragement can go a long way.

- Thanks to John Vlissides for his thoughtful comments and tough questions.

Special thanks from Jim:

- Dr. Karen Gardner, a mentor and wise teacher in patterns of human thought.

- Dr. Marel Norwood and Arthur Murphy, my initial collaborators in KADS and pattern-based analysis.

- Brad VanBeek who gave me the space to grow in this discipline.

- Alex Sidey who coached me in the discipline and mysteries of technical writing.

PART I

An Introduction to Object-Oriented Software Development

Part Overview

This part introduces you to a method for developing object-oriented software that is based on *patterns*—the insights and best practices learned by designers and users over the years—and on the modeling language (UML) that supports it.

In this part

This will not follow the object-oriented paradigm of the 1980s, where developers were simply told to find the nouns in the requirement statements and make them into objects. In that paradigm, encapsulation was defined as data-hiding and objects were defined as things with data and methods used to access that data. This is a limited view, constrained as it is by a focus on how to implement objects. It is incomplete.

This part discusses a version of the object-oriented paradigm that is based on an expanded definition of these concepts. These expanded definitions are the result of strategies and principles that arise from the design and implementation of design patterns. It reflects a more complete mindset of object orientation.

Chapter	Discusses These Topics
1	An introduction to the latest understanding of objects.
2	The Unified Modeling Language (UML) will then be presented. The UML gives us the tools to describe object-oriented designs in a graphical, more readily understood manner.

CHAPTER 1

The Object-Oriented Paradigm

Overview

This chapter introduces you to the object-oriented paradigm by comparing and contrasting it with something familiar: standard structured programming.

In this chapter

The object-oriented paradigm grew out of a need to meet the challenges of past practices using standard structured programming. By being clear about these challenges, we can better see the advantages of object-oriented programming, as well as gain a better understanding of this mechanism.

This chapter will not make you an expert on object-oriented methods. It will not even introduce you to all of the basic object-oriented concepts. It will, however, prepare you for the rest of this book, which will explain the proper use of object-oriented design methods as practiced by the experts.

In this chapter,

- I discuss a common method of analysis, called functional decomposition.

- I address the problem of requirements and the need to deal with change (the scourge of programming!).

- I describe the object-oriented paradigm and show its use in action.

- I point out special object methods.

- I provide a table of important object terminology used in this chapter on page 21.

Before The Object-Oriented Paradigm: Functional Decomposition

Functional decomposition is a natural way to deal with complexity

Let's start out by examining a common approach to software development. If I were to give you the task of writing code to access a description of shapes that were stored in a database and then display them, it would be natural to think in terms of the steps required. For example, you might think that you would solve the problem by doing the following:

1. Locate the list of shapes in the database.

2. Open up the list of shapes.

3. Sort the list according to some rules.

4. Display the individual shapes on the monitor.

You could take any one of these steps and further break down the steps required to implement it. For example, you could break down Step 4 as follows:

For each shape in the list, do the following:

4a. Identify type of shape.

4b. Get location of shape.

4c. Call appropriate function that will display shape, giving it the shape's location.

This is called *functional decomposition* because the analyst breaks down (decomposes) the problem into the functional steps that compose it. You and I do this because it is easier to deal with smaller pieces than it is to deal with the problem in its entirety. It is the same approach I might use to write a recipe for making lasagna, or instructions to assemble a bicycle. We use this approach so often and so naturally that we seldom question it or ask if there are other alternatives.

The problem with functional decomposition is that it does not help us prepare the code for possible changes in the future, for a graceful evolution. When change is required, it is often because I want to add a new variation to an existing theme. For example, I might have to deal with new shapes or new ways to display shapes. If I have put all of the logic that implements the steps into one large function or module, then virtually any change to the steps will require changes to that function or module.

The challenge with this approach: dealing with change

And change creates opportunities for mistakes and unintended consequences. Or, as I like to say,

> *Many bugs originate with changes to code.*

Verify this assertion for yourself. Think of a time when you wanted to make a change to your code, but were afraid to put it in because you knew that modifying the code in one place could break it somewhere else. Why might this happen? Must the code pay attention to all of its functions and how they might be used? How might the functions interact with one another? Were there too many details for the function to pay attention to, such as the logic it was trying to implement, the things with which it was interacting, the data it was using? As it is with people, trying to focus on too many things at once begs for errors when anything changes.

And no matter how hard you try, no matter how well you do your analysis, you can never get all of the requirements from the user. Too much is unknown about the future. Things change. They always do . . .

> *And nothing you can do will stop change. But you do not have to be overcome by it.*

The Problem of Requirements

Requirements always change

Ask software developers what they know to be true about the requirements they get from users. They will often say:

- Requirements are incomplete.

- Requirements are usually wrong.

- Requirements (and users) are misleading.

- Requirements do not tell the whole story.

One thing you will never hear is, "not only were our requirements complete, clear, and understandable, but they laid out all of the functionality we were going to need for the next five years!"

In my thirty years of experience writing software, the main thing I have learned about requirements is that . . .

> *Requirements always change.*

I have also learned that most developers think this is a bad thing. But few of them write their code to handle changing requirements well.

Requirements change for a very simple set of reasons:

- The users' view of their needs change as a result of their discussions with developers and from seeing new possibilities for the software.

- The developers' view of the users' problem domain changes as they develop software to automate it and thus become more familiar with it.

- The environment in which the software is being developed changes. (Who anticipated, five years ago, Web development as it is today?)

This does not mean you and I can give up on gathering good requirements. It does mean that we must write our code to accommodate change. It also means we should stop beating ourselves up (or our customers, for that matter) for things that will naturally occur.

Change happens! Deal with it.

- In all but the simplest cases, requirements will always change, no matter how well we do the initial analysis!

- Rather than complaining about changing requirements, we should change the development process so that we can address change more effectively.

Dealing with Changes: Using Functional Decomposition

Look a little closer at the problem of displaying shapes. How can I write the code so that it is easier to handle shifting requirements? Rather than writing one large function, I could make it more modular.

Using modularity to contain variation

For example, in Step 4c on page 4, where I *"Call appropriate function that will display shape, giving it the shape's location,"* I could write a module like that shown in Example 1-1.

Example 1-1 Using Modularity to Contain Variation

```
function: display shape
input: type of shape, description of shape
action:
   switch (type of shape)
      case square: put display function for square here
      case circle: put display function for circle here
```

Then, when I receive a requirement to be able to display a new type of shape—a triangle, for instance—I only need to change this module (hopefully!).

Problems with modularity in a functional decomposition approach

There are some problems with this approach, however. For example, I said that the inputs to the module were the type of shape and a description of the shape. Depending upon how I am storing shapes, it may or may not be possible to have a consistent description of shapes that will work well for all shapes. What if the description of the shape is sometimes stored as an array of points? Would that still work?

Modularity definitely helps to make the code more understandable, and understandability makes the code easier to maintain. But modularity does not always help code deal with all of the variation it might encounter.

Low cohesion, tight coupling

With the approach that I have used so far, I find that I have two significant problems, which go by the terms *low cohesion* and *tight coupling*. In his book *Code Complete*, Steve McConnell gives an excellent description of both cohesion and coupling. He says,

- *Cohesion* refers to how "closely the operations in a routine are related."[1]

I have heard other people refer to cohesion as *clarity* because the more that operations are related in a routine (or a class), the easier it is to understand things.

- *Coupling* refers to "the strength of a connection between two routines. Coupling is a complement to cohesion. Cohesion describes how strongly the internal contents of a routine are

---

1. McConnell, S., *Code Complete: A Practical Handbook of Software Construction,* Redmond: Microsoft Press, 1993, p. 81. (Note: McConnell did not invent these terms, we just happen to like his definitions of them best.)

related to each other. Coupling describes how strongly a routine is related to other routines. The goal is to create routines with internal integrity (strong cohesion) and small, direct, visible, and flexible relations to other routines (loose coupling)."[2]

Most programmers have had the experience of making a change to a function or piece of data in one area of the code that then has an unexpected impact on other pieces of code. This type of bug is called an "unwanted side effect." That is because while we get the impact we want (the change), we also get other impacts we don't want—bugs! What is worse, these bugs are often difficult to find because we usually don't notice the relationship that caused the side effects in the first place (if we had, we wouldn't have changed it the way we did).

Changing a function, or even data used by a function, can wreak havoc on other functions

In fact, bugs of this type lead me to a rather startling observation:

We really do not spend much time fixing bugs.

I think fixing bugs takes a short period of time in the maintenance and debugging process. The overwhelming amount of time spent in maintenance and debugging is on *finding* bugs and taking the time to avoid unwanted side effects. The actual fix is relatively short!

Since unwanted side effects are often the hardest bugs to find, having a function that touches many different pieces of data makes it more likely that a change in requirements will result in a problem.

---

2. ibid, p. 87.

> ### The devil is in the side effects.
>
> - A focus on functions is likely to cause side effects that are difficult to find.
>
> - Most of the time spent in maintenance and debugging is not spent on fixing bugs, but in *finding* them and seeing how to avoid unwanted side effects from the fix.

Functional decomposition focuses on the wrong thing

With functional decomposition, changing requirements causes my software development and maintenance efforts to thrash. I am focused primarily on the functions. Changes to one set of functions or data impact other sets of functions and other sets of data, which in turn impact other functions that must be changed. Like a snowball that picks up snow as it rolls downhill, a focus on functions leads to a cascade of changes from which it is difficult to escape.

Dealing with Changing Requirements

How do people do things?

To figure out a way around the problem of changing requirements and to see if there is an alternative to functional decomposition, let's look at how people do things. Let's say that you were an instructor at a conference. People in your class had another class to attend following yours, but didn't know where it was located. One of your responsibilities is to make sure everyone knows how to get to their next class.

If you were to follow a structured programming approach, you might do the following:

1. Get list of people in the class.

2. For each person on this list:

   a. Find the next class they are taking.

   b. Find the location of that class.

c. Find the way to get from your classroom to the person's next class.

d. Tell the person how to get to their next class.

To do this would require the following procedures:

1. A way of getting the list of people in the class

2. A way of getting the schedule for each person in the class

3. A program that gives someone directions from your classroom to any other classroom

4. A control program that works for each person in the class and does the required steps for each person

I doubt that you would actually follow this approach. Instead, you would probably post directions to go from this classroom to the other classrooms and then tell everyone in the class, "I have posted the locations of the classes following this in the back of the room, as well as the locations of the other classrooms. Please use them to go to your next classroom." You would expect that everyone would know what their next class was, that they could find the classroom they were to go to from the list, and could then follow the directions for going to the classrooms themselves.

Doubtful you'd follow this approach

What is the difference between these approaches?

• In the first one—giving explicit directions to everyone—you have to pay close attention to a lot of details. No one other than you is responsible for anything. You will go crazy!

• In the second case, you give general instructions and then expect that each person will figure out how to do the task himself or herself.

Shifting responsibility from yourself to individuals . . .

The biggest difference is this **shift of responsibility**. In the first case, you are responsible for everything; in the second case, students are responsible for their own behavior. In both cases, the same things must be implemented, but the organization is very different.

What is the impact of this?

To see the effect of this reorganization of responsibilities, let's see what happens when some new requirements are specified.

Suppose I am now told to give special instructions to graduate students who are assisting at the conference. Perhaps they need to collect course evaluations and take them to the conference office before they can go to the next class. In the first case, I would have to modify the control program to distinguish the graduate students from the undergraduates, and then give special instructions to the graduate students. It's possible that I would have to modify this program considerably.

. . . can minimize changes

However, in the second case—where people are responsible for themselves—I would just have to write an additional routine for graduate students to follow. The control program would still just say, "Go to your next class." Each person would simply follow the instructions appropriate for himself or herself.

Why the difference?

This is a significant difference for the control program. In one case, it would have to be modified every time there was a new category of students with special instructions that they might be expected to follow. In the other one, new categories of students have to be responsible for themselves.

What makes it happen?

There are three different things going on that make this happen. They are:

- The people are responsible for themselves, instead of the control program being responsible for them. (Note that to accomplish this, a person must also be aware of what type of student he or she is.)

- The control program can talk to different types of people (graduate students and regular students) as if they were exactly the same.

- The control program does not need to know about any special steps that students might need to take when moving from class to class.

To fully understand the implications of this, it's important to establish some terminology. In *UML Distilled*, Martin Fowler describes three different perspectives in the software development process.[3] These are described in Table 1-1.

Different perspectives

Table 1-1   Perspectives in the Software Development Process

Perspective	Description
Conceptual	This perspective "represents the concepts in the domain under study. . . . a conceptual model should be drawn with little or no regard for the software that might implement it . . ."
Specification	"Now we are looking at software, but we are looking at the interfaces of the software, not the implementation."
Implementation	At this point we are at the code itself. "This is probably the most often-used perspective, but in many ways the specification perspective is often a better one to take."

3. Fowler, M., Scott, K., *UML Distilled: A Brief Guide to the Standard Object Modeling Language, 2nd Edition*, Reading, Mass.: Addison-Wesley, 1999, pp. 51–52.

How perspectives help

Look again at the previous example of "Go to your next class." Notice that you—as the instructor—are communicating with the people at the *conceptual level*. In other words, you are telling people what you want, not how to do it. However, the way they go to their next class is very specific. They are following specific instructions and in doing so are working at the *implementation level*.

Communicating at one level (conceptually) while performing at another level (implementation) results in the requestor (the instructor) not knowing exactly what is happening, only knowing conceptually what is happening. This can be very powerful. Let's see how to take these notions and write programs that take advantage of them.

The Object-Oriented Paradigm

Using objects shifts responsibility to a more local level

The object-oriented paradigm is centered on the concept of the object. Everything is focused on objects. I write code organized around objects, not functions.

What is an object? Objects have traditionally been defined as data with *methods* (the object-oriented term for functions). Unfortunately, this is a very limiting way of looking at objects. I will look at a better definition of objects shortly (and again in Chapter 8, "Expanding Our Horizons"). When I talk about the data of an object, these can be simple things like numbers and character strings, or they can be other objects.

The advantage of using objects is that I can define things that are responsible for themselves. (See Table 1-2.) Objects inherently know what type they are. The data in an object allow it to know what state it is in and the code in the object allows it to function properly (that is, do what it is supposed to do).

Table 1-2   Objects and Their Responsibilities

This Object . . .	Is Responsible For . . .
Student	Knowing which classroom they are in Knowing which classroom they are to go to next Going from one classroom to the next
Instructor	Telling people to go to next classroom
Classroom	Having a location
Direction giver	Given two classrooms, giving directions from one classroom to the other

In this case, the objects were identified by looking at the entities in the problem domain. I identified the responsibilities (or methods) for each object by looking at what these entities need to do. This is consistent with the technique of finding objects by looking for the nouns in the requirements and finding methods by looking for verbs. I find this technique to be quite limiting and will show a better way throughout the book. For now, it is a way to get us started.

The best way to think about what an object is, is to think of it as something with responsibilities. A good design rule is that objects should be responsible for themselves and should have those responsibilities clearly defined. This is why I say one of the responsibilities of a student object is knowing how to go from one classroom to the next.

How to think about objects

I can also look at objects using the framework of Fowler's perspectives:

Or, taking Fowler's perspective

- At the *conceptual level*, an object is a set of responsibilities.[4]

---

4. I am roughly paraphrasing Bertrand Meyer's work of Design by Contract as outlined in *Object-Oriented Software Construction*, Upper Saddle River, N.J.: Prentice Hall, 1997, p. 331.

- At the *specification level*, an object is a set of methods that can be invoked by other objects or by itself.

- At the *implementation level*, an object is code and data.

Unfortunately, object-oriented design is often taught and talked about only at the implementation level—in terms of code and data—rather than at the conceptual or specification level. But there is great power in thinking about objects in these latter ways as well!

Objects have interfaces for other objects to use

Since objects have responsibilities and objects are responsible for themselves, there has to be a way to tell objects what to do. Remember that objects have data to tell the object about itself and methods to implement functionality. Many methods of an object will be identified as callable by other objects. The collection of these methods is called the object's *public interface*.

For example, in the classroom example, I could write the **Student** object with the method gotoNextClassroom(). I would not need to pass any parameters in because each student would be responsible for itself. That is, it would know:

- What it needs to be able to move

- How to get any additional information it needs to perform this task

Organizing objects around the class

Initially, there was only one kind of student—a regular student who goes from class to class. Note that there would be many of these "regular students" in my classroom (my system). But what if I want to have more *kinds* of students? It seems inefficient for each student type to have its own set of methods to tell it what it can do, especially for tasks that are common to all students.

A more efficient approach would be to have a set of methods associated with all students that each one could use or tailor to their own needs. I want to define a "general student" to contain the definitions of these common methods. Then, I can have all manner of specialized students, each of whom has to keep track of his or her own private information.

In object-oriented terms, this general student is called a *class*. A class is a definition of the behavior of an object. It contains a complete description of:

- The data elements the object contains
- The methods the object can do
- The way these data elements and methods can be accessed

Since the data elements an object contains can vary, each object of the same type may have different data but will have the same functionality (as defined in the methods).

To get an object, I tell the program that I want a new object of this type (that is, the class that the object belongs to). This new object is called an *instance* of the class. Creating instances of a class is called *instantiation*.

Objects are instances of classes

Writing the "Go to the next classroom" example using an object-oriented approach is much simpler. The program would look like this:

Working with objects in the example

1. Start the control program.
2. Instantiate the collection of students in the classroom.
3. Tell the collection to have the students go to their next class.
4. The collection tells each student to go to their next class.
5. Each student:
   a. Finds where his next class is
   b. Determines how to get there

    c. Goes there

4. Done.

The need for an
abstract type

This works fine until I need to add another student type, such as the graduate student.

I have a dilemma. It appears that I must allow any type of student into the collection (either regular or graduate student). The problem facing me is how do I want the collection to refer to its constituents? Since I am talking about implementing this in code, the collection will actually be an array or something of some type of object. If the collection were named something like, **Regular-Students**, then I would not be able to put **GraduateStudents** into the collection. If I say that the collection is just a group of objects, how can I be sure that I do not include the wrong type of object (that is, something that doesn't do "Go to your next class")?

The solution is straightforward. I need a general type that encompasses more than one specific type. In this case, I want a **Student** type that includes both **RegularStudent**s and **GraduateStudent**s. In object-oriented terms, we call **Student** an *abstract class*.

Abstract classes
define what a set of
classes can do

Abstract classes define what other, related, classes can do. These "other" classes are classes that represent a particular type of related behavior. Such a class is often called a *concrete class* because it represents a specific, or nonchanging, implementation of a concept.

In the example, the abstract class is **Student**. There are two types of **Student**s represented by the concrete classes, **Regular-Student**s and **GraduateStudent**s. **RegularStudent** is one kind of **Student** and **GraduateStudent** is also a kind of **Student**.

This type of relationship is called an *is-a* relationship, which is formally called *inheritance*. Thus, the **RegularStudent** class *inherits from* **Student**. Other ways to say this would be, the **Graduate-Student** *derives from, specializes,* or *is a subclass of* **Student**.

Going the other way, "the **Student** class is the *base class, generalizes,* or is the *superclass of* **GraduateStudent** and of **RegularStudent**.

Abstract classes act as placeholders for other classes. I use them to define the methods their derived classes must implement. Abstract classes can also contain common methods that can be used by all derivations. Whether a derived class uses the default behavior or replaces it with its own variation is up to the derivation (this is consistent with the mandate that objects be responsible for themselves).

Abstract classes act as placeholders for other classes

This means that I can have the controller contain **Student**s. The reference type used will be **Student**. The compiler can check that anything referred to by this **Student** reference is, in fact, a kind of **Student**. This gives the best of both worlds:

- The collection only needs to deal with **Student**s (thereby allowing the instructor object just to deal with students).

- Yet, I still get type checking (only **Student**s that can "Go to their next classroom" are included).

- And, each kind of **Student** is left to implement its functionality in its own way.

Abstract classes are more than classes that do not get instantiated.

Abstract classes are often described as classes that do not get instantiated. This definition is accurate—at the implementation level. But that is too limited. It is more helpful to define abstract classes at the conceptual level. Thus, at the conceptual level, abstract classes are simply placeholders for other classes.

That is, they give us a way to assign a name to a set of related classes. This lets us treat this set as one concept.

In the object-oriented paradigm, you must constantly think about your problem from all three levels of perspective.

Visibility

Since the objects are responsible for themselves, there are many things they do not need to expose to other objects. Earlier, I mentioned the concept of the *public interface*—those methods that are accessible by other objects. In object-oriented systems, the main types of accessibility are:

- *Public*—Anything can see it.

- *Protected*—Only objects of this class and derived classes can see it.

- *Private*—Only objects from this class can see it.

Encapsulation

This leads to the concept of *encapsulation*. Encapsulation has often been described simply as hiding data. Objects generally do not expose their internal data members to the outside world (that is, their visibility is protected or private).

But encapsulation refers to more than hiding data. In general, encapsulation means *any kind of hiding*.

In the example, the instructor did not know which were the regular students and which were the graduate students. The type of student is hidden from the instructor (I am encapsulating the type of student). As you will see later in the book, this is a very important concept.

Polymorphism

Another term to learn is *polymorphism*.

In object-oriented languages, we often refer to objects with one type of reference that is an abstract class type. However, what we are actually referring to are specific instances of classes derived from their abstract classes.

Thus, when I tell the objects to do something conceptually through the abstract reference, I get different behavior, depending upon the specific type of derived object I have. Polymorphism derives from *poly* (meaning many) and *morph* (meaning form). Thus, it means *many forms*. This is an appropriate name because I have many different forms of behavior for the same call.

In the example, the instructor tells the students to "Go to your next classroom." However, depending upon the type of student, they will exhibit different behavior (hence polymorphism).

Review of Object-Oriented Terminology

Term	Description
Object	An entity that has responsibilities. I implement these by writing a class (in code) that defines data members (the variables associated with the objects) and methods (the functions associated with the objects).
Class	The repository of methods. Defines the data members of objects. Code is organized around the class.
Encapsulation	Typically defined as data-hiding, but better thought of as any kind of hiding.
Inheritance	Having one class be a special kind of another class. These specialized classes are called derivations of the base class (the initial class). The base class is sometimes called the superclass while the derived classes are sometimes called the subclasses.
Instance	A particular example of a class (it is always an object).
Instantiation	The process of creating an instance of a class.
Polymorphism	Being able to refer to different derivations of a class in the same way, but getting the behavior appropriate to the derived class being referred to.
Perspectives	There are three different perspectives for looking at objects: *conceptual*, *specification*, and *implementation*. These distinctions are helpful in understanding the relationship between abstract classes and their derivations. The abstract class defines how to solve things conceptually. It also gives the specification for communicating with any object derived from it. Each derivation provides the specific implementation needed.

Object-Oriented Programming in Action

New example

Let's re-examine the shapes example discussed at the beginning of the chapter. How would I implement it in an object-oriented manner? Remember that it has to do the following:

1. Locate the list of shapes in the database.

2. Open up the list of shapes.

3. Sort the list according to some rules.

4. Display the individual shapes on the monitor.

To solve this in an object-oriented manner, I need to define the objects and the responsibilities they would have.

Using objects in the Shape program

The objects I would need are:

Class	Responsibilities (Methods)
ShapeDataBase	*getCollection*—get a specified collection of shapes
Shape (an abstract class)	*display*—defines interface for Shapes *getX*—return X location of Shape (used for sorting) *getY*—return Y location of Shape (used for sorting)
Square (derived from Shape)	*display*—display a square (represented by this object)
Circle (derived from Shape)	*display*—display a circle (represented by this object)
Collection	*display*—tell all contained shapes to display *sort*—sort the collection of shapes
Display	*drawLine*—draw a line on the screen *drawCircle*—draw a circle on the screen

The main program would now look like this:

Running the program

1. Main program creates an instance of the database object.

2. Main program asks the database object to find the set of shapes I am interested in and to instantiate a collection object containing all of the shapes (actually, it will instantiate circles and squares that the collection will hold).

3. Main program asks the collection to sort the shapes.

4. Main program asks the collection to display the shapes.

5. The collection asks each shape it contains to display itself.

6. Each shape displays itself (using the **Display** object) according to the type of shape I have.

Let's see how this helps to handle new requirements (remember, requirements always change). For example, consider the following new requirements:

Why this helps—handling new requirements

- **Add new kinds of shapes (such as a triangle).** To introduce a new kind of shape, only two steps are required:

  - Create a new derivation of **Shape** that defines the shape.

  - In the new derivation, implement a version of the display method that is appropriate for that shape.

- **Change the sorting algorithm.** To change the method for sorting the shapes, only one step is required:

  - Modify the method in **Collection**. Every shape will use the new algorithm.

Bottom line: The object-oriented approach has limited the impact of changing requirements.

Encapsulation revisited

There are several advantages to encapsulation. The fact that it hides things from the user directly implies the following:

- Using things is easier because the user does not need to worry about implementation issues.

- Implementations can be changed without worrying about the caller. (Since the caller didn't know how it was implemented in the first place, there shouldn't be any dependencies.)

- The insides of an object are unknown to outside objects—they are used by the object to help implement the function specified by the object's interface.

Benefit: reduced side effects

Finally, consider the problem of unwanted side effects that arise when functions are changed. This kind of bug is addressed effectively with encapsulation. The internals of objects are unknown to other objects. If I use encapsulation and follow the strategy that objects are responsible for themselves, then the only way to affect an object will be to call a method on that object. The object's data and the way it implements its responsibilities are shielded from changes caused by other objects.

Encapsulation saves us.

- The more I make my objects responsible for their own behaviors, the less the controlling programs have to be responsible for.

- Encapsulation makes changes to an object's internal behavior transparent to other objects.

- Encapsulation helps to prevent unwanted side effects.

Special Object Methods

Creating and destroying

I have talked about methods that are called by other objects or possibly used by an object itself. But what happens when objects are created? What happens when they go away? If objects are self-contained units, then it would be a good idea to have methods to handle these situations.

These special methods do, in fact, exist and are called *constructors* and *destructors*.

A constructor is a special method that is automatically called when the object is created. Its purpose is to handle starting up the object. This is part of an object's mandate to be responsible for itself. The constructor is the natural place to do initializations, set default information, set up relationships with other objects, or do anything else that is needed to make a well-defined object. All object-oriented languages look for a constructor method and execute it when the object is created.

Constructors initialize, or set up, an object

By using constructors properly it is easier to eliminate (or at least minimize) uninitialized variables. This type of error usually occurs from carelessness on the part of the developer. By having a set, consistent place for all initializations throughout your code (that is, the constructors of your objects) it is easier to ensure that initializations take place. Errors caused by uninitialized variables are easy to fix but hard to find, so this convention (with the automatic calling of the constructor) can increase the efficiency of programmers.

A destructor is a special method that helps an object clean up after itself when the object goes out of existence; that is, when the object is destroyed. All object-oriented languages look for a destructor method and execute it when the object is being deleted. As with the constructor, the use of the destructor is part of the object's mandate to be responsible for itself.

Destructors clean up an object when it is no longer needed (when it has been deleted)

Destructors are typically used for releasing resources when objects are no longer needed. Since Java has garbage collection (auto-cleanup of objects no longer in use), destructors are not as important in Java as they are in C++. In C++, it is common for an object's destructor also to destroy other objects that are used only by this object.

Summary

In this chapter

In this chapter, I have shown how object orientation helps us minimize consequences of shifting requirements on a system and how it contrasts with functional decomposition.

I covered a number of the essential concepts in object-oriented programming and have introduced and described the primary terminology. These are essential to understanding the concepts in the rest of this book. (See Tables 1-3 and 1-4.)

Table 1-3   Object-Oriented Concepts

Concept	Review
Functional decomposition	Structured programmers usually approach program design with *functional decomposition.* Functional decomposition is the method of breaking down a problem into smaller and smaller functions. Each function is subdivided until it is manageable.
Changing requirements	Changing requirements are inherent to the development process. Rather than blaming users or ourselves about the seemingly impossible task of getting good and complete requirements, we should use development methods that deal with changing requirements more effectively.
Objects	Objects are defined by their responsibilities. Objects simplify the tasks of programs that use them by being responsible for themselves.
Constructors and destructors	An object has special methods that are called when it is created and deleted. These special methods are: • *Constructors*, which initialize or set up an object. • *Destructors*, which clean up an object when it is deleted. All object-oriented languages use constructors and destructors to help manage objects.

Table 1-4   Object-Oriented Terminology

Term	Definition
Abstract class	Defines the methods and common attributes of a set of classes that are conceptually similar. Abstract classes are never instantiated.
Attribute	Data associated with an object (also called a data member).
Class	Blueprint of an object—defines the methods and data of an object of its type.
Constructor	Special method that is invoked when an object is created.
Derived class	A class that is specialized from a superclass. Contains all of the attributes and methods of the superclass but may also contain other attributes or different method implementations.
Destructor	Special method that is invoked when an object is deleted.
Encapsulation	Any kind of hiding. Objects encapsulate their data. Abstract classes encapsulate their derived concrete classes.
Functional decomposition	A method of analysis in which a problem is broken into smaller and smaller functions.
Inheritance	The way that a class is specialized, used to relate derived classes from their abstractions.
Instance	A particular object of a class.
Instantiation	The process of creating an instance of a class.
Member	Either data or method of a class.
Method	Functions that are associated with an object.
Object	An entity with responsibilities. A special, self-contained holder of both data and methods that operate on that data. An object's data are protected from external objects.
Polymorphism	The ability of related objects to implement methods that are specialized to their type.
Superclass	A class from which other classes are derived. Contains the master definitions of attributes and methods that all derived classes will use (and possibly will override).

CHAPTER 2

The UML—The Unified Modeling Language

Overview

This chapter gives a brief overview of the Unified Modeling Language (UML), which is the modeling language of the object-oriented community. If you do not already know the UML, this chapter will give you the minimal understanding you will need to be able to read the diagrams contained in this book.

In this chapter

In this chapter,

- I describe what the UML is and why to use it.
- I discuss the UML diagrams that are essential to this book:
    - The Class Diagram
    - The Interaction Diagram

What Is the UML?

The UML is a visual language (meaning a drawing notation with semantics) used to create models of programs. By models of programs, I mean a diagrammatic representation of the programs in which one can see the relationships between the objects in the code.

UML offers many kinds of modeling diagrams

The UML has several different diagrams—some for analysis, others for design, and still others for implementation (or more accurately, for the dissemination, that is, the distribution of the code) (see Table 2-1). Each diagram shows the relationships among the different sets of entities, depending upon the purpose of the diagram.

Table 2-1   UML Diagrams and Their Purposes

When You Are...	Use the UML Diagram...
In the analysis phase	• **Use Case Diagrams**, which involve entities interacting with the system (say, users and other systems) and the function points that I need to implement.
	• **Activity Diagrams**, which focus on workflow of the problem domain (the actual space where people and other agents are working, the subject area of the program) rather than the logic flow of the program.
	Note: Since this book is principally focused on design, I will not cover Use Case Diagrams or Activity Diagrams here.
Looking at *object* interactions	• **Interaction Diagrams**, which show how specific objects interact with each other. Since they deal with *specific* cases rather than general situations, they are helpful both when checking requirements and when checking designs. The most popular kind of Interaction Diagram is the **Sequence Diagram**.
In the design phase	• **Class Diagrams**, which detail the relationships between the classes.
Looking at an object's *behaviors* that differ based upon the state that the object is in	• **State Diagrams**, which detail the different states an object may be in as well as the transitions between these states.
In the deployment phase	• **Deployment Diagrams**, which show how different modules will be deployed. I will not talk about these diagrams here.

Why Use the UML?

The UML is used primarily for communication—with myself, my team members, and with my customers. Poor requirements (either incomplete or inaccurate) are ubiquitous in the field of software development. The UML gives us tools to gather better requirements.

Principally for communications

The UML gives a way to determine if my understanding of the system is the same as others'. Because systems are complex and have different types of information that must be conveyed, it offers different diagrams specializing in the different types of information.

For clarity

One easy way to see the value of the UML is to recall your last several design reviews. If you have ever been in a review where someone starts talking about their code and describes it without a modeling language like the UML, almost certainly their talk was both confusing as well as being much longer than necessary. The UML is not only a better way of describing object-oriented designs, it also forces the designer to think through his or her approach (since it must be written down).

For precision

The Class Diagram

The most basic of UML diagrams is the Class Diagram. It both describes classes and shows the relationships between them. The types of relationships that are possible are

The basic modeling diagram

- When one class is a "kind of" another class: the *is-a* relationship
- When there are associations between two classes
  - One class "contains" another class: the *has-a* relationship
  - One class "uses" another class

There are variations on these themes. For example, to say something contains something else can mean that

- The contained item is a part of the containing item (like an engine in a car).

- I have a collection of things that can exist on their own (like airplanes at an airport).

The first example is called *composition* while the second is called *aggregation*.[1]

Different ways of showing class information

Figure 2-1 illustrates several important things. First, each rectangle represents a class. In the UML, I can represent up to three things in a class:

- The name of the class

- The data members of the class

- The methods (functions) of the class

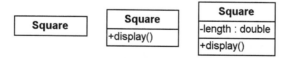

Figure 2-1   The Class Diagram—its three variations.

I have three different ways of showing these.

- The *leftmost rectangle* shows just the class' name. I would use this type of class representation when more detailed information is not needed.

---

1. Gamma, Helm, Johnson, and Vlissides (the Gang of Four) call the first "aggregation" and the second "composition"—exactly the reverse of the UML. However, the Gang of Four book was written before the UML was finalized. The presented definition is, in fact, consistent with the UML's. This illustrates some of the motivation for the UML; before it came out there were several different modeling languages, each with its own notation and terms.

- The *middle rectangle* shows both the name and the methods of the class. In this case, the **Square**[2] has the method *display*. The plus sign (+) in front of *display* (the name of the method) means that this method is public—that is, objects other than objects of this class can call it.

- The *rightmost rectangle* shows what I had before (the name and methods of the class) as well as data members of the class. In this case, the minus sign (–) before the data member *length* (which is of type double) indicates that this data member's value is private, that is it is unavailable to anything other than the object to which it belongs.[3]

UML notation for access.

You can control the accessibility of a class' data and method members. You can use the UML to notate which accessibility you want each member to have. The three types of accessibility available in most object-oriented languages are as follows:

- **Public:** notated with a plus sign (+).
  This means all objects can access this data or method.

- **Protected:** notated with a pound sign (#).
  This means only this class and all of its derivations (including derivations from its derivations) can access this data or method.

- **Private:** notated with a minus sign (–).
  This means that only methods of this class can access this data or method. (Note: Some languages further restrict this to the particular object.)

---

2. Whenever we refer to a class name, we will bold it as done here.
3. In some languages, objects of the same type can share each other's private data.

Class Diagrams also show relationships

Class Diagrams can also show relationships between different classes. Figure 2-2 shows the relationship between the **Shape** class and several classes that derive from it.

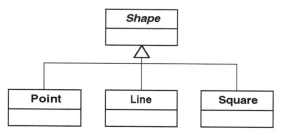

Figure 2-2   The Class Diagram showing the *is-a* relationships.

Showing the is-a *relationship*

Figure 2-2 represents several things. First, the arrowhead under the **Shape** class means that those classes pointing to **Shape** derive from **Shape**. Furthermore, since **Shape** is *italicized* that means it is an abstract class. An abstract class is a class that is used to define an interface for the classes that derive from it.

Showing the has-a *relationship*

There are actually two different kinds of *has-a* relationships. One object can have another object where the contained object is a part of the containing object—or not. In Figure 2-3, I show **Airports** "having" **Aircraft**. **Aircraft** are not part of **Airports**, but I can still say the **Airport** has them. This type of relationship is called *aggregation*.

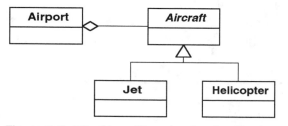

Figure 2-3   The Class Diagram showing the *has-a* relationship.

In this diagram, I also show that an **Aircraft** is either a **Jet** or a **Helicopter**. I can see that **Aircraft** is an abstract class because its name is shown in italics. That means that an **Airport** will have either **Jet** or **Helicopter** but will treat them the same (as **Aircraft**). The open (unfilled) diamond on the right of the **Airport** class indicates the aggregation relationship.

Aggregation

The other type of *has-a* relationship is where the containment means the contained object is a part of the containing object. This type of relationship is also called *composition*.

Composition

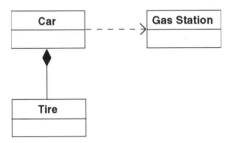

Figure 2-4   The Class Diagram showing composition and the *uses* relationship.

Figure 2-4 shows that a **Car** has **Tire**s as parts (that is, the **Car** is made up of **Tire**s and other things). This type of *has-a* relationship, called composition, is depicted by the filled in diamond. This diagram also shows that a **Car** uses a **GasStation**. The *uses* relationship is depicted by a dashed line with an arrow. This is also called a dependency relationship.

Composition and uses

Both composition and aggregation involve one object containing one or more objects. Composition, however, implies the contained object is a part of the containing object, whereas aggregation means the contained objects are more like a collection of things. We can consider composition to be an unshared association, with

Composition versus aggregation

the contained object's lifetime being controlled by its containing object. The appropriate use of constructor and destructor methods is useful here to help facilitate object creation and destruction.

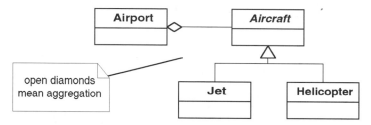

Figure 2-5 The Class Diagram with a Note.

Notes in the UML.

In Figure 2-5, there is a new symbol: the Note. The box containing the message "open diamonds mean aggregation" is a note. They are meant to look like pieces of paper with the right corner folded back. You often see them with a line connecting them to a particular class indicating they relate just to that class.

Indicating the number of things another object has

Class Diagrams show the relationships between classes. With composition and aggregation, however, the relationship is more specifically about objects of that type of class. For example, it is true **Airport**s have **Aircraft**, but more specifically, specific airports have specific aircraft. The question may arise—"how many aircraft does an airport have?" This is called the *cardinality* of the relationship. I show this in Figures 2-6 and 2-7.

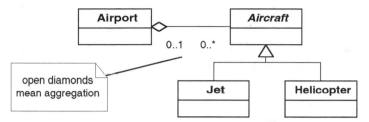

Figure 2-6 The cardinality of the `Airport-Aircraft` relationship.

Figure 2-6 tells us that when I have an **Airport**, it has from 0 to   *Cardinality*
any number (represented by an asterisk here, but sometimes by the
letter "n") of **Aircraft**. The "0..1" on the **Airport** side means that
when I have an **Aircraft**, it can be contained by either 0 or 1
Airport (it may be in the air).

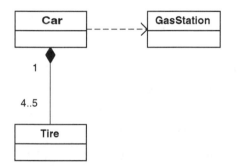

Figure 2-7 The cardinality of the `Car-Tire` relationship.

Figure 2-7 tells us that when I have a **Car**, it has either 4 or 5 tires   *Cardinality*
(it may or may not have a spare). Tires are on exactly one car. I   *continued*
have heard some people assume no specification of cardinality
assumes that there is one object. That is not correct. If cardinality is
not specified there is no assumption made as to how many objects
there are.

Dashes show
dependence

As before, the dashed line between **Car** and **GasStation** in Figure 2-7 shows that there is a dependency between the two. The UML uses a dashed arrow to indicate semantic relationships (meanings) between two model elements.

Interaction Diagrams

Sequence Diagram

Class Diagrams show static relationships between classes. In other words, they do not show us any activity. Although very useful, sometimes I need to show how the objects instantiated from these classes actually work together.

The UML diagrams that show how objects interact with each other are called *Interaction Diagrams*. The most common type of Interaction Diagram is the Sequence Diagram, such as shown in Figure 2-8.

How to read the
Sequence Diagram

Sequence Diagrams are read from top to bottom.

- Each rectangle at the top represents a particular object. Although many of the rectangles have class names in them, notice how there is a colon in front of the class name. Some of the rectangles have other names—for example, **shape1:Square**.

- The boxes at the top give the class name (to the right of the colon) and optionally, a name of the object (before the colon).

- The vertical lines represent the lifespan of the objects. Unfortunately, most UML drawing programs don't support this and draw the lines from the top to the bottom, leaving it unclear when an object actually comes into existence.

- I show objects sending messages to each other with horizontal lines between these vertical lines.

- Sometimes returned values and/or objects are explicitly shown and sometimes it is just understood that they are returned.

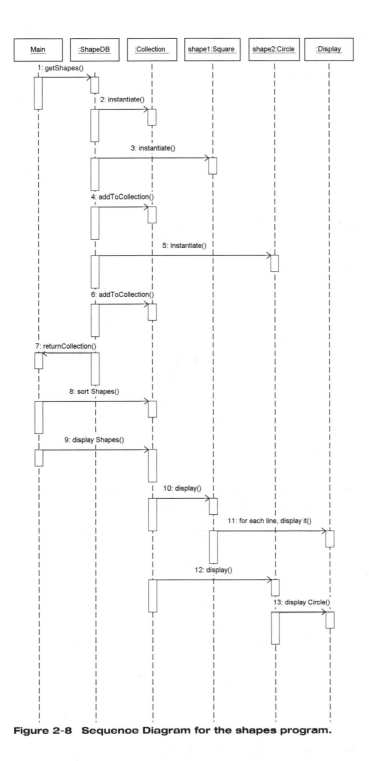

Figure 2-8 Sequence Diagram for the shapes program.

For example, in Figure 2-8,

- At the top I see that **Main** sends a "get shapes" message to the **ShapeDB** object (which isn't named). After being asked to "get shapes," the **ShapeDB**:
  - Instantiates a collection
  - Instantiates a square
  - Adds the square to the collection
  - Instantiates a circle
  - Adds the circle to the collection
  - Returns the collection to the calling routine (the Main)

I read the rest of the diagram in this top-down fashion to see the rest of the action. This diagram is called a Sequence Diagram because it depicts the sequence of operations.

Object:Class notation.

In some UML diagrams, you want to refer to an object with the class from which it is derived. This is done by connecting them with a colon. In Figure 2-8, I show **shape1:Square** refers to the **shape1** object which is instantiated from the **Square** class.

Summary

In this chapter

The purpose of the UML is to both flesh out your designs and to communicate them. Do not worry so much about creating diagrams the "right" way. Think about the best way to communicate the concepts in your design. In other words,

- If you think something needs to be said, use a Note to say it.

- If you aren't sure about an icon or a symbol and you have to look it up to find out its meaning, include a note to explain it since others may be unclear about its meaning, too.

- Go for clarity.

Of course, this means you should not use the UML in nonstandard ways—that does not communicate properly either. Just consider what you are trying to communicate as your draw your diagrams.

PART II

The Limitations of Traditional Object-Oriented Design

Part Overview

In this part, I solve a real-world problem using standard object-oriented methods. This was a problem I worked on when I was just beginning to learn design patterns.

In this section

Chapter	Discusses These Topics
3	• A description of the CAD/CAM problem: extract information from a large computer-aided design/computer-aided manufacturing (CAD/CAM) database to feed a complex and expensive analysis program. • Because the CAD/CAM system continues to evolve, the problem cries out for flexible code.
4	• My first solution to the CAD/CAM problem, using standard object-oriented methods. • At the time I actually worked on this problem, I hadn't yet learned the essence of the principles behind many design patterns. This resulted in an initial solution that over-relied on inheritance. It was easy to design and the initial solution worked, but I ended up with too many special cases. • My solution had significant problems—difficult maintenance and inflexibility—just the things I hoped to avoid with object-oriented design. • Later, in Part IV, I will revisit the problem in Chapter 12, "Solving the CAD/CAM Problem with Patterns." I will solve the problem again using design patterns to orchestrate the application's architecture and its implementation details. By doing this, I create a solution that is much easier to maintain and is much more flexible.

Why read this part   This part is important to read because it illustrates a typical problem that results in traditional object-oriented design—taller-than-necessary inheritance hierarchies that have tight coupling and low cohesion.

CHAPTER 3

A Problem That Cries Out for Flexible Code

Overview

This chapter gives an overview of a problem we want to solve: extracting information from a large CAD/CAM database to feed a complex and expensive analysis program. Because the CAD/CAM system continues to evolve, the problem cries out for flexible code.

In this chapter

In this chapter, I give an overview of the CAD/CAM problem, the vocabulary of the domain, and important features of the problem.

Extracting Information from a CAD/CAM System

I am now going to review a past design of mine that got me on the road to the insights contained in this book.

The problem: extract information for an expert system

I was supporting a design center in which engineers used a CAD/ CAM system to make drawings of sheet metal parts. An example of one of these parts is shown in Figure 3-1.

My problem was to write a computer tool to extract information from the CAD/CAM system so that an expert system could use it in a particular way. The expert system needed this information in order to conrol the manufacturing of the part. Since the expert system was complex to modify and would have a longer life than the current version of the CAD/CAM system, I wanted to write the information-extracting tool so that it could easily be adapted to new revisions of the CAD/CAM system.

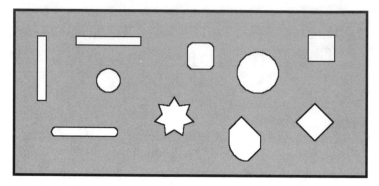

Figure 3-1   Example of a piece of sheet metal.

What are expert systems?

An *expert system* is a special computer system that uses the rules of a human expert(s) to make automated decisions. Building expert systems involves two steps. First, acquire and model the set of rules that experts use to make decisions and accomplish the task. Second, implement this set of rules in the computer system; this step usually uses some sort of commercially available expert system tool. The first step is by far the more difficult assignment for the analyst.

Understand the Vocabulary

Terminology: classifying the shapes cut from the sheet metal

The first task in analysis is to understand the vocabulary used by the users and the experts in the problem domain. The most important terms used are those that describe the dimensions and geometry in the sheet metal.

As shown in Figure 3-1, a piece of sheet metal is cut to a particular size and has shapes cut out inside it. Experts call these cutouts by the general name "feature." A piece of sheet metal can be fully specified by its external dimensions and the features contained in it.

The types of shapes—features—that may be found in a piece of sheet metal are described in Table 3-1. These are the shapes the system will have to address.

Table 3-1   Shapes Found in a Piece of Sheet Metal

Shape	Description
Slot	Straight cuts in the metal of constant width that terminate with either squared or rounded edges. Slots may be oriented to any angle. They are usually cut with a router bit. Figure 3-1 has three slots on the left side; one is oriented vertically while the others are oriented horizontally.
Hole	Circles cut into the sheet metal. Typically they are cut with drill bits of varying width. Figure 3-1 has a hole toward the left surrounded by the three slots and has a larger hole toward the right of the sheet metal.
Cutout	Squares with either squared or rounded edges. These are cut by a high-powered punch hitting the metal with great impact. Figure 3-1 has three cutouts; the lower right one is oriented at 45 degrees.
Special	Preformed shapes that are not slots, holes, or cutouts. In these cases, a special punch has been made to create these quickly. Electrical outlets are a common "special" case. The star shape in Figure 3-1 is a special shape.
Irregular	Anything else. They are formed by using a combination of tools. The irregularly shaped object toward the bottom right of Figure 3-1 is an irregular shape.

CAD/CAM experts also use additional terminology that is important to understand, as described in Table 3-2.

Additional terminology

Table 3-2   Additional CAD/CAM Terminology

Term	Description
Geometry	The description of how a piece of sheet metal looks: the location of each of the features and their dimensions and the external shape of the sheet metal.
Part	The piece of sheet metal itself. I need to be able to store the geometry of each of the parts.
Dataset or model	The set of records in the CAD/CAM database that stores the geometry of a part.
NC machine and NC set	Numerically controlled (NC) machine. A special manufacturing tool that cuts metal using a variety of cutting heads that are controlled by a computer program. Usually, the computer program is fed the geometry of the part. This computer program is composed of commands called the NC set.

Describe the Problem

High-level description of the system's tasks

I need to design a program that will allow the expert system to open and read a model containing the geometry of a part that I want to analyze and then to generate the commands for the numerically controlled (NC) machine to build the piece of sheet metal.

I am only concerned about sheet metal parts in this example. However, the CAD/CAM system can handle many other kinds of parts.

At a high level, I want the system to perform the following steps:

- Analyze pieces of sheet metal.

- See how they should be made, based on the features they contain.

- Generate a set of instructions that are readable by manufacturing equipment. This set of instructions is called an NC set or a numerical control set.

- Give these instructions to manufacturing equipment when I want to make any of these parts

The difficulty with my programming task is that I cannot simply extract the features from the dataset and generate NC set commands. The type of commands to use and the order of these commands depend upon the features and their relation to other features.

The expert system's task is not trivial

For example, take a shape that is made up of several features: a shape made up of a cutout with two slots. One of the slots runs vertically through the cutout while the other runs horizontally through it. This is shown in Figure 3-2.

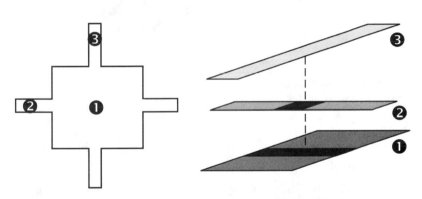

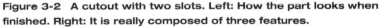

Figure 3-2   A cutout with two slots. Left: How the part looks when finished. Right: It is really composed of three features.

It is important to realize that I am actually given the three features on the right to make up the shape on the left. That is because the engineers using the CAD/CAM system typically think in terms of the features to make up more complex shapes because they know that doing so will enable quicker manufacturing of the parts.

. . . because it must determine the order of the features

The problem is, I cannot just generate the NC set commands for the three features independently of one another and hope the part comes out properly—there is often a particular order that must be used. In the example, if I do the slots first and then the cutout, as shown in Figure 3-3, when the cutout is made (remember a cutout is created by using a high-impact punch), the sheet metal will bend because the slots will have weakened the metal.

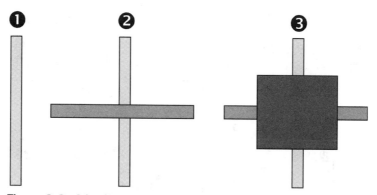

Figure 3-3 A bad approach to cutting out the openings. This sequence results in weakened, bent sheet metal.

I must create the shape shown in Figure 3-2 by punching out the cutout first, then doing the slots. This works because the slots are created using a router, which applies sideways pressure. Making the cutout first actually makes the job easier, not harder. This is shown in Figure 3-4.

Fortunately, someone had already worked out the rules for the expert system. I did not have to worry about that. I took the time to explain these challenges so that you could understand the type of information needed by the expert system.

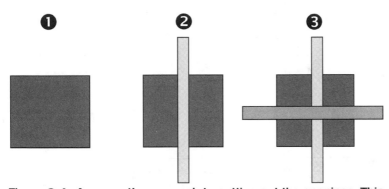

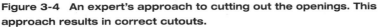

Figure 3-4 An expert's approach to cutting out the openings. This approach results in correct cutouts.

The Essential Challenges and Approaches

The CAD/CAM system is constantly evolving, changing. My real problem was to make it possible for the company to continue to use its expensive expert system while the CAD/CAM system changed.

Challenge: allow the expert system to work with a constantly changing CAD/CAM system

In my situation, they were currently using one version of the CAD/CAM system, Version 1 (V1), and a new version, Version 2 (V2), was coming out shortly. Although one vendor made both versions, the two versions were not compatible.

For a variety of technical and administrative reasons, it was not possible to translate the models from one version to the next. Thus, the expert system needed to be able to support both versions of the CAD/CAM system.

In fact, the situation was even a little worse than just having to accomodate two different versions of the CAD/CAM system. I knew a third version was coming out before long, but did not know when that would happen. In order to preserve the investment in the company's expert system, I wanted a system architecture approximately like the one diagrammed in Figure 3-5.

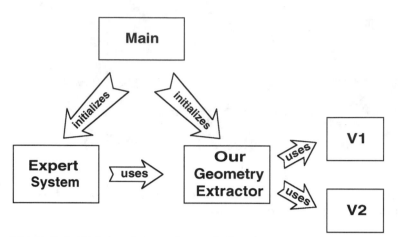

Figure 3-5 High-level view of my solution.

In other words, the application can initalize everything so that the expert system uses the appropriate CAD/CAM system. However, the expert system has to be able to use either version. Hence, I need to make V1 and V2 look the same to the expert system.

Polymorphism isn't needed at all levels

Although polymorphism is definitely needed at the geometry extractor level, it will not be needed at the feature level. This is because the expert system needs to know what type of features it is dealing with. However, we don't want to make any changes to the expert system when Version 3 of the CAD/CAM system comes out.

High-level class diagram

A basic understanding of object-oriented design implies that I will have a high-level class diagram similar to the one shown in Figure 3-6.

In other words, the expert system relates to the CAD/CAM systems through the **Model** class. The **Main** class takes care of instantiating the correct version of the **Model** (that is, **V1Model** or **V2Model**).

A more detailed look at the CAD/CAM systems

Now, I will describe the CAD/CAM systems and how they work. Unfortunately, the two are very different beasts.

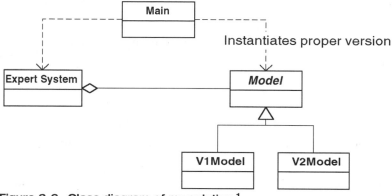

Figure 3-6 Class diagram of my solution.[1]

Version 1 is essentially a collection of subroutine libraries. To get information from a model, a series of calls must be made. A typical set of queries would be the following:

Step	Do this in CAD/CAM Version 1
1.	Open model XYZ and return a handle to it
2.	Store this handle as H
3.	For model, referred to by H, tell me how many features are present, store as N
4.	For each feature in the model referred to by H (from 1 to N)
4a.	for model referred to by H, tell me the ID of the ith element and store as ID
4b.	for model referred to by H, tell me the feature type of ID and store as T
4c.	for model referred to by H, tell me the X coordinate of ID and store as X (use T to determine the proper routine to call, based on type)
...	...

---

1. This and all other class diagrams in this book use the Unified Modeling Language (UML) notation. See Chapter 2, "The UML—The Unified Modeling Language" for a description of UML notation.

CAD/CAM V1 is clearly not object-oriented

This system is painful to deal with and clearly not object-oriented. Whoever is using the system must maintain the context for every query manually. Each call about a feature must know what kind of feature it has.

CAD/CAM V2 is object-oriented

The CAD/CAM vendor realized the inherent limitations of this type of system. The primary motivation for building V2 was to make it object-oriented. The geometry in V2 is therefore stored in objects. When a system requests a model, it gets back an object which represents the model. This model object contains a set of objects, each representing a feature. Since the problem domain is based on features, it is not surprising that the classes V2 uses to represent these features correspond exactly to the ones I have mentioned already: slots, holes, cutouts, specials, and irregulars.

Therefore, in V2, I can get a set of objects that correspond to the features that exist in the sheet metal. The UML diagram in Figure 3-7 shows the classes for the features.

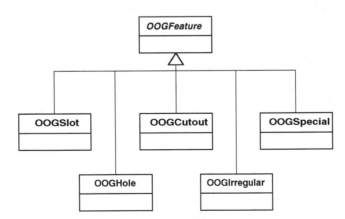

Figure 3-7 Feature classes of V2.

The OOG stands for object-oriented geometry, just as a reminder that V2 is an object-oriented system.

Summary

In this chapter, I described the CAD/CAM problem.

- I must extract information from different CAD/CAM systems in the same way. This will allow a system in which the company has a great investment (an expert system) to continue working without expensive modifications every time the CAD/CAM systems changes.

- I have two systems that are implemented in completely different ways, even though they contain essentially the same information.

This task has many similarities to other problems I have run across in projects. There are different specific implementations of systems, but I want to allow other objects to communicate with these different implementations in the same way.

In this chapter

CHAPTER 4

A Standard Object-Oriented Solution

Overview

This chapter gives an initial solution to the problem discussed in Chapter 3, "A Problem That Cries Out for Flexible Code." It is a reasonable first attempt at a solution and gets the job done quickly. However, it misses an important system requirement: flexibility as the CAD/CAM system continues to evolve.

In this chapter

In this chapter, I describe a solution based on object orientation. It is not a great solution, but it is a solution that would work.

Note: I will only show Java code examples in the main body of this chapter. The equivalent C++ code examples can be found at the end of this chapter.

Solving with Special Cases

Given the two different CAD/CAM systems described in Chapter 3, "A Problem That Cries Out for Flexible Code," how do I build an information-extraction system that will look the same to a client object regardless of which CAD/CAM system that I have?

Getting to a solution: special subclasses for each version

In thinking how to solve this problem, I reasoned that if I can solve it for slots, I can use that same solution for cutouts, holes, etc. In thinking about slots, I saw that I could easily specialize each case. That is, I'd have a `Slot` class and make a derivation for `Slot`s when I had the V1 system and another derivation when I had a V2 system. I show this in Figure 4-1.

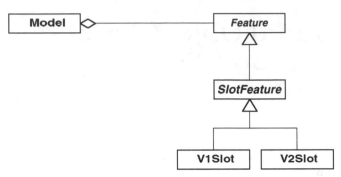

Figure 4-1 The design for slots.

Completing the solution

I complete this solution by extending it for each of the feature types, as shown in Figure 4-2.

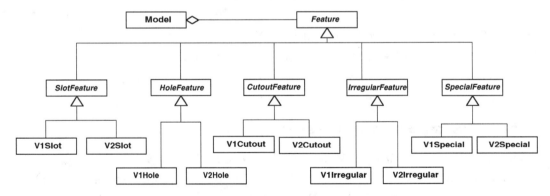

Figure 4-2 Original solution to the problem of extracting information.

Of course, Figure 4-2 is pretty high-level. Each of the **V1xxx** classes would communicate with the corresponding V1 library. Each of the **V2xxx** classes would communicate with the corresponding object in the V2 model.

This is easier to visualize by looking at each class individually.

- **V1Slot** would be implemented by remembering the model it belongs to and its ID in the V1 system when it is instantiated. Then, whenever one of the **V1Slot** methods is called to get information about it, the method would have to call a sequence of subroutine calls in V1 to get that information.

- **V2Slot** would be implemented in a similar fashion, except that, in this case, each **V2Slot** object would contain the slot object corresponding to it in the V2 system. Then, whenever the object was asked for information, it would simply pass this request on to the **OOGSlot** object and pass the response back to the client object that originally requested it.

A more detailed diagram incorporating the V1 and V2 systems is shown in Figure 4-3.

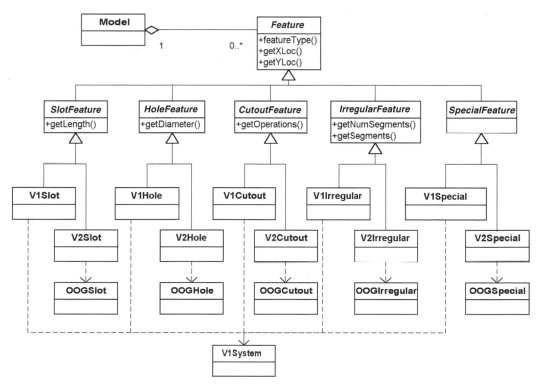

Figure 4-3   A first solution.

Code fragments help to understand the design

I am going to provide code examples for a couple of the classes in this design. These examples are just to help you understand how this design could be implemented. If you feel comfortable that you could implement this design, feel free to skip the following Java code examples (C++ code examples appear at the end of this chapter).

Example 4-1 Java Code Fragments: Instantiating the V1 Features

```
// segment of code that instantiates the features
// no error checking provided--for illustration
// purposes only

// each feature object needs to know the model number
// and feature ID it corresponds to in order to retrieve
// information when requested. Note how this information
// is passed into each object's constructor

   // open model
   V1Model myModel= V1OpenModel( modelName);

   nElements = V1GetNumberofElements(myModel);

   Feature features[]= new Feature[MAXFEATURES];

   // do for each feature in the model
   for (i= 0; i < nElements; i++) {
      // determine feature present and create
      // appropriate feature object
      switch( V1GetType( myModel, i)) {
         case SLOT:
            features[i]=
               new V1Slot( myModel,
                           V1GetID( myModel, i));
            break;

         case HOLE:

            features[i]=
               new V1Hole( myModel,
                           V1GetID( myModel, i));
            break;

         . . .

      }
   }
```

Example 4-2 Java Code Fragments:
Implementation of V1 Methods

```
// myModel and myID are private members containing
// information about the model and feature (in V1) this
// feature corresponds to

class V1Slot {
  double getX () {
    // call appropriate method for V1 to get needed
    // information. Note: this method may actually
    // call several methods in V1
    // to get the information.
    return V1GetXforSlot( myModel, myID);
  }
}

class V1Hole {
  double getX () {
    // call appropriate method for V1 to get needed
    // information. Note: this method may actually
    // call several methods in V1
    // to get the information.
    return V1GetXforHole( myModel, myID);
  }
}
```

Example 4-3 Java Code Fragments:
Instantiating the V2 Features

```
// segment of code that instantiates the features
// no error checking provided--for illustration
// purposes only

// each feature object needs to know the feature in the
// V2 system it corresponds to in order to retrieve
// information when requested. Note how this information
// is passed into each object's constructor

    // open model
    V2Model myModel= V2OpenModel( modelName);

  nElements= myModel.getNumElements();
    Feature features[]= new Feature[MAXFEATURES];
```

(continued)

Example 4-3   Java Code Fragments:
Instantiating the V2 Features *(continued)*

```java
OOGFeature oogF;
// do for each feature in the model
for (i= 0; i < nElements; i++) {
    // determine feature present and create
    // appropriate feature object
    oogF= myModel.getElement(i);

    switch( oogF.myType()) {
       case SLOT:
           features[i]= new V2Slot( oogF);
           break;

       case HOLE:

           features[i]= new V2Hole( oogF);
           break;

       ...

    }
  }
```

Example 4-4   Java Code Fragments:
Implementation of V2 Methods

```java
// oogF is a reference to the feature object in V2 that
// the object containing it corresponds to

class V2Slot {
   double getX () {
      // call appropriate method on oogF to get needed
      // information.
      return oogF.getX();
   }
}

class V2Hole {
   double getX () {
      // call appropriate method on oogF to get needed
      // information.
      return oogF.getX();
   }
}
```

In Figure 4-3, I have added a few of the methods that are needed by the features. Note how they differ depending upon the type of feature. This means I do not have polymorphism across features. This is not a problem, however, since the expert system needs to know what type of feature it has anyway. This is because the expert system needs different kinds of information from different types of features.

This solution satisfies one goal: a common API

This brings up the point that I am not so interested in polymorphism of the features. Rather, I need the ability to plug-and-play different CAD/CAM systems without changing the expert system.

What I am trying to do—handle multiple CAD/CAM versions transparently—gives me several clues that this solution is not a good one:

but contains many challenges

- *Redundancy amongst methods*—I can easily imagine that the methods that are making calls to the V1 system will have many similarities between them. For example, the V1getX for **Slot** and V1getX for **Hole** will be very similar.

- *Messy*—This is not always a good predictor, but it is another factor that reinforces my discomfort with the solution.

- *Tight coupling*—This solution has tight coupling because the features are related to each other indirectly. These relationships manifest themselves as the likely need to modify all of the features if the following occurs:

  - A new CAD/CAM system is required.

  - An existing CAD/CAM system is modified.

- *Low cohesion*—Cohesion is fairly low since methods to perform core functions are scattered amongst the classes.

However, my greatest concern comes from looking into the future. Imagine what will happen when the third version of the CAD/CAM system arrives. The combinatorial explosion will kill us! Look at the third row of the class diagram in Figure 4-3.

- There are five types of features.

- Each type of feature has a pair of classes, one for each CAD/ CAM system.

- When I get the third version, I will have groups of three, not groups of two.

- Instead of ten classes, I will have fifteen.

This is certainly not a system I will have fun maintaining!

A pitfall of analysis:
too much attention to details too early.

One common problem that we analysts can have is that we dive into the details too early in the development process. It is natural because it is easy to work with these details. Solutions for the details are usually apparent, but are not necessarily the best thing to start with. Delay as long as you can before you commit to the details.

In this case, I achieved one objective: a common API for feature information. Also, I defined my objects from a responsibility point of view. However, I did this at the price of creating special cases for everything. When I get new special cases, I will have to implement them as such. Hence, the high maintenance costs.

. . . and intuition says there must be a better solution

This was my first-blush solution and I immediately disliked it. My dislike grew more from my intuition than from the more logical reasons I gave above. I felt that there were problems.

In this case, I felt strongly that a better solution existed. Yet, two hours later, this was still the best I could come up with. The problem, it turned out, was my general approach, as will be seen later in this book.

Pay attention to your instincts.

Gut instinct is a surprisingly powerful indicator of the quality of a design. I suggest that developers learn to listen to their instincts.

By gut instinct, I mean the sensation in your stomach when you see something you do not like. I know this sounds unscientific (and it is), but my experience has shown me consistently that when I have an instinctive dislike for a design, a better one lies around the corner. Of course, there are sometimes several different corners nearby and I'm not always sure where the solution is.

Summary

I showed how easy it is to solve this problem by special-casing everything. The solution is straightforward. It allows me to add additional methods without changing what I already have. However, there are several disadvantages to it: high redundancy, low cohesion, and class explosion (from future changes).

In this chapter

The overreliance on inheritance will result in higher maintenance costs than should occur (or at least, than I *feel* should occur).

Supplement: C++ Code Examples

Example 4-5   C++ Code Fragments:
Instantiating the V1 Features

```cpp
// segment of code that instantiates the features
// no error checking provided--for illustration
// purposes only

// each feature object needs to know the model number
// and feature ID it corresponds to in order to retrieve
// information when requested. Note how this information
// is passed into each object's constructor

    // open model
    myModel= V1OpenModel( modelName);

    nElements= V1GetNumberofElements(myModel);

    Feature *features[MAXFEATURES];

    // do for each feature in the model
    for (i= 0; i < nElements; i++) {
        // determine feature present and create
        // appropriate feature object
        switch( V1GetType( myModel, i)) {
            case SLOT:
                features[i]=
                    new V1Slot( myModel,
                                V1GetID( myModel, i));
                break;

            case HOLE:

                features[i]=
                    new V1Hole( myModel,
                                V1GetID( myModel, i));
                break;
            ...
        }
    }
```

Example 4-6   C++ Code Fragments:
Implementation of V1 Methods

```
// myModel and myID are private members containing
// information about the model and feature (in V1) this
// feature corresponds to

double V1Slot::getX () {
   // call appropriate method for V1 to get needed
   // information. Note: this method may actually
   // call several methods in V1
   // to get the information.
   return V1GetXforSlot( myModel, myID);
}

double V1Hole::getX () {
   // call appropriate method for V1 to get needed
   // information. Note: this method may actually
   // call several methods in V1
   // to get the information.
   return V1GetXforHole( myModel, myID);
}
```

Example 4-7   C++ Code Fragments:
Instantiating the V2 Features

```
// segment of code that instantiates the features
// no error checking provided--for illustration
// purposes only

// each feature object needs to know the feature in the
// V2 system it corresponds to in order to retrieve
// information when requested. Note how this information
// is passed into each object's constructor

   // open model
   myModel= V2OpenModel( modelName);

   nElements= myModel->getNumElements();
   Feature *features[MAXFEATURES];

   OOGFeature *oogF;
   // do for each feature in the model
   for (i= 0; i < nElements; i++) {
```

(continued)

Example 4-7 C++ Code Fragments:
Instantiating the V2 Features *(continued)*

```
            // determine feature present and create
            // appropriate feature object
            oogF= myModel->getElement(i);

            switch( oogF->myType()) {
               case SLOT:
                  features[i]= new V2Slot( oogF);
                  break;

               case HOLE:

                  features[i]= new V2Hole( oogF);
                  break;
               ...

            }
         }
}
```

Example 4-8 C++ Code Fragments:
Implementation of V2 Methods

```
// oogF is a reference to the feature object in V2 that
// the object containing it corresponds to

double V2Slot::getX () {
  // call appropriate method on oogF to get needed
  // information.
  return oogF->getX();
}

double V2Hole::getX () {
  // call appropriate method on oogF to get needed
  // information.
  return oogF->getX();
}
```

PART III

Design Patterns

Part Overview

This part introduces design patterns: what they are and how to *In this part* use them. Four patterns pertinent to the CAD/CAM problem (Chapter 3, "A Problem That Cries Out for Flexible Code") are described. They are presented individually and then related to the earlier problem. In learning these patterns, I emphasize the object-oriented strategies espoused by the Gang of Four (as the authors Gamma, Helm, Johnson, and Vlissides are often referred to) in their seminal work, *Design Patterns: Elements of Reusable Object-Oriented Software*.

Chapter	Discusses These Topics
5	• An introduction to design patterns. • The concept of design patterns, their origins in architecture, and how they apply in the discipline of software design. • The motivations for studying design patterns.
6	• The **Facade pattern**: what it is, where it is used, and how it is implemented. • How the Facade pattern relates to the CAD/CAM problem.
7	• The **Adapter pattern**: what it is, where it is used, and how it is implemented. • Comparison between the Adapter pattern and the Facade pattern. • How the Adapter pattern relates to the CAD/CAM problem.

8
- Some important concepts in object-oriented programming: polymorphism, abstraction, classes, and encapsulation. It uses what has been learned in Chapters 5–7.

9
- The **Bridge pattern**. This pattern is quite a bit more complex than the previous patterns. It is also much more useful; therefore, I go into great detail with the Bridge pattern.
- How the Bridge pattern relates to the CAD/CAM problem.

10
- The **Abstract Factory pattern**, which focuses on creating families of objects. What the pattern is, how it is used and implemented.
- How the Abstract Factory pattern relates to the CAD/ CAM problem.

Objectives

At the end of this section, the reader will understand what design patterns are, why they are useful, and will be familiar with four specific patterns. The reader will also see how these patterns relate to the earlier CAD/CAM problem. This information, however, may not be enough to create a better design than we arrived at by over-relying on inheritance. However, the stage is set for using patterns in a way different from the way most design pattern practitioners use them.

CHAPTER 5

An Introduction
to Design Patterns

Overview

This chapter introduces the concept of design patterns.

In this chapter

In this chapter,

- I discuss the origins of design patterns in architecture and how they apply in the discipline of software design.
- I discuss the motivations for studying design patterns.

Design patterns are part of the cutting edge of object-oriented technology. Object-oriented analysis tools, books, and seminars are incorporating design patterns. Study groups on design patterns abound. It is often suggested that people learn design patterns only after they have mastered basic object-oriented skills. I have found that the opposite is true: learning design patterns early in the learning of object-oriented skills greatly helps to improve understanding of object-oriented analysis and design.

Design patterns and object-oriented design reinforce each other

Throughout the rest of the book, I will discuss not only design patterns, but also how they reveal and reinforce good object-oriented principles. I hope to improve both your understanding of these principles and illustrate why the design patterns being discussed here represent good designs.

Some of this material may seem abstract or philosophical. But give it a chance! This chapter lays the foundation for your understanding of design patterns. Understanding this material will enhance your ability to understand and work with new patterns.

Give this a chance

I have taken many of my ideas from Christopher Alexander's *The Timeless Way of Building*.[1] I will discuss these ideas throughout this book.

Design Patterns Arose from Architecture and Anthropology

Is quality objective?   Years ago, an architect named Christopher Alexander asked himself, "Is quality objective?" Is beauty truly in the eye of the beholder or would people agree that some things are beautiful and some are not? Now, the particular form of beauty that Alexander was interested in was one of architectural quality: what makes us know when an architectural design is good? For example, if a person were going to design an entryway for a house, how would he or she know that the design was good? Can we know good design? Is there an objective basis for such a judgment? A basis for describing our common consensus?

Alexander postulates that there is such an objective basis within architectural systems. The judgment that a building is beautiful is not simply a matter of taste. We can describe beauty through an objective basis that can be measured.

The discipline of cultural anthropology discovered the same thing. That body of work suggests that within a culture, individuals will agree to a large extent on what is considered to be a good design, what is beautiful. Cultures make judgments on good design that transcend individual beliefs. I believe that there are transcending patterns that serve as objective bases for judging design. A major branch of cultural anthropology looks for such patterns to describe the behaviors and values of a culture.[2]

---

1. Alexander, C., Ishikawa, S., Silverstein, M., *The Timeless Way of Building*, New York: Oxford University Press, 1979.
2. The anthropologist Ruth Benedict is a pioneer in pattern-based analysis of cultures. For examples, see Benedict, R., *The Chrysanthemum and the Sword*, Boston: Houghton Mifflin, 1946.

The proposition behind design patterns is that the quality of software systems can also be measured objectively.

If you accept the idea that it is possible to recognize and describe a good quality design, then how do you go about creating one? I can imagine Alexander asking himself,

How do you get good quality repeatedly?

> *What is present in a good quality design that is not present in a poor quality design?*

and

> *What is present in a poor quality design that is not present in a good quality design?*

These questions spring from Alexander's belief that if quality in design is objective, then we should be able to identify what makes designs good and what makes designs bad.

Alexander studied this problem by making many observations of buildings, towns, streets, and virtually every other aspect of living spaces that human beings have built for themselves. He discovered that, for a particular architectural creation, good constructs had things in common with each other.

Look for the commonalties

Architectural structures differ from each other, even if they are of the same type. Yet even though they are different, they can still be of high quality.

. . . especially commonality in the features of the problem to be solved

For example, two porches may appear structurally different and yet both may still be considered high quality. They might be solving different problems for different houses. One porch may be a transition from the walkway to the front door. Another porch might be a place for shade on a hot day. Or two porches might solve a common problem (transition) in different ways.

Alexander understood this. He knew that structures couldn't be separated from the problem they are trying to solve. Therefore, in his quest to identify and describe the consistency of quality in design, Alexander realized that he had to look at different structures that were designed to solve the same problem. For example, Figure 5-1 illustrates two solutions to the problem of demarking an entryway.

Figure 5-1 Structures may look different but still solve a common problem.

This led to the concept of a pattern

Alexander discovered that by narrowing his focus in this way—by looking at structures that solve similar problems—he could discern similarities between designs that were high quality. He called these similarities, *patterns*.

He defined a pattern as "a solution to a problem in a context."

> Each pattern describes a problem which occurs over and over again in our environment and then describes the core of the solution to that problem, in such a way that you can use this solution a million times over, without ever doing it the same way twice.[3]

---

3. Alexander, C., Ishikawa, S., Silverstein, M., *A Pattern Language*, New York: Oxford University Press, 1977, p. x.

Let's review some of Alexander's work to illustrate this. In Table 5-1 I will present an excerpt from his *The Timeless Way of Building*,[4] an excellent book that presents the philosophy of patterns succinctly.

Table 5-1   Excerpt from *The Timeless Way of Building*

Alexander Says . . .	My Comments . . .
In the same way, a courtyard, which is properly formed, helps people come to life in it.	A pattern always has a name and has a purpose. Here, the pattern's name is Courtyard and its purpose is to help people to come to life in it.
Consider the forces at work in a courtyard. Most fundamental of all, people seek some kind of private outdoor space, where they can sit under the sky, see the stars, enjoy the sun, perhaps plant flowers. This is obvious.	Although it might be obvious sometimes, it is important to state explicitly the problem being solved, which is the reason for having the pattern in the first place. This is what Alexander does here for Courtyard.
But there are more subtle forces too. For instance, when a courtyard is too tightly enclosed, has no view out, people feel uncomfortable, and tend to stay away . . . they need to see out into some larger and more distant space.	He points out a difficulty with the simplified solution and then gives us a way to solve the problem that he has just pointed out.
Or again, people are creatures of habit. If they pass in and out of the courtyard, every day, in the course of their normal lives, the courtyard becomes familiar, a natural place to go . . . and it is used.	Familiarity sometimes keeps us from seeing the obvious. The value of a pattern is that those with less experience can take advantage of what others have learned before them: both what must be included to have a good design, and what must be avoided to keep from a poor design.
But a courtyard with only one way in, a place you only go when you "want" to go there, is an unfamiliar place, tends to stay unused . . . people go more often to places which are familiar.	

(continued)

---

4. Alexander, C., Ishikawa, S., Silverstein, M., *The Timeless Way of Building*, New York: Oxford University Press, 1979.

Table 5-1   Excerpt from *The Timeless Way of Building* (continued)

Alexander Says . . .	My Comments . . .
Or again, there is a certain abruptness about suddenly stepping out, from the inside, directly to the outside . . . it is subtle, but enough to inhibit you.	
If there is a transitional space—a porch or a veranda, under cover, but open to the air—this is psychologically half way between indoors and outdoors, and makes it much easier, more simple, to take each of the smaller steps that brings you out into the courtyard . . .	He proposes a solution to a possibly overlooked challenge to building a great courtyard.
When a courtyard has a view out to a larger space, has crossing paths from different rooms, and has a veranda or a porch, these forces can resolve themselves. The view out makes it comfortable, the crossing paths help generate a sense of habit there, the porch makes it easier to go out more often . . . and gradually the courtyard becomes a pleasant customary place to be.	Alexander is telling us how to build a great courtyard . . . . . . and then tells us why it is great.

The four compo-
nents required of
every pattern
description

To review, Alexander says that a description of a pattern involves four items:

- The name of the pattern
- The purpose of the pattern, the problem it solves
- How we could accomplish this
- The constraints and forces we have to consider in order to accomplish it

Alexander postulated that patterns can solve virtually every archi-   *Patterns exist for*
tectural problem that one will encounter. He further postulated that   *almost any design*
patterns could be used together to solve complex architectural   *problem*
problems.

How patterns work together will be discussed later in this book. For   *. . . and may be*
now, I want to focus on his claim that patterns are useful to solve   *combined to solve*
specialized problems.   *complex problems*

Moving from Architectural to Software Design Patterns

What does all of this architectural stuff have to do with us software
developers?

Well, in the early 1990s some smart developers happened upon   *Adapting Alexander*
Alexander's work in patterns. They wondered if what was true for   *for software*
architectural patterns would also be true for software design.[5]

- Were there problems in software that occur over and over again
  that could be solved in somewhat the same manner?

- Was it possible to design software in terms of patterns, creating
  specific solutions based on these patterns only after the patterns
  had been identified?

The group felt the answer to both of these questions was "unequiv-
ocally yes." The next step was to identify several patterns and
develop standards for cataloging new ones.

---

5. The ESPRIT consortium in Europe was doing similar work in the 1980s. ESPRIT's
   Project 1098 and Project 5248 developed a pattern-based design methodology
   called Knowledge Analysis and Design Support (KADS) that was focused on patterns for creating expert systems. Karen Gardner extended the KADS analysis
   patterns to object orientation. See Gardner, K., *Cognitive Patterns: Problem-Solving
   Frameworks for Object Technology*, New York: Cambridge University Press, 1998.

The Gang of Four did the early work on Design Patterns

Although many people were working on design patterns in the early 1990s, the book that had the greatest influence on this fledging community was *Design Patterns: Elements of Reusable Object-Oriented Software*[6] by Gamma, Helm, Johnson, and Vlissides. In recognition of their important work, these four authors are commonly and affectionately known as the Gang of Four.

This book served several purposes:

- It applied the idea of design patterns to software design.
- It described a structure within which to catalog and describe design patterns.
- It cataloged 23 such patterns.
- It postulated object-oriented strategies and approaches based on these design patterns.

It is important to realize that the authors did not create the patterns described in the book. Rather, the authors identified these patterns as already existing within the software community, patterns that reflected what had been learned about high-quality designs for specific problems (note the similarity to Alexander's work).

Today, there are several different forms for describing design patterns. Since this is not a book about writing design patterns, I will not offer an opinion on the best structure for describing patterns; however, the following items listed in Table 5-2 need to be included in any description.

For each pattern that I present in this book, I present a one-page summary of the key features that describes that pattern.

---

6. Gamma, E., Helm, R., Johnson, R., Vlissides, J., *Design Patterns: Elements of Reusable Object-Oriented Software*, Reading, Mass.: Addison-Wesley, 1995.

Table 5-2   Key Features of Patterns

Item	Description
Name	All patterns have a unique name that identifies them.
Intent	The purpose of the pattern.
Problem	The problem that the pattern is trying to solve.
Solution	How the pattern provides a solution to the problem in the context in which it shows up.
Participants and Collaborators	The entities involved in the pattern.
Consequences	The consequences of using the pattern. Investigates the forces at play in the pattern.
Implementation	How the pattern can be implemented. *Note*: Implementations are just concrete manifestations of the pattern and should not be construed as the pattern itself.
GoF Reference	Where to look in the Gang of Four text to get more information.

Consequences/Forces

The term *consequences* is used in design patterns and is often misunderstood. In everyday usage, consequences usually carries a negative connotation. (You never hear someone say, "I won the lottery! As a *consequence*, I now do not have to go to work!") Within the design pattern community, on the other hand, consequences simply refers to cause and effect. That is, if you implement this pattern in such-and-such a way, this is how it will affect and be affected by the forces present.

Why Study Design Patterns?

*Design patterns help
with reuse and
communication*

Now that you have an idea about what design patterns are, you may still be wondering, "Why study them?" There are several reasons that are obvious and some that are not so obvious.

The most commonly stated reasons for studying patterns are because patterns allow us to:

- *Reuse solutions*—By reusing already established designs, I get a head start on my problems and avoid *gotchas*. I get the benefit of learning from the experience of others. I do not have to reinvent solutions for commonly recurring problems.

- *Establish common terminology*—Communication and teamwork require a common base of vocabulary and a common viewpoint of the problem. Design patterns provide a common point of reference during the analysis and design phase of a project.

*Design patterns give
a higher perspective
on analysis and
design*

However, there is a third reason to study design patterns:

Patterns give you a higher-level perspective on the problem and on the process of design and object orientation. This frees you from the tyranny of dealing with the details too early.

By the end of this book, I hope you will agree that this is one of the greatest reasons to study design patterns. It will shift your mindset and make you a more powerful analyst.

To illustrate this advantage, I want to relate a conversation between two carpenters about how to build the drawers for some cabinets.[7]

---

7. This section is inspired by a talk given by Ralph Johnson and is adapted by the authors.

Consider two carpenters discussing how to build the drawers for some cabinets.

Example of the tyranny of details: carpenters making a set of drawers

Carpenter 1: How do you think we should build these drawers?

Carpenter 2: Well, I think we should make the joint by cutting straight down into the wood, and then cut back up 45 degrees, and then going straight back down, and then back up the other way 45 degrees, and then going straight back down, and then . . .

Now, your job is to figure out what they are talking about!

Isn't that a confusing description? What is Carpenter 2 prescribing? The details certainly get in the way! Let's try to draw out his description.

The details may confuse the solution

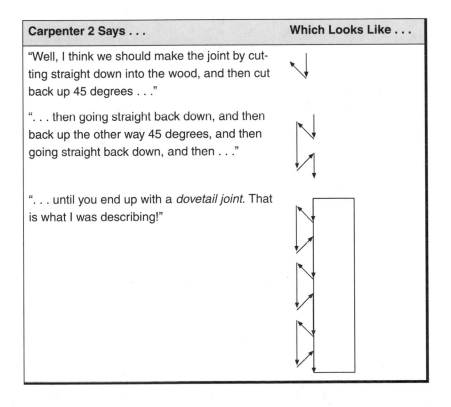

Carpenter 2 Says . . .	Which Looks Like . . .
"Well, I think we should make the joint by cutting straight down into the wood, and then cut back up 45 degrees . . ."	
". . . then going straight back down, and then back up the other way 45 degrees, and then going straight back down, and then . . ."	
". . . until you end up with a *dovetail joint*. That is what I was describing!"	

This sounds like so many code reviews: details, details, details

Doesn't this sound like code reviews you have heard? The one where the programmer describes the code in terms such as,

> And then, I use a WHILE LOOP here to do . . . followed by a series of IF statements to do . . . and here I use a SWITCH to handle . . .

You get a description of the details of the code, but you have no idea *what the program is doing and why it is doing it!*

Carpenters do not really talk at that level of detail

Of course, no self-respecting carpenter would talk like this. What would really happen is something like:

> **Carpenter 1:** Should we use a dovetail joint or a miter joint?

Already we see a qualitative difference. The carpenters are discussing differences in the quality of solutions to a problem; their discussion is at a higher level, a more abstract level. They avoid getting bogged down in the details of a particular solution.

When the carpenter speaks of a miter joint, he or she has the following characteristics of the solution in mind:

- *It is a simpler solution*—A miter joint is a simple joint to make. You cut the edges of the joining pieces at 45 degrees, abut them, and then nail or glue them together (see Figure 5-2).

- *It is lightweight*—A miter joint is weaker than a dovetail. It cannot hold together under great stress.

- *It is inconspicuous*—The miter joint's single cut is much less noticeable than the dovetail joint's multiple cuts.

Figure 5-2   A miter joint

When the carpenter speaks of a dovetail joint (which we described how to make on page 81), he or she has other characteristics of the solution in mind. These characteristics may not be obvious to a layman, but would be clearly understood by any carpenter.

- *It is a more complex solution*—It is more involved to make a dovetail joint. Thus, it is more expensive.

- *It is impervious to temperature and humidity*—As these change, the wood expands or contracts. However, the dovetail joint will remain solid.

- *It is independent of the fastening system*—In fact, dovetail joints do not even depend upon glue to work.

- *It is a more aesthetically pleasing joint*—It is beautiful to look at when made well.

In other words, the dovetail joint is a strong, dependable, beautiful joint that is complex (and therefore expensive) to make.

So, when Carpenter 1 asked,

> Should we use a dovetail joint or a miter joint?

the real question that was being asked was,

There is a meta-level conversation going on

Should we use a joint that is expensive to make but is both beautiful and durable, or should we just make a quick and dirty joint that will last at least as long until the check clears?

We might say the carpenters' discussion really occurs at two levels: the surface level of their words, and the *real* conversation, which occurs at a higher level (a *meta-level*) that is hidden from the layman and which is much richer in meaning. This higher level is the level of "carpenter patterns" and reflects the real design issues for the carpenters.

In the first case, Carpenter 2 obscures the real issues by discussing the details of the implementations of the joints. In the second case, Carpenter 1 wants to decide which joint to use based on costs and quality of the joint.

Who is more efficient? Who would you rather work with?

Patterns help us see the forest and the trees

This is one thing I mean when I say that patterns can help raise the level of your thinking. You will learn later in the book that when you raise your level of thinking like this, new design methods become available. This is where the real power of patterns lies.

Other Advantages to Studying Design Patterns

Improve team communications and individual learning

My experience with development groups working with design patterns is that design patterns helped both individual learning and team development. This occurred because the more junior team members saw that the senior developers who knew design patterns had something of value and these junior members wanted it. This provided motivation for them to learn some of these powerful concepts.

Most design patterns also make software more modifiable. The reason for this is that they are time-tested solutions. Therefore, they have evolved into structures that can handle change more readily than what often first comes to mind as a solution.

Improved modifiability of code

Design patterns, when they are taught properly, can be used to greatly increase the understanding of basic object-oriented design principles. I have seen this countless times in the introductory object-oriented courses I teach. In those classes, I start with a brief introduction to the object-oriented paradigm. I then proceed to teach design patterns, using them to illustrate the basic object-oriented concepts (encapsulation, inheritance, and polymorphism). By the end of the three-day course, although we've been talking mostly about patterns, these concepts—which were just introduced to many of the participants—feel like they are old friends.

Design patterns illustrate basic object-oriented principles

The Gang of Four suggests a few strategies for creating good object-oriented designs. In particular, they suggest the following:

Adoption of improved strategies— even when patterns aren't present

- Design to interfaces.
- Favor composition over inheritance.
- Find what varies and encapsulate it.

These strategies were employed in most of the design patterns discussed in this book. Even if you do not learn a lot of design patterns, studying a few should enable you to learn why these strategies are useful. With that understanding comes the ability to apply them to your own design problems even if you do not use design patterns directly.

Another advantage is that design patterns allow you or your team to create designs for complex problems that do not require large inheritance hierarchies. Again, even if design patterns are not used directly, avoiding large inheritance hierarchies will result in improved designs.

Learn alternatives to large inheritance hierarchies

Summary

In this chapter   In this chapter, I described what design patterns are. Christopher Alexander says "patterns are solutions to a problem in a context." They are more than a kind of template to solve one's problems. They are a way of describing the motivations by including both what we want to have happen along with the problems that are plaguing us.

I looked at reasons for studying design patterns. Such study helps to

- Reuse existing, high-quality solutions to commonly recurring problems.

- Establish common terminology to improve communications within teams.

- Shift the level of thinking to a higher perspective.

- Decide whether I have the right design, not just one that works.

- Improve individual learning and team learning.

- Improve the modifiability of code.

- Facilitate adoption of improved design alternatives, even when patterns are not used explicitly.

- Discover alternatives to large inheritance hierarchies.

CHAPTER 6

The Facade Pattern

Overview

I will start the study of design patterns with a pattern that you have probably implemented in the past but may not have had a name for: the Facade pattern.

In this chapter

In this chapter,

- I explain what the Facade pattern is and where it is used.

- I present the key features of the pattern.

- I present some variations on the Facade pattern.

- I relate the Facade pattern to the CAD/CAM problem.

Introducing the Facade Pattern

According to Gang of Four, the intent of the Facade pattern is to:

Intent: a unified, high-level interface

> "Provide a unified interface to a set of interfaces in a subsystem. Facade defines a higher-level interface that makes the subsystem easier to use." [1]

Basically, this is saying that we need a new way to interact with a system that is easier than the current way, or we need to use the system in a particular way (such as using a 3-D drawing program in a 2-D way). We can build such a method of interaction because we only need to use a subset of the system in question.

---

1. Gamma, E., Helm, R., Johnson, R., Vlissides, J., *Design Patterns: Elements of Reusable Object-Oriented Software*, Reading, Mass.: Addison-Wesley, 1995, p. 185.

Learning the Facade Pattern

A motivating example: learn how to use our complex system!

Once, I worked as a contractor for a large engineering and manufacturing company. My first day on the job, the technical lead of the project was not in. Now, this client did not want to pay me by the hour and not have anything for me to do. They wanted me to be doing something, even if it was not useful! Haven't you had days like this?

So, one of the project members found something for me to do. She said, "You are going to have to learn the CAD/CAM system we use some time, so you might as well start now. Start with these manuals over here." Then she took me to the set of documentation. I am not making this up: there were *8 feet* of manuals for me to read . . . each page 8½ × 11 inches and in small print! This was one complex system!

Figure 6-1   Eight feet of manuals = one complex system!

I want to be insulated from this

Now, if you and I and say another four or five people were on a project that needed to use this system, not all of us would have to learn the entire thing. Rather than waste everyone's time, we would probably draw straws, and the *loser* would have to write routines that the rest of us would use to interface with the system.

This person would determine how I and others on our team were going to use the system and what API would be best for our particular needs. She would then create a new class or classes that had the interface we required. Then, I and the rest of the programming community could use this new interface without having to learn the entire complicated system (see Figure 6-2).

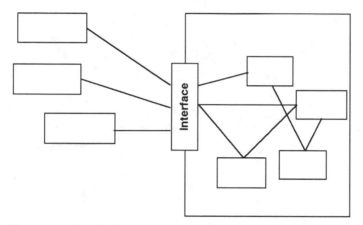

Figure 6-2 Insulating clients from the subsystem.

Now, this approach only works when using a subset of the system's capabilities or when interacting with it in a particular way. If everything in the system needs to be used, it is unlikely that I can come up with a simpler interface (unless the original designers did a poor job).

Works with subsets

This is the Facade pattern. It enables us to use a complex system more easily, either to use just a subset of the system or use the system in a particular way. We have a complicated system of which we need to use only a part. We end up with a simpler, easier-to-use system or one that is customized to our needs.

This is the Facade pattern

Most of the work still needs to be done by the underlying system. The Facade provides a collection of easier-to-understand methods. These methods use the underlying system to implement the newly defined functions.

The Facade Pattern: Key Features

Intent	You want to simplify how to use an existing system. You need to define your own interface.
Problem	You need to use only a subset of a complex system. Or you need to interact with the system in a particular way.
Solution	The Facade presents a new interface for the client of the existing system to use.
Participants and Collaborators	It presents a specialized interface to the client that makes it easier to use.
Consequences	The Facade simplifies the use of the required subsystem. However, since the Facade is not complete, certain functionality may be unavailable to the client.
Implementation	• Define a new class (or classes) that has the required interface. • Have this new class use the existing system.
GoF Reference	Pages 185–193.

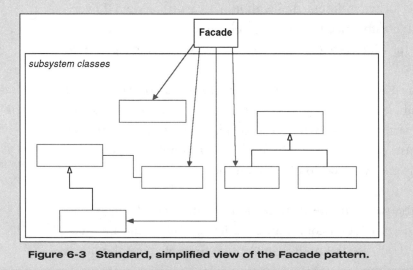

Figure 6-3 Standard, simplified view of the Facade pattern.

Field Notes: The Facade Pattern

Facades can be used not only to create a simpler interface in terms of method calls, but also to reduce the number of objects that a client object must deal with. For example, suppose I have a **Client** object that must deal with **Database**s, **Model**s, and **Element**s. The **Client** must first open the **Database** and get a **Model**. Then it queries the **Model** to get an **Element**. Finally, it asks the **Element** for information. It might be a lot easier to create a **Database-Facade** that could be queried by the **Client** (see Figure 6-4).

Variations on Facade: reduce the number of objects a client must work with

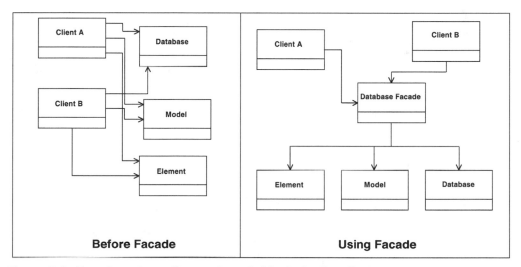

Figure 6-4   Facade reduces the number of objects for the client.

Suppose that in addition to using functions that are in the system, I also need to provide some new functionality. In this case, I am going beyond a simple subset of the system.

Variations on Facade: supplement existing functions with new routines

In this case, the methods I write for the Facade class may be supplemented by new routines for the new functionality. This is still the Facade pattern, but expanded with new functionality.

The Facade pattern sets the general approach; it got me started. The Facade part of the pattern is the fact that I am creating a new interface for the client to use instead of the existing system's interface. I can do this because the **Client** object does not need to use all of the functions in my original system.

Patterns set a general approach.

A pattern just sets the general approach. Whether or not to add new functions depends upon the situation at hand. Patterns are blueprints to get you started; they are not carved in stone.

Variations on Facade: an "encapsulating" layer

The Facade can also be used to hide, or encapsulate, the system. The Facade could contain the system as private members of the Facade class. In this case, the original system would be linked in with the Facade class, but not presented to users of the Facade class.

There are a number of reasons to encapsulate the system:

- *Track system usage*—By forcing all accesses to the system to go through the Facade, I can easily monitor system usage.

- *Swap out systems*—I may need to change out systems in the future. By making the original system a private member of the Facade class, I can switch out the system for a new one with minimal effort. There may still be a significant amount of effort required, but at least I will only have to change the code in one place (the Facade class).

Relating the Facade Pattern to the CAD/CAM Problem

Encapsulate the V1 system

Think of the example above. The Facade pattern could be useful to help **V1Slot**s, **V1Hole**s, etc., use the **V1System**. I will do just that in the solution in Chapter 12, "Solving the CAD/CAM Problem with Patterns."

Summary

The Facade pattern is so named because it puts up a new front (a *In this chapter* facade) in front of the original system.

The Facade pattern applies when

- You do not need to use all of the functionality of a complex system and can create a new class that contains all of the rules for accessing that system. If this is a subset of the original system, as it usually is, the API that you create in new class should be much simpler than the original system's API.

- You want to encapsulate or hide the original system.

- You want to use the functionality of the original system and want to add some new functionality as well.

- The cost of writing this new class is less than the cost of everybody learning how to use the original system or is less than you would spend on maintenance in the future.

CHAPTER 7

The Adapter Pattern

Overview

I will continue our study of design patterns with the Adapter pattern. The Adapter pattern is a very common pattern, and, as you will see, it is used with many other patterns.

In this chapter

In this chapter,

- I explain what the Adapter pattern is, where it is used, and how it is implemented.

- I present the key features of the pattern.

- I use the pattern to illustrate polymorphism.

- I illustrate how the UML can be used at different levels of detail.

- I present some observations on the Adapter pattern from my own practice, including a comparison of the Adapter pattern and the Facade pattern.

- I relate the Adapter pattern to the CAD/CAM problem.

Note: I will only show Java code examples in the main body of this chapter. The equivalent C++ code examples can be found at the end of this chapter.

Introducing the Adapter Pattern

Intent: create a new interface

According to the Gang of Four, the intent of the Adapter pattern is to

> Convert the interface of a class into another interface that the clients expect. Adapter lets classes work together that could not otherwise because of incompatible interfaces.[1]

Basically, this is saying that we need a way to create a new interface for an object that does the right stuff but has the wrong interface.

Learning the Adapter Pattern

A motivating example: free the client object from knowing details

The easiest way to understand the intent of the Adapter pattern is to look at an example of where it is useful. Let's say I have been given the following requirements:

- Create classes for points, lines, and squares that have the behavior "display."
- The client objects should not have to know whether they actually have a point, a line, or a square. They just want to know that they have one of these shapes.

In other words, I want to encompass these specific shapes in a higher-level concept that I will call a "displayable shape."

Now, as I work through this simple example, try to imagine other situations that you have run into that are similar, such as

- You have wanted to use a subroutine or a method that someone else has written because it performs some function that you need.

---

1. Gamma, E., Helm, R., Johnson, R., Vlissides, J., *Design Patterns: Elements of Reusable Object-Oriented Software*, Reading, Mass.: Addison-Wesley, 1995, p. 185.

- You cannot incorporate the routine directly into your program.

- The interface or the way of calling the code is not exactly equivalent to the way that its related objects need to use it.

In other words, although the system will *have* points, lines, and squares, I want the client objects to *think* I have only *shapes.*

. . . so that it can treat details in a common way

- This allows the client objects to deal with all these objects in the same way—freed from having to pay attention to their differences.

- It also enables me to add different kinds of shapes in the future without having to change the clients (see Figure 7-1).

What we have
(points, lines, squares)

What the client sees
(shapes)

Figure 7-1   The objects we have . . . should all look just like "shapes."

I will make use of polymorphism; that is, I will have different objects in my system, but I want the clients of these objects to interact with them in a common way.

How to do this: use derived classes polymorphically

In this case, the client object will simply tell a point, line, or square to do something such as display itself or undisplay itself. Each point, line, and square is then responsible for knowing the way to carry out the behavior that is appropriate to its type.

To accomplish this, I will create a **Shape** class and then derive from it the classes that represent points, lines, and squares (see Figure 7-2).

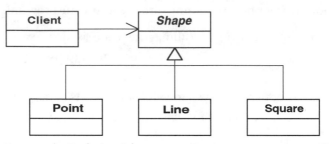

Figure 7-2 Points, Lines, and Squares are types of Shape.[2]

How to do this: define the interface and then implement in derived classes

First, I must specify the particular behavior that **Shape**s are going to provide. To accomplish this, I define an interface in the **Shape** class for the behavior and then implement the behavior appropriately in each of the derived classes.

The behaviors that a **Shape** needs to have are:

- Set a **Shape**'s location.
- Get a **Shape**'s location.
- Display a **Shape**.
- Fill a **Shape**.
- Set the color of a **Shape**.
- Undisplay a **Shape**.

I show these in Figure 7-3.

Now, add a new shape

Suppose I am now asked to implement a circle, a new kind of **Shape** (remember, requirements always change!). To do this, I will want to create a new class—**Circle**—that implements the shape "circle" and derive it from the **Shape** class so that I can still get polymorphic behavior.

---

2. This and all other class diagrams in this book use the Unified Modeling Language (UML) notation. See Chapter 2, "The UML—The Unified Modeling Language," for a description of UML notation.

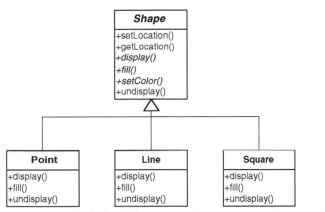

Figure 7-3 Points, Lines, and Squares showing methods.

Now, I am faced with the task of having to write the *display*, *fill* and *undisplay* methods for **Circle**. That could be a pain.

... but use behavior from outside ‑

Fortunately, as I scout around for an alternative (as a good coder always should), I discover that Jill down the hall has already written a class she called **XXCircle** that deals with circles already (see Figure 7-4). Unfortunately, she didn't ask me what she should name the methods (and I did not ask her!). She named the methods

- *displayIt*
- *fillIt*
- *undisplayIt*

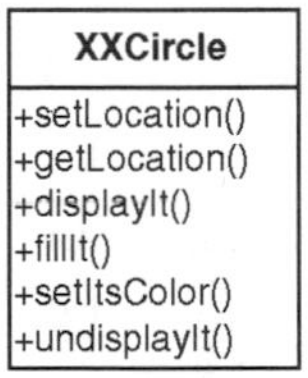

Figure 7-4 Jill's XXCircle class.

I cannot use
XXCircle directly

I cannot use **XXCircle** directly because I want to preserve poly-morphic behavior with **Shape**. There are two reasons for this:

- *I have different names and parameter lists*—The method names and parameter lists are different from **Shape**'s method names and parameter lists.

- *I cannot derive it*—Not only must the names be the same, but the class must be derived from **Shape** as well.

It is unlikely that Jill will be willing to let me change the names of her methods or derive **XXCircle** from **Shape**. To do so would require her to modify all of the other objects that are currently using **XXCircle**. Plus, I would still be concerned about creating unanticipated side effects when I modify someone else's code.

I have what I want almost within reach, but I cannot use it and I do not want to rewrite it. What can I do?

Rather than change
it, I adapt it

I can make a new class that *does* derive from **Shape** and therefore implements **Shape**'s interface but avoids rewriting the circle imple-mentation in **XXCircle** (see Figure 7-5).

- Class **Circle** derives from **Shape**.
- **Circle** contains **XXCircle**.
- **Circle** passes requests made to the **Circle** object on through to the **XXCircle** object.

How to implement

The diamond at the end of the line between **Circle** and **XXCircle** in Figure 7-5 indicates that **Circle** contains an **XXCircle**. When a **Circle** object is instantiated, it must instantiate a corresponding **XXCircle** object. Anything the **Circle** object is told to do will get passed on to the **XXCircle** object. If this is done consistently, and if the **XXCircle** object has the complete functionality the **Circle** object needs (I will discuss shortly what happens if this is not the case), the **Circle** object will be able to manifest its behavior by let-ting the **XXCircle** object do the job.

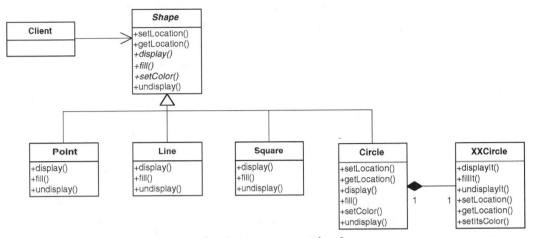

Figure 7-5 The Adapter pattern: `Circle` "wraps" `XXCircle`.

An example of wrapping is shown in Example 7-1.

Example 7-1   Java Code Fragments: Implementing the Adapter Pattern

```
class Circle extends Shape {
   ...
   private XXCircle pxc;
   ...
   public Circle () {
     pxc= new XXCircle();
   }

   void public display() {
      pxc.displayIt();
   }
}
```

Using the Adapter pattern allowed me to continue using polymorphism with **Shape**. In other words, the client objects of **Shape** do not know what types of shapes are actually present. This is also an example of our new thinking of encapsulation as well—the class **Shape** encapsulates the specific shapes present. The Adapter pattern is most commonly used to allow for polymorphism. As we shall see in later chapters, it is often used to allow for polymorphism required by other design patterns.

What we accomplished

The Adapter Pattern: Key Features

Intent	Match an existing object beyond your control to a particular interface.
Problem	A system has the right data and behavior but the wrong interface. Typically used when you have to make something a derivative of an abstract class we are defining or already have.
Solution	The Adapter provides a wrapper with the desired interface.
Participants and Collaborators	The **Adapter** adapts the interface of an **Adaptee** to match that of the **Adapter**'s **Target** (the class it derives from). This allows the **Client** to use the **Adaptee** as if it were a type of **Target**.
Consequences	The Adapter pattern allows for preexisting objects to fit into new class structures without being limited by their interfaces.
Implementation	Contain the existing class in another class. Have the containing class match the required interface and call the methods of the contained class.
GoF Reference	Pages 139–150.

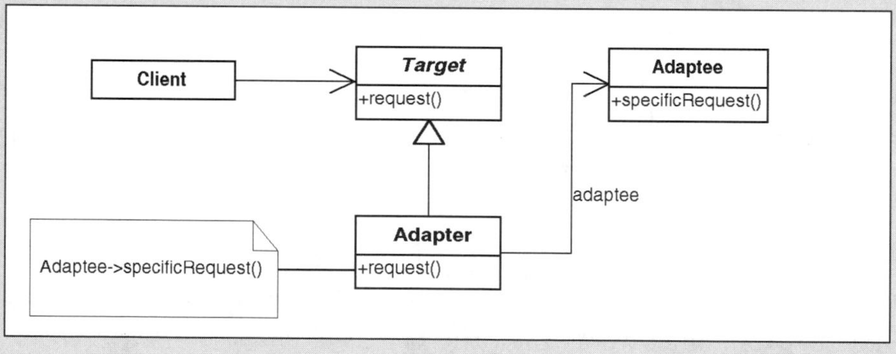

Figure 7-6 Standard, simplified view of the Adapter pattern.

Field Notes: The Adapter Pattern

Often, I will be in a situation similar to the one above, but the object being adapted does not do all the things I need.

You can do more than wrapping

In this case, I can still use the Adapter pattern, but it is not such a perfect fit. In this case,

- Those functions that are implemented in the existing class can be adapted.

- Those functions that are not present can be implemented in the wrapping object.

This does not give me quite the same benefit, but at least I do not have to implement all of the required functionality.

The Adapter pattern frees me from worrying about the interfaces of existing classes when I am doing a design. If I have a class that does what I need, at least conceptually, then I know that I can always use the Adapter pattern to give it the correct interface.

Adapter frees you from worrying about existing interfaces

This will become more important as you learn a few more patterns. Many patterns require certain classes to derive from the same class. If there are preexisting classes, the Adapter pattern can be used to adapt it to the appropriate abstract class (as **Circle** adapted **XXCircle** to **Shape**).

There are actually two types of Adapter patterns:

Variations: Object Adapter, Class Adapter

- *Object Adapter pattern*—The Adapter pattern I have been using is called an Object Adapter because it relies on one object (the adapting object) containing another (the adapted object).

- *Class Adapter pattern*—Another way to implement the Adapter pattern is with multiple inheritance. In this case, it is called a Class Adapter pattern.

The decision of which Adapter pattern to use is based on the different forces at work in the problem domain. At a conceptual level, I may ignore the distinction; however, when it comes time to implement it, I need to consider more of the forces involved.[3]

Comparing the Adapter with the Facade

In my classes on design patterns, someone almost always states that it sounds as if both the Adapter pattern and the Facade pattern are the same. In both cases there is a preexisting class (or classes) that does not have the interface that is needed. In both cases, I create a new object that has the desired interface (see Figure 7-7).

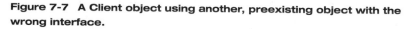

which pattern?

Figure 7-7 A Client object using another, preexisting object with the wrong interface.

Both are wrappers

Wrappers and object wrappers are terms that you hear a lot about. It is popular to think about wrapping legacy systems with objects to make them easier to use.

At this high view, the Facade and the Adapter patterns do seem similar. They are both wrappers. But they are different kinds of wrappers. You need to understand the differences, which can be subtle. Finding and understanding these more subtle differences gives insight into a pattern's properties. Let's look at some different forces involved with these patterns (see Table 7-1).

---

3. For help in deciding between Object Adapter and Class Adapter, see pages 142–144 in the Gang of Four book.

Table 7-1   Comparing the Facade Pattern with the Adapter Pattern

	Facade	Adapter
Are there preexisting classes?	Yes	Yes
Is there an interface we must design to?	No	Yes
Does an object need to behave polymorphically?	No	Probably
Is a simpler interface needed?	Yes	No

Table 7-1 tells us the following:

- In both the Facade and Adapter pattern I have preexisting classes.

- In the Facade, however, I do not have an interface I must design to, as I do in the Adapter pattern.

- I am not interested in polymorphic behavior in the Facade, while in the Adapter, I probably am. (There are times when we just need to design to a particular API and therefore must use an Adapter. In this case, polymorphism may not be an issue— that's why I say "probably").

- In the case of the Facade pattern, the motivation is to simplify the interface. With the Adapter, while simpler is better, I am trying to design to an existing interface and cannot simplify things even if a simpler interface were otherwise possible.

Sometimes people draw the conclusion that another difference between the Facade and the Adapter pattern is that the Facade hides multiple classes behind it while the Adapter only hides one. While this is often true, it is not part of the pattern. It is possible that a Facade could be used in front of a very complex object while an Adapter wrapped several small objects that between them implemented the desired function.

Not all differences are part of the pattern

Bottom line: A Facade *simplifies* an interface while an Adapter *converts* the interface into a preexisting interface.

Relating the Adapter Pattern to the CAD/CAM Problem

Adapter lets me communicate with OOGFeature

In the CAD/CAM problem (Chapter 3, "A Problem That Cries Out for Flexible Code"), the features in the V2 model will be represented by **OOGFeature** objects. Unfortunately, these objects do not have the correct interface (from my perspective) because I did not design them. I cannot make them derive from the **Feature** classes, yet, when I use the V2 system, they would do our job perfectly.

In this case, the option of writing new classes to implement this function is not even present—I must communicate with the **OOGFeature** objects. The easiest way to do this is with the Adapter pattern.

Summary

In this chapter

The Adapter pattern is a very useful pattern that converts the interface of a class (or classes) into another interface, which we need the class to have. It is implemented by creating a new class with the desired interface and then wrapping the original class methods to effectively contain the adapted object.

Supplement: C++ Code Example

Example 7-2   C++ Code Fragments: Implementing the Adapter Pattern

```cpp
class Circle : public Shape {
   .  .  .
  private:
    XXCircle *pxc;
   .  .  .
}
Circle::Circle () {
   .  .  .
   pxc= new XXCircle;
}
void Circle::display () {
   pxc->displayIt();
}
```

CHAPTER 8

Expanding Our Horizons

Overview

In previous chapters, I discussed three fundamental concepts of object-oriented design: objects, encapsulation, and abstract classes. How a designer views these concepts is important. The traditional ways are simply too limiting. In this chapter I step back and reflect on topics discussed earlier in the book. My intent is to describe a new way of seeing object-oriented design, which comes from the perspective that design patterns create.

In this chapter

In this chapter,

- I compare and contrast the traditional way of looking at objects—as a bundle of data and methods—with the new way—as things with responsibilities.

- I compare and contrast the traditional way of looking at encapsulation—as hiding data—with the new way—as the ability to hide anything. Especially important is to see that encapsulation can be used to contain variation in behavior.

- I compare and contrast the traditional way of using inheritance—for specialization and reuse—with the new way—as a method of classifying objects.

- The new viewpoints allow for containing variation of behaviors in objects.

- I show how the conceptual, specification, and implementation perspectives relate to an abstract class and its derived classes.

Acknowledgment

Perhaps this new perspective is not all that original. I believe that this perspective is one that many developers of the design patterns held when they developed what ended up being called a pattern. Certainly, it is a perspective that is consistent with the writings of Christopher Alexander, Jim Coplien, and the Gang of Four.

While it may not be original, it has also not been expressed in quite the way I do in this chapter and in this book. I have had to distill this way of looking at patterns from the way design patterns behave and how they have been described by others.

When I call it a new perspective, what I mean is that it is most likely a new way for most developers to view object orientation. It was certainly new to me when I was learning design patterns for the first time.

Objects: the Traditional View and the New View

The traditional view: data with methods

The traditional view of objects is that they are data with methods. One of my teachers called them "smart data." It is just a step up from a database. This view comes from looking at objects from an implementation perspective.

The new view: things with responsibilities

While this definition is accurate, as explained in Chapter 1, "The Object-Oriented Paradigm," it is based on the implementation perspective. A more useful definition is one based on the conceptual perspective—an object is an entity that has responsibilities. These responsibilities give the object its behavior. Sometimes, I also think of an object as an entity that has specific behavior.

This is a better definition because it helps to focus on what the objects are supposed to *do*, not simply on how to implement them. This enables me to build the software in two steps:

1. Make a preliminary design without worrying about all of the details involved.

2. Implement the design achieved.

Ultimately, this perspective allows for better object selection and definition (in a sense, the main point of design anyway). Object definition is more flexible; by focusing on what an object does, inheritance allows us to use different, specific behaviors when needed. A focus on implementation may achieve this, but flexibility typically comes at a higher price.

It is easier to think in terms of responsibilities because that helps to define the object's public interface. If an object has a responsibility, there must be some way to ask it to perform its responsibility. However, it does not imply anything about what is *inside* the object. The information for which the object is responsible may not even be inside the object itself.

For example, suppose I have a **Shape** object and its responsibilities are

- To know where it is located
- To be able to draw itself on a display
- To be able to remove itself from a display

These responsibilities imply that a particular set of method calls must exist:

- `getLocation( ... )`
- `drawShape( ... )`
- `unDrawShape( ... )`

There is no implication about what is inside of **Shape**. I only care that **Shape** is responsible for its own behaviors. It may have attributes inside it or it may have methods that calculate or even refer to other objects. Thus, **Shape** might contain attributes about its location or it might refer to another database object to get its location. This gives you the flexibility you need to meet your modeling objectives.

Interestingly, you will find that focusing on motivation rather than on implementation is a recurring theme in design patterns.

Look at objects this way. Make it your basic viewpoint for objects. If you do, you will have superior designs.

Encapsulation: the Traditional View and the New View

My object-oriented umbrella

In my classes on pattern-oriented design, I often ask my students, "Who has heard encapsulation defined as 'data hiding'?" Almost everyone raises his or her hand.

Then I proceed to tell a story about my umbrella. Keep in mind that I live in Seattle, which has a reputation for being wetter than it is, but is still a pretty wet place in the fall, winter, and spring. Here, umbrellas and hooded coats are personal friends!

Let me tell you about my great umbrella. It is large enough to get into! In fact, three or four other people can get in it with me. While we are in it, staying out of the rain, I can move it from one place to another. It has a stereo system to keep me entertained while I stay dry. Amazingly enough, it can also condition the air to make it warmer or colder. It is one cool umbrella.

My umbrella is convenient. It sits there waiting for me. It has wheels on it so that I do not have to carry it around. I don't even have to push it because it can propel itself. Sometimes, I will open the top of my umbrella to let in the sun. (Why I am using my umbrella when it is sunny outside is beyond me!)

In Seattle, there are hundreds of thousands of these umbrellas in all kinds of colors.

Most people call them *cars*.

But I think of mine as an umbrella because an umbrella is something you use to keep out of the rain. Many times, while I am waiting outside for someone to meet me, I sit in my "umbrella" to stay dry!

Of course, a car isn't really an umbrella. Yes, you can use it to say out of the rain, but that is too limited a view of a car. In the same way, encapsulation isn't just for hiding data. That is too limited a view of encapsulation. To think of it that way constrains my mind when I design.

Definitions can be limitations

Encapsulation should be thought of as "any kind of hiding." In other words, it *can* hide data. But it can also hide implementations, derived classes, or any number of things. Consider the diagram shown in Figure 8-1. You might recollect this diagram from Chapter 7, "The Adapter Pattern."

How to think about encapsulation

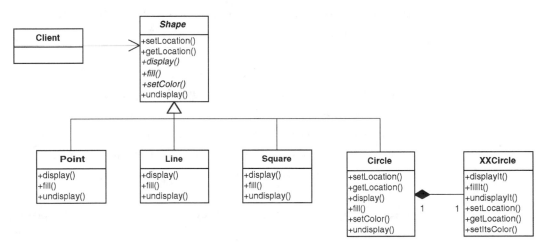

Figure 8-1 Adapting XXCircle with Circle.

Multiple levels of encapsulation

Figure 8-1 shows many kinds of encapsulation:

- *Encapsulation of data*—The data in **Point**, **Line**, **Square**, and **Circle** are hidden from everything else.

- *Encapsulation of methods*—For example, **Circle**'s setLocation.

- *Encapsulation of subclasses*—Clients of **Shape** do not see **Point**s, **Line**s, **Square**s, or **Circle**s.

- *Encapsulation of other objects*—Nothing but **Circle** is aware of **xxCircle**.

One type of encapsulation is thus achieved when there is an abstract class that behaves polymorphically without the client of the abstract class knowing what kind of derived class actually is present. Furthermore, adapting interfaces hides what is behind the adapting object.

The advantage of this new definition

The advantage of looking at encapsulation this way is that it gives me a better way to split up (decompose) my programs. The encapsulating layers become the interfaces I design to. By encapsulating different kinds of **Shape**s, I can add new ones without changing any of the client programs using them. By encapsulating **XXCircle** behind **Circle**, I can change this implementation in the future if I choose to or need to.

Inheritance as a concept versus inheritance for reuse

When the object-oriented paradigm was first presented, reuse of classes was touted as being one of its big benefits. This reuse was usually achieved by creating classes and then deriving new classes based on these base classes. Hence the term *specialized* classes for those subclasses that were derived from other classes (which were called *generalized* classes).

I am not arguing with the accuracy of this, rather I am proposing what I believe to be a more powerful way of using inheritance. In the example above, I can do my design based on different special types of **Shape**s (that is, **Point**s, **Line**s, **Square**s and **Circle**s). However, this will probably not have me hide these special cases when I think about using **Shape**s—I will probably take advantage of the knowledge of these concrete classes.

If, however, I think about **Shape**s as a way of classifying **Point**s, **Line**s, **Square**s and **Circle**s, I can more easily think about them as a whole. This will make it more likely I will design to an interface (**Shape**s). It also means if I get a new **Shape**, I will be less likely to have designed myself into a difficult maintenance position (because no client object knows what kind of **Shape** it is dealing with anyway).

Find What Is Varying and Encapsulate It

In *Design Patterns: Elements of Reusable Object-Oriented Software*, the Gang of Four suggests the following:

Using inheritance this way in design patterns

> *Consider what should be variable in your design.* This approach is the opposite of focusing on the cause of redesign. Instead of considering what might *force* a change to a design, consider what you want to be *able* to change without redesign. The focus here is on *encapsulating the concept that varies,* a theme of many design patterns.[1]

Or, as I like to rephrase it, "Find what varies and encapsulate it."

These statements seem odd if you only think about encapsulation as data-hiding. They are much more sensible when you think of encapsulation as hiding classes using abstract classes. Using composition of a reference to an abstract class hides the variations.

---

1. Gamma, E., Helm, R., Johnson, R., Vlissides, J., *Design Patterns: Elements of Reusable Object-Oriented Software*, Reading, Mass.: Addison-Wesley, 1995, p. 29.

In effect, many design patterns use encapsulation to create layers between objects—enabling the designer to change things on different sides of the layers without adversely affecting the other side. This promotes loose-coupling between the sides.

This way of thinking is very important in the Bridge pattern, which will be discussed in Chapter 9, "The Bridge Pattern." However, before proceeding, I want to show a bias in design that many developers have.

Containing variation in data versus containing variation in behavior

Suppose I am working on a project that models different characteristics of animals. My requirements are the following:

- Each type of animal can have a different number of legs.
  - Animal objects must be able to remember and retrieve this information.
- Each type of animal can have a different type of movement.
  - Animal objects must be able to return how long it will take to move from one place to another given a specified type of terrain.

A typical approach of handling the variation in the number of legs would be to have a data member containing this value and having methods to set and get it. However, one typically takes a different approach to handling variation in behavior.

Suppose there are two different methods for moving: walking and flying. These requirements need two different pieces of code: one to handle walking and one to handle flying; a simple variable won't work. Given that I have two different methods, I seem to be faced with a choice of approach:

- Having a data member that tells me what type of movement my object has.

- Having two different types of **Animal**s (both derived from the base **Animal** class)—one for walking and one for flying.

Unfortunately, both of these approaches have problems:

- *Tight coupling*—The first approach (using a flag with presumably a switch based on it) may lead to tight coupling if the flag starts implying other differences. In any event, the code will likely be rather messy.

- *Too many details*—The second approach requires that I also manage the subtype of **Animal**. And I cannot handle **Animal**s that can both walk and fly.

A third possibility exists: have the **Animal** class contain an object that has the appropriate movement behavior. I show this in Figure 8-2.

Handling variation in behavior with objects

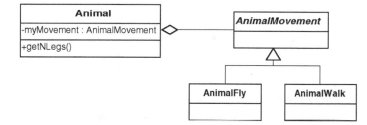

Figure 8-2 Animal containing AnimalMovement object.

This may seem like overkill at first. However, it's nothing more than an **Animal** containing an object that contains the movement behavior of the **Animal**. This is very analogous to having a member containing the number of legs—in which case an intrinsic type object is containing the number of legs. I suspect these appear more different in concept than they really are, because Figures 8-2 and 8-3 appear to be different.

Overkill?

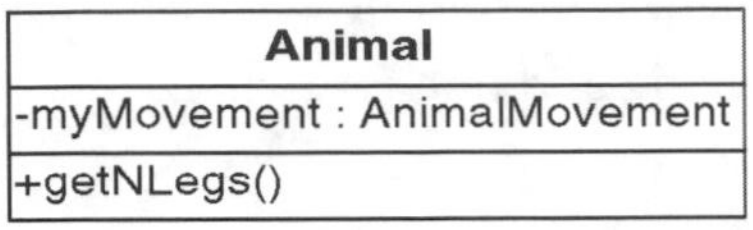

Animal
-myMovement : AnimalMovement
+getNLegs()

Figure 8-3 Showing containment as a member.

Comparing the two Many developers tend to think that one object containing another object is inherently different from an object having a mere data member. But data members that appear not to be objects (integers and doubles, for example) really are. In object-oriented programming, *everything* is an object, even these intrinsic data types, whose behavior is arithmetic.

Using objects to contain variation in attributes and using objects to contain variation in behavior are very similar; this can be most easily shown through an example. Let's say I am writing a point-of-sale system. In this system, there is a sales receipt. On this sales receipt there is a total. I could start out by making this total be a type **double**. However, if I am dealing with an international application, I quickly realize I need to handle monetary conversions, and so forth. I might therefore make a **Money** class that contains an amount and a currency. Total can now be of type **Money**.

Using the **Money** class this way appears to be using an object just to contain more data. However, when I need to convert **Money** from one currency to the next, it is the **Money** object itself that should do the conversion, because objects should be responsible for themselves. At first it may appear that this conversion can be done by simply having another data member that specifies what the conversion factor is.

However, it may be more complicated than this. For example, perhaps I need to be able to convert currency based on past dates. In that case, if I add behaviors to the **Money** or **Currency** classes I am essentially adding different behaviors to the **SalesReceipt** as well, based upon which **Money** objects (and therefore which **Currency** objects) it contains.

I will demonstrate this strategy of using contained objects to perform required behavior in the next few design patterns.

Commonality/Variability and Abstract Classes

Consider Figure 8-4. It shows the relationship between

Object-oriented design captures all three perspectives

- Commonality/variability analysis

- The conceptual, specification, and implementation perspectives

- An abstract class, its interface, and its derived classes

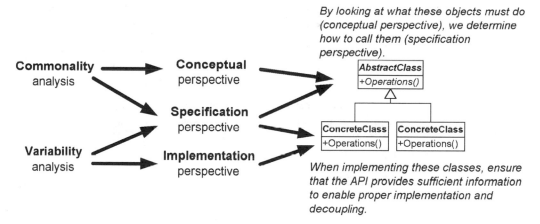

Figure 8-4 The relationship between commonality/variability analysis, perspectives, and abstract classes.

As you can see in Figure 8-4, commonality analysis relates to the conceptual view of the problem domain and variability analysis relates to the implementation, that is, to specific cases.

*Now, specification
gives a better under-
standing of abstract
classes*

The specification perspective lies in the middle. Both commonality and variability are involved in this perspective. The specification describes how to communicate with a set of objects that are conceptually similar. Each of these objects represents a variation of the common concept. This specification becomes an abstract class or an interface at the implementation level.

In the new perspective of object-oriented design, I can now say the following:

Mapping with Abstract Classes	Discussion
Abstract class → the central binding concept	An abstract class represents the core concept that binds together all of the derivatives of the class. This core concept is what defines the commonality.
Commonality → which abstract classes to use	The commonalities define the abstract classes I need to use.
Variations → derivation of an abstract class	The variations identified *within* that commonality become derivations of the abstract classes.
Specification → interface for abstract class	The interface for these classes corresponds to the specification level.

This simplifies the design process of the classes into a two-step procedure:

When Defining . . .	You Must Ask Yourself. . .
An abstract class (commonality)	What *interface* is needed to handle all of the *responsibilities* of this class?
Derived classes	Given this particular implementation (this variation), how can I implement it with the given specification?

The relationship between the specification perspective and the conceptual perspective is this: *It identifies the interface I need to use to handle all of the cases of this concept (that is, the commonality).*

The relationship between the specification perspective and the implementation perspective is this: *Given this specification, how can I implement this particular case (this variation)?*

Summary

The traditional way of thinking about objects, encapsulation, and inheritance is very limiting. Encapsulation exists for so much more than simply hiding data. By expanding the definition to include any kind of hiding, I can use encapsulation to create layers between objects—enabling me to change things on one side of a layer without adversely affecting the other side.

In this chapter

Inheritance is better used as a method of consistently dealing with different concrete classes that are conceptually the same rather than as a means of specialization.

The concept of using objects to hold variations in behavior is not unlike the practice of using data members to hold variations in data. Both allow for the encapsulation (and therefore extension) of the data/behavior being contained.

CHAPTER 9

The Bridge Pattern

Overview

I will continue our study of design patterns with the Bridge pattern. The Bridge pattern is quite a bit more complex than the other patterns you just learned; it is also much more useful.

In this chapter

In this chapter,

- I derive the Bridge pattern by working through an example. I will go into great detail to help you learn this pattern.
- I present the key features of the pattern.
- I present some observations on the Bridge pattern from my own practice.

Introducing the Bridge Pattern

According to the Gang of Four, the intent of the Bridge pattern is to "De-couple an abstraction from its implementation so that the two can vary independently."[1]

Intent: decouple abstraction from implementation

I remember exactly what my first thoughts were when I read this:

This is hard to understand

>   Huh?

---

1. Gamma, E., Helm, R., Johnson, R., Vlissides, J., *Design Patterns: Elements of Reusable Object-Oriented Software*, Reading, Mass.: Addison-Wesley, 1995, p. 151.

And then,

> *How come I understand every word in this sentence but I have*
> *no idea what it means?!*

I knew that

- *De-couple* means to have things behave independently from each other or at least explicitly state what the relationship is, and

- *Abstraction* is how different things are related to each other conceptually.

And I thought that *implementations* were the way to build the abstractions; but I was confused about how I was supposed to separate abstractions from the specific ways that implemented them.

It turns out that much of my confusion was due to misunderstanding what implementations meant. *Implementations* here means the objects that the abstract class and its derivations use to implement themselves with (not the derivations of the abstract class, which are called concrete classes). But to be honest, even if I had understood it properly, I am not sure how much it would have helped. The concept expressed in this sentence is just hard to understand at first.

If you are also confused about the Bridge pattern at this point, that is okay. If you understand the stated intent, then you are that much ahead.

It is a challenging pattern to learn because it is so powerful

The Bridge pattern is one of the toughest patterns to understand in part because it is so powerful and applies to so many situations. Also, it goes against a common tendency to handle special cases with inheritance. However, it is also an excellent example of following two of the mandates of the design pattern community: "find what varies and encapsulate it" and "favor object composition over class inheritance" (as you will see).

Learning the Bridge Pattern: An Example

To learn the thinking behind the Bridge pattern and what it is trying to do, I will work through an example from scratch. Starting with requirements, I will derive the pattern and then see how to apply it.

Learn why it exists, then derive the pattern

Perhaps this example will seem basic. But look at the concepts discussed in this example and then try to think of situations that you have encountered that are similar, having

- Variations in abstractions of a concept, and

- Variations in how these concepts are implemented.

You will see that this example has many similarities to the CAD/CAM problem discussed earlier. But rather than give you all the requirements up front, I am going to give them a little at a time, just as they were given to me. You can't always see the variations at the beginning of the problem.

Bottom line: During requirements definition, explore for variations early and often!

Suppose I have been given the task of writing a program that will draw rectangles with either of two drawing programs. I have been told that when I instantiate a rectangle, I will know whether I should use drawing program 1 (**DP1**) or drawing program 2 (**DP2**).

Start with a simple problem: drawing shapes

The rectangles are defined as two pairs of points, as represented in Figure 9-1. The differences between the drawing programs are summarized in Table 9-1.

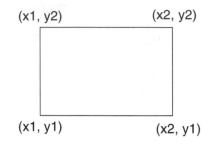

(x1, y2)   (x2, y2)

(x1, y1)   (x2, y1)

Figure 9-1   Positioning the rectangle.

Table 9-1   Different Drawing Programs

	DP1	DP2
Used to draw a line	`draw_a_line( x1, y1, x2, y2)`	`drawline( x1, x2, y1, y2)`
Used to draw a circle	`draw_a_circle( x, y, r)`	`drawcircle( x, y, r)`

Proper use of inheritance

My customer told me that the collection (the client of the rectangles) does not want to worry about what type of drawing program it should use. It occurs to me that since the rectangles are told what drawing program to use when instantiated, I can have two different kinds of rectangle objects: one that uses **DP1** and one that uses **DP2**. Each would have a draw method but would implement it differently. I show this in Figure 9-2.

A note on the implementation

By having an abstract class **Rectangle**, I take advantage of the fact that the only difference between the different types of **Rectangle**s are how they implement the *drawLine* method. The **V1Rectangle** is implemented by having a reference to a **DP1** object and using that object's *draw_a_line* method. The **V2Rectangle** is implemented by having a reference to a **DP2** object and using that object's *drawline* method. However, by instantiating the right type of **Rectangle**, I no longer have to worry about this difference.

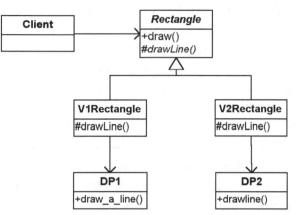

Figure 9-2 Design for rectangles and drawing programs (DP1 and DP2).

Example 9-1 Java Code Fragments

```
class Rectangle {
  public void draw () {
    drawLine(_x1,_y1,_x2,_y1);
    drawLine(_x2,_y1,_x2,_y2);
    drawLine(_x2,_y2,_x1,_y2);
    drawLine(_x1,_y2,_x1,_y1);
  }
  abstract protected void
    drawLine ( double x1, double y1,
               double x2, double y2);
}

class V1Rectangle extends Rectangle {
  drawLine( double x1, double y1,
            double x2, double y2) {
    DP1.draw_a_line( x1,y1,x2,y2);
  }
}
class V2Rectangle extends Rectangle {
  drawLine( double x1, double y1,
            double x2, double y2) {
    // arguments are different in DP2
    // and must be rearranged
    DP2.drawline( x1,x2,y1,y2);
  }
}
```

But, though requirements always change

Now, suppose that after completing this code, one of the *inevitable three* (death, taxes, and changing requirements) comes my way. I am asked to support another kind of shape—this time, a circle. However, I am also given the mandate that the collection object does not want to know the difference between **Rectangle**s and **Circle**s.

. . . I can still have a simple implementation

It occurs to me that I can simply extend the approach I've already started by adding another level to my class hierarchy. I only need to add a new class, called **Shape**, from which I will derive the **Rectangle** and **Circle** classes. This way, the **Client** object can just refer to **Shape** objects without worrying about what kind of **Shape** it has been given.

Designing with inheritance

As a beginning object-oriented analyst, it might seem natural to implement these requirements using only inheritance. For example, I could start out with something like Figure 9-2, and then, for each kind of **Shape**, implement the shape with each drawing program, deriving a version of **DP1** and a version of **DP2** for **Rectangle** and deriving a version of **DP1** and a version of **DP2** one for **Circle**. I would end up with Figure 9-3.

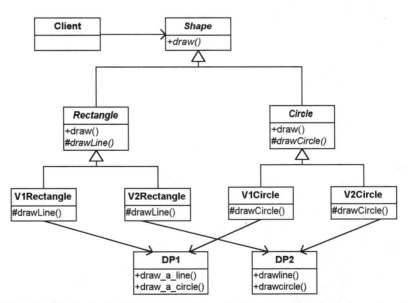

Figure 9-3 A straightforward approach: implementing two shapes and two drawing programs.

I implement the **Circle** class the same way that I implemented the **Rectangle** class. However, this time, I implement *draw* by using *drawCircle* instead of *drawLine*.

Example 9-2   Java Code Fragments

```
abstract class Shape {
  abstract public void draw ();
}
abstract class Rectangle extends Shape {
  public void draw () {
    drawLine(_x1,_y1,_x2,_y1);
    drawLine(_x2,_y1,_x2,_y2);
    drawLine(_x2,_y2,_x1,_y2);
    drawLine(_x1,_y2,_x1,_y1);
  }
  abstract protected void
    drawLine(
      double x1, double y1,
      double x2, double y2);
}
class V1Rectangle extends Rectangle {
  protected void drawLine (
    double x1, double y1,
    double x2, double y2) {
      DP1.draw_a_line( x1,y1,x2,y2);
  }
}
class V2Rectangle extends Rectangle {
  protected void drawLine (
    double x1, double x2,
    double y1, double y2) {
    DP2.drawline( x1,x2,y1,y2);
  }
}
abstract class Circle extends Shape {
  public void draw () {
    drawCircle( x,y,r);
  }
  abstract protected void
    drawCircle (
      double x, double y, double r);
}
```

(continued)

Example 9-2   Java Code Fragments *(continued)*

```
class V1Circle extends Circle {
  protected void drawCircle() {
    DP1.draw_a_circle( x,y,r);
  }
}
class V2Circle extends Circle {
  protected void drawCircle() {
    DP2.drawcircle( x,y,r);
  }
}
```

Understanding the design

To understand this design, let's walk through an example. Consider what the *draw* method of a **V1Rectangle** does.

- **Rectangle**'s *draw* method is the same as before (calling *drawLine* four times as needed).

- *drawLine* is implemented by calling **DP1**'s *draw_a_line*.

In action, this looks like Figure 9-4.

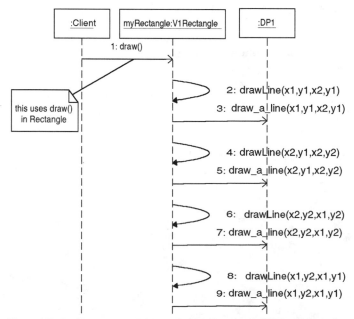

Figure 9-4 Sequence Diagram when have a V1Rectangle.

Reading a Sequence Diagram.

As I discussed in Chapter 2, "The UML—The Unified Modeling Language," the diagram in Figure 9-4 is a special kind of interaction diagram called a *Sequence Diagram*. It is a common diagram in the UML. Its purpose is to show the interaction of objects in the system.

- Each box at the top represents an object. It may be named or not.

- If an object has a name, it is given to the left of the colon.

- The class to which the object belongs is shown to the right of the colon. Thus, the middle object is named **myRectangle** and is an instance of **V1Rectangle**.

You read the diagram from the top down. Each numbered statement is a message sent from one object to either itself or to another object.

- The sequence starts out with the unnamed **Client** object calling the *draw* method of **myRectangle**.

- This method calls its own *drawLine* method four times (shown in steps 2, 4, 6, and 8). Note the arrow pointing back to the **myRectangle** in the timeline.

- *drawLine* calls **DP1**'s *draw_a_line*. This is shown in steps 3, 5, 7 and 9.

Even though the Class Diagram makes it look like there are many objects, in reality, I am only dealing with three objects (see Figure 9-5):

- The client using the rectangle

- The **V1Rectangle** object

- The **DP1** drawing program

When the client object sends a message to the **V1Rectangle** object (called **myRectangle**) to perform *draw*, it calls **Rectangle**'s *draw* method resulting in steps 2 through 9.

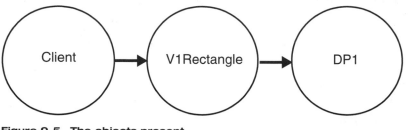

Figure 9-5   The objects present.

This solution suffers from combinatorial explosion

Unfortunately, this approach introduces new problems. Look at Figure 9-3 and pay attention to the third row of classes. Consider the following:

- The classes in this row represent the four specific types of **Shape**s that I have.

- What happens if I get another drawing program, that is, another variation in implementation? I will have *six* different kinds of **Shape**s (two **Shape** concepts times three drawing programs).

- Imagine what happens if I then get another type of **Shape**, another variation in concept. I will have *nine* different types of **Shape**s (three **Shape** concepts times three drawing programs).

. . . because of tight coupling

The class explosion problem arises because in this solution, the abstraction (the kinds of **Shape**s) and the implementation (the drawing programs) are tightly coupled. Each type of shape must know what type of drawing program it is using. I need a way to separate the variations in abstraction from the variations in implementation so that the number of classes only grows linearly (see Figure 9-6).

This is exactly the intent of the Bridge pattern: [to] de-couple an abstraction from its implementation so that the two can vary independently.[2]

Abstraction 1   Implementation A
Abstraction 2   Implementation B
Abstraction 3   Implementation C
. . .   . . .

Figure 9-6 The Bridge pattern separates variations in abstraction and implementation.

Before showing a solution and deriving the Bridge pattern, I want to mention a few other problems (beyond the combinatorial explosion).

Looking at Figure 9-3, ask yourself what else is poor about this design.

There are several other problems. Our poor approach to design gave us this mess!

- Does there appear to be redundancy?

- Would you say things have high cohesion or low cohesion?

- Are things tightly or loosely coupled?

- Would you want to have to maintain this code?

The overuse of inheritance.

As a beginning object-oriented analyst, I had a tendency to solve the kind of problem I have seen here by using special cases, taking advantage of inheritance. I loved the idea of inheritance because it seemed new and powerful. I used it whenever I could. This seems to be normal for many beginning analysts, but it is naive: given this new "hammer," everything seems like a nail.

---

2. Gamma, E., Helm, R., Johnson, R., Vlissides, J., *Design Patterns: Elements of Reusable Object-Oriented Software*, Reading, Mass.: Addison-Wesley, 1995, p. 151.

Unfortunately, many approaches to teaching object-oriented design focus on data abstraction—making designs overly based on the "*is*-ness" of the objects. As I became an experienced object-oriented designer, I was still stuck in the paradigm of designing based on inheritance—that is, looking at the characteristics of my classes based on their "*is*-ness." Characteristics of objects should be based on their responsibilities, not on what they might contain or be. Objects, of course, may be responsible for giving information about themselves; for example, a customer object may need to be able to tell you its name. Think about objects in terms of their responsibilities, not in terms of their structure.

Experienced object-oriented analysts have learned to use inheritance selectively to realize its power. Using design patterns will help you move along this learning curve more quickly. It involves a transition from using a different specialization for each variation (inheritance) to moving these variations into used or owned objects (composition).

An alternative approach

When I first looked at these problems, I thought that part of the difficulty might have been that I simply was using the wrong kind of inheritance hierarchy. Therefore, I tried the alternate hierarchy shown in Figure 9-7.

Not really a lot better, just bad in a different way

I still have the same four classes representing all of my possible combinations. However, by first deriving versions for the different drawing programs, I eliminated the redundancy between the **DP1** and **DP2** packages.

Unfortunately, I am unable to eliminate the redundancy between the two types of **Rectangle**s and the two types of **Circle**s, each pair of which has the same *draw* method.

In any event, the class explosion that was present before is still present here.

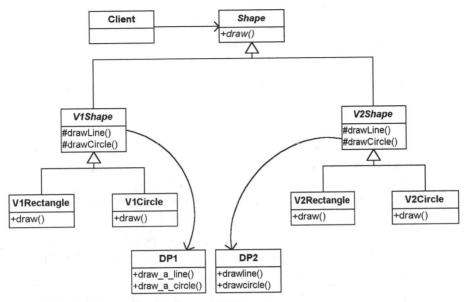

Figure 9-7 An alternative implementation.

The sequence diagram for this solution is shown in Figure 9-8.

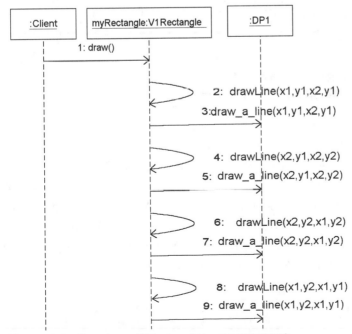

Figure 9-8 Sequence Diagram for new approach.

It still has scaling problems

While this may be an improvement over the original solution, it still has a problem with scaling. It also still has some of the original cohesion and coupling problems.

Bottom line: I do not want to have to maintain this version either! There must be a better way.

Look for alternatives in initial design.

Although my alternative design here was not significantly better than my original design, it is worth pointing out that finding alternatives to an original design is a good practice. Too many developers take what they first come up with and go with that. I am not endorsing an in-depth study of all possible alternatives (another way of getting "paralysis by analysis"). However, stepping back and looking at how we can overcome the design deficiencies in our original design is a great practice. In fact, it was just this stepping back, a refusal to move forward with a known, poor design, that led me to understanding the powerful methods of using design patterns that this entire book is about.

An Observation About Using Design Patterns

A new way to look at design patterns

When people begin to look at design patterns, they often focus on the solutions the patterns offer. This seems reasonable because they are advertised as providing good solutions to the problems at hand.

However, this is starting at the wrong end. When you learn patterns by focusing on the solutions they present, it makes it hard to determine the situations in which a pattern applies. This only tells us *what to do* but not *when to use it* or *why to do it*.

I find it much more useful to focus on the context of the pattern—the problem it is trying to solve. This lets me know the *when* and the *why*. It is more consistent with the philosophy of Alexander's patterns: "Each pattern describes a problem which occurs over and over again in the environment, and then describes the core of the solution to that problem . . ."[3]

What I have done here is a case in point. What is the problem being solved by the Bridge pattern?

> *The Bridge pattern is useful when you have an abstraction that has different implementations. It allows the abstraction and the implementation to vary independently of each other.*

The characteristics of the problem fit this nicely. I can know that I ought to be using the Bridge pattern even though I do not know yet how to implement it. Allowing for the abstraction to vary independently from the implementation would mean I could add new abstractions without changing my implementations and vice versa.

The current solution does not allow for this independent variation. I can see that it would be better if I could create an implementation that would allow for this.

It is very important to realize that, without even knowing how to implement the Bridge pattern, you can determine that it would be useful in this situation. You will find that this is generally true of design patterns. That is, you can identify when to apply them to your problem domain before knowing exactly how to implement them.

The bottom line

---

3. Alexander, C., Ishikawa, S., Silverstein, M., *A Pattern Language: Towns/Buildings/ Construction*, New York: Oxford University Press, 1977, p. x.

Learning the Bridge Pattern: Deriving It

Deriving a solution

Now that you have been through the problem, we are in a position to derive the Bridge pattern together. Doing the work to derive the pattern will help you to understand more deeply what this complex and powerful pattern does.

Let's apply some of the basic strategies for good object-oriented design and see how they help to develop a solution that is very much like the Bridge pattern. To do this, I will be using the work of Jim Coplien[4] on commonality and variability analysis.

Design patterns are solutions that occur again and again.

Design patterns are solutions that have recurred in several problems and have therefore proven themselves over time to be good solutions. The approach I am taking in this book is to *derive* the pattern in order to teach it so that you can understand its characteristics.

In this case, I know the pattern I want to derive—the Bridge pattern—because I was shown it by the Gang of Four and have seen how it works in my own problem domains. It is important to note that patterns are not really derived. By definition, they must be recurring—having been demonstrated in at least three independent cases—to be considered patterns. What I mean by "derive" is that we will go through a design process where you create the pattern as if you did not know it. This is to illustrate some key principles and useful strategies.

First, use commonality/ variability analysis

Coplien's work on commonality/variability analysis tells us how to find variations in the problem domain and identify what is common across the domain. Identify where things vary (commonality analysis) and then identify how they vary (variability analysis).

---

4. Coplein, J., *Multi-Paradigm Design for C++*. Reading, Mass.: Addison-Wesley, 1998.

According to Coplien, "Commonality analysis is the search for common elements that helps us understand how family members are the same."[5] Thus, the process of finding out how things are common defines the family in which these elements belong (and hence, where things vary).

Variability analysis reveals how family members vary. Variability only makes sense within a given commonality.

> Commonality analysis seeks structure that is unlikely to change over time, while variability analysis captures structure that is likely to change. Variability analysis makes sense only in terms of the context defined by the associated commonality analysis . . . From an architectural perspective, commonality analysis gives the architecture its longevity; variability analysis drives its fitness for use.[6]

In other words, if variations are the specific concrete cases in the domain, commonality defines the concepts in the domain that tie them together. The common concepts will be represented by abstract classes. The variations found by variability analysis will be implemented by the concrete classes (that is, classes derived from the abstract class with specific implementations).

It is almost axiomatic with object-oriented design methods that the designer is supposed to look in the problem domain, identify the nouns present, and create objects representing them. Then, the designer finds the verbs relating to those nouns (that is, their actions) and implement them by adding methods to the objects. This process of focusing on nouns and verbs typically leads to larger class hierarchies than we might want. I suggest that using commonality/variability analysis as a primary tool in creating objects is a better approach than looking at just nouns and verbs (actually, I believe this is a restatement of Jim Coplien's work).

---

5. ibid, p. 63.
6. ibid, pp. 60, 64.

Strategies to handle variations

There are two basic strategies to follow in creating designs to deal with the variations:

- Find what varies and encapsulate it.

- Favor composition over inheritance.

In the past, developers often relied on extensive inheritance trees to coordinate these variations. However, the second strategy says to try composition when possible. The intent of this is to be able to contain the variations in independent classes, thereby allowing for future variations without affecting the code. One way to do this is to have each variation contained in its own abstract class and then see how the abstract classes relate to each other.

Reviewing encapsulation.

Most object-oriented developers learned that "encapsulation" is data-hiding. Unfortunately, this is a very limiting definition. True, encapsulation does hide data, but it can be used in many other ways. If you look back at Figure 7-2, you will see encapsulation operates at many levels. Of course, it works at hiding data for each of the particular **Shape**s. However, notice that the **Client** object is not aware of the particular kinds of shapes. That is, the **Client** object has no idea that the **Shape**s it is dealing with are **Rectangle**s and **Circle**s. Thus, the concrete classes that **Client** deals with are hidden (or encapsulated) from **Client**. This is the kind of encapsulation that the Gang of Four is talking about when they say, "find what varies and encapsulate it". They are finding what varies, and encapsulating it "behind" an abstract class (see Chapter 8, "Expanding Our Horizons").

Try it: identify what is varying

Follow this process for the rectangle drawing problem.

First, identify what it is that is varying. In this case, it is different types of **Shape**s and different types of drawing programs. The common concepts are therefore shapes and drawing programs. I represent this in Figure 9-9 (note that the class names are shown in italics because the classes are abstract).

Figure 9-9   What is varying.

At this point, I mean for **Shape** to encapsulate the concept of the types of shapes that I have. Shapes are responsible for knowing how to draw themselves. **Drawing** objects, on the other hand, are responsible for drawing lines and circles. I represent these responsibilities by defining methods in the classes.

The next step is to represent the specific variations that are present. For **Shape**, I have rectangles and circles. For drawing programs, I will have a program that is based on **DP1** (**V1Drawing**) and one based on **DP2** (**V2Drawing**), respectively. I show this in Figure 9-10.

Try it: represent the variations

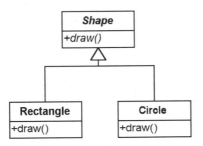
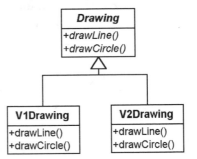

Figure 9-10   Represent the variations.

At this point, the diagram is simply notional. I know that **V1Drawing** will use **DP1** and **V2Drawing** will use **DP2** but I have not said *how*. I have simply captured the concepts of the problem domain (shapes and drawing programs) and have shown the variations that are present.

Tying the classes together: who uses whom?

Given these two sets of classes, I need to ask how they will relate to one another. I do not want to come up with a new set of classes based on an inheritance tree because I know what happens if I do that (look at Figures 9-3 and 9-7 to refresh your memory). Instead, I want to see if I can relate these classes by having one use the other (that is, follow the mandate to favor composition over inheritance). The question is, which class uses the other?

Consider these two possibilities: either **Shape** uses the **Drawing** programs or the **Drawing** programs use **Shape**.

Consider the latter case first. If drawing programs could draw shapes directly, then they would have to know some things about shapes in general: what they are, what they look like. But this violates a fundamental principle of objects: an object should only be responsible for itself.

It also violates encapsulation. **Drawing** objects would have to know specific information about the **Shape**s (that is, the kind of **Shape**) in order to draw them. The objects are not really responsible for their own behaviors.

Now, consider the first case. What if I have **Shape**s use **Drawing** objects to draw themselves? **Shape**s wouldn't need to know what type of **Drawing** object it used since I could have **Shape**s refer to the **Drawing** class. **Shape**s also would be responsible for controlling the drawing.

This looks better to me. Figure 9-11 shows this solution.

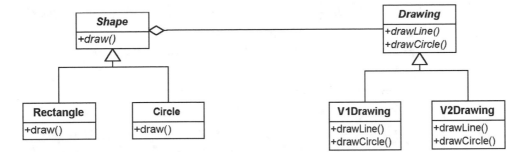

Figure 9-11   Tie the classes together.

In this design, **Shape** uses **Drawing** to manifest its behavior. I left out the details of **V1Drawing** using the **DP1** program and **V2Drawing** using the **DP2** program. In Figure 9-12, I add this as well as the protected methods *drawLine* and *drawCircle* (in **Shape**), which calls **Drawing**'s *drawLine*, and *drawCircle*, respectively.

Expanding the design

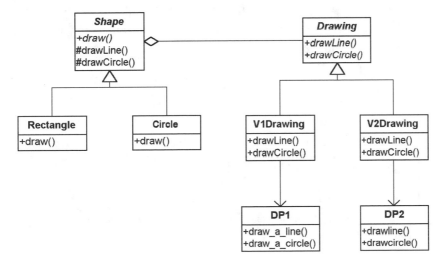

Figure 9-12   Expanding the design.

One rule, one place.

A very important implementation strategy to follow is to have only one place where you implement a rule. In other words, if you have a rule how to do things, only implement that once. This typically results in code with a greater number of smaller methods. The extra cost is minimal, but it eliminates duplication and often prevents many future problems. Duplication is bad not only because of the extra work in typing things multiple times, but because of the likelihood of something changing in the future and then forgetting to change it in all of the required places.

While the *draw* method or **Rectangle** could directly call the *drawLine* method of whatever **Drawing** object the **Shape** has, I can improve the code by continuing to follow the one rule, one place strategy and have a *drawLine* method in **Shape** that calls the *drawLine* method of its **Drawing** object.

I am not a purist (at least not in most things), but if there is one place where I think it is important to always follow a rule, it is here. In the example below, I have a *drawLine* method in **Shape** because that describes my rule of drawing a line with **Drawing**. I do the same with *drawCircle* for circles. By following this strategy, I prepare myself for other derived objects that might need to draw lines and circles.

Where did the one rule, one place strategy come from? While many have documented it, it has been in the folklore of object-oriented designers for a long time. It represents a best practice of designers. Most recently, Kent Beck called this the "once and only once rule."[*]

---

[*] Beck, K., *Extreme Programming Explained: Embrace Change*, Reading, Mass.: Addison Wesley, 2000, pp. 108–109.

He defines it as part of his constraints:

- The system (code and tests together) must communicate everything you want to communicate.

- The system must contain no duplicate code. (1 and 2 together constitute the Once and Only Once rule).

Figure 9-13 illustrates the separation of the **Shape** abstraction from the **Drawing** implementation.

The pattern llustrated

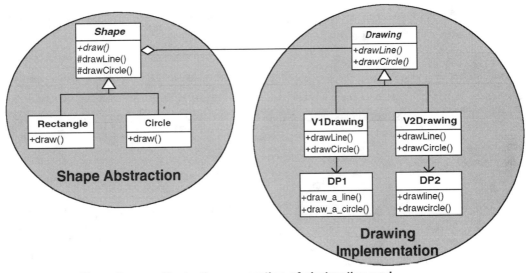

Figure 9-13 Class diagram illustrating separation of abstraction and implementation.

From a method point of view, this looks fairly similar to the inheritance-based implementation (such as shown in Figure 9-3). The biggest difference is that the methods are now located in different objects.

Relating this to the inheritance-based design

I said at the beginning of this chapter that my confusion over the Bridge pattern was due to my misunderstanding of the term "implementation." I thought that implementation referred to how I implemented a particular abstraction.

The Bridge pattern let me see that viewing the implementation as something outside of my objects, something that is *used by* the objects, gives me much greater freedom by hiding the variations in implementation from my calling program. By designing my objects this way, I also noticed how I was containing variations in separate class hierarchies. The hierarchy on the left side of Figure 9-13 contains the variations in my abstractions. The hierarchy on the right side of Figure 9-13 contains the variations in how I will implement those abstractions. This is consistent with the new paradigm for creating objects (using commonality/variability analysis) that I mentioned earlier.

From an object perspective

It is easiest to visualize this when you remember that there are only three objects to deal with at any one time, even though there are several classes (see Figure 9-14).

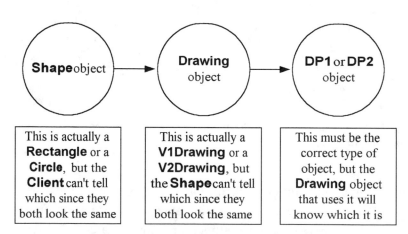

Figure 9-14 There are only three objects at a time.

A reasonably complete code example is shown in Example 9-3 for   *Code examples*
Java and in the Examples beginning on page 157 for C++.

Example 9-3   Java Code Fragments

```java
class Client {
  public static void main
    (String argv[]) {
      Shape r1, r2;
      Drawing dp;

      dp= new V1Drawing();
      r1= new Rectangle(dp,1,1,2,2);

      dp= new V2Drawing ();
      r2= new Circle(dp,2,2,3);

      r1.draw();
      r2.draw();
  }
}

abstract class Shape {
  abstract public draw() ;
  private Drawing _dp;

  Shape (Drawing dp) {
    _dp= dp;
  }
  protected void drawLine (
    double x1,double y1,
    double x2,double y2) {
      _dp.drawLine(x1,y1,x2,y2);
  }

  protected void drawCircle (
    double x,double y,double r) {
      _dp.drawCircle(x,y,r);
  }
}

abstract class Drawing {
  abstract public void drawLine (
    double x1, double y1,
    double x2, double y2);
```

(continued)

Example 9-3 Java Code Fragments *(continued)*

```java
  abstract public void drawCircle (
    double x,double y,double r);
}

class V1Drawing extends Drawing {
  public void drawLine (
    double x1,double y1,
    double x2,double y2) {
    DP1.draw_a_line(x1,y1,x2,y2);
  }
  public void drawCircle (
    double x,double y,double r) {
    DP1.draw_a_circle(x,y,r);
  }
}

class V2Drawing extends Drawing {
  public void drawLine (
    double x1,double y1,
    double x2,double y2) {
    // arguments are different in DP2
    // and must be rearranged
    DP2.drawline(x1,x2,y1,y2);
  }
  public void drawCircle (
    double x, double y,double r) {
    DP2.drawcircle(x,y,r);
  }
}

class Rectangle extends Shape {
  private double _x1, _x2, _y1, _y2;
  public Rectangle (
    Drawing dp,
    double x1,double y1,
    double x2,double y2) {
      super( dp) ;
      _x1= x1; _x2= x2 ;
      _y1= y1; _y2= y2;
  }

  public void draw () {
   drawLine(_x1,_y1,_x2,_y1);
   drawLine(_x2,_y1,_x2,_y2);
```

(continued)

Example 9-3 Java Code Fragments *(continued)*

```java
    drawLine(_x2,_y2,_x1,_y2);
    drawLine(_x1,_y2,_x1,_y1);
   }
}

class Circle extends Shape {
  private double _x, _y, _r;
  public Circle (
    Drawing dp,
    double x,double y,double r) {
      super( dp) ;
      _x= x; _y= y; _r= r ;
  }

  public void draw () {
   drawCircle(_x,_y,_r);
  }
}

// We've been given the implementations for DP1 and DP2

class DP1 {
  static public void draw_a_line (
    double x1,double y1,
    double x2,double y2) {
      // implementation
  }
  static public void draw_a_circle(
    double x,double y,double r) {
      // implementation
  }
}

class DP2 {
  static public void drawline (
    double x1,double x2,
    double y1,double y2) {
      // implementation
  }
  static public void drawcircle (
    double x,double y,double r) {
      // implementation
  }
}
```

The Bridge Pattern in Retrospect

The essence of the
pattern

Now that you've seen how the Bridge pattern works, it is worth looking at it from a more conceptual point of view. As shown in Figure 9-13, the pattern has an abstraction part (with its derivations) and an implementation part. When designing with the Bridge pattern, it is useful to keep these two parts in mind. The implementation's interface should be designed considering the different derivations of the abstract class that it will have to support. Note that a designer shouldn't necessarily put in an interface that will implement all possible derivations of the abstract class (yet another possible route to paralysis by analysis). Only those derivations that actually are being built need be supported. Time and time again, the authors have seen that the mere consideration of flexibility at this point often greatly improves a design.

Note: In C++, the Bridge pattern's implementation must be implemented with an abstract class defining the public interface. In Java, either an abstract class or an interface can be used. The choice depends upon whether implementations share common traits that abstract classes can take advantage of. See Peter Coad's *Java Design*, discussed on page 316 of the Bibliography, for more on this.

Field Notes: Using the Bridge Pattern

The Bridge pattern
often incorporates
the Adapter pattern

Note that the solution presented in Figures 9-12 and 9-13 integrates the Adapter pattern with the Bridge pattern. I do this because I was given the drawing programs that I must use. These drawing programs have preexisting interfaces with which I must work. I must use the Adapter to adapt them so that they can be handled in the same way.

While it is very common to see the Adapter pattern incorporated into the Bridge pattern, the Adapter pattern is not part of the Bridge pattern.

The Bridge Pattern: Key Features

Intent	Decouple a set of implementations from the set of objects using them.
Problem	The derivations of an abstract class must use multiple implementations without causing an explosion in the number of classes.
Solution	Define an interface for all implementations to use and have the derivations of the abstract class use that.
Participants and Collaborators	The **Abstraction** defines the interface for the objects being implemented. The **Implementor** defines the interface for the specific implementation classes. Classes derived from the **Abstraction** use classes derived from the **Implementor** without knowing which particular **ConcreteImplementor** is in use.
Consequences	The decoupling of the implementations from the objects that use them increases extensibility. Client objects are not aware of implementation issues.
Implementation	• Encapsulate the implementations in an abstract class. • Contain a handle to it in the base class of the abstraction being implemented. *Note:* In Java, you can use interfaces instead of an abstract class for the implementation.
GoF Reference	Pages 151–162.

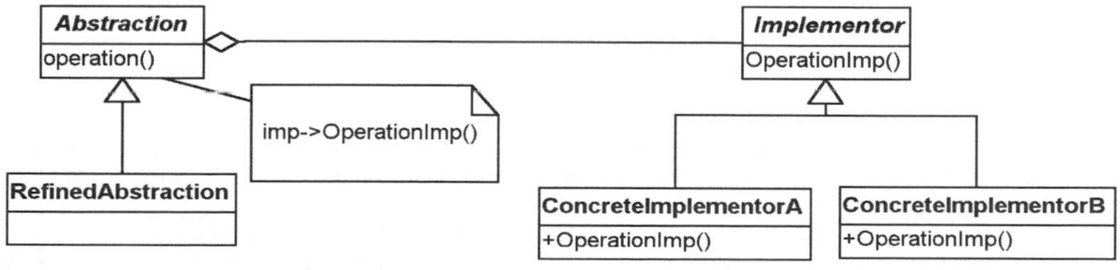

Figure 9-15 Standard, simplified view of the Bridge pattern.

Compound design patterns

When two or more patterns are tightly integrated (like my Bridge and Adapter), the result is called a composite design pattern.[7,8] It is now possible to talk about patterns of patterns!

Instantiating the objects of the Bridge pattern

Another thing to notice is that the objects representing the abstraction (the **Shape**s) were given their implementation while being instantiated. This is not an inherent part of the pattern, but it is very common.

Now that you understand the Bridge pattern, it is worth reviewing the Gang of Four's Implementation section in their description of the pattern. They discuss different issues relating to how the abstraction creates and/or uses the implementation.

An advantage of Java over C++ in the Bridge pattern

Sometimes when using the Bridge pattern, I will share the implementation objects across several abstraction objects.

- In Java, this is no problem; when all the abstraction objects go away, the garbage collector will realize that the implementation objects are no longer needed and will clean them up.

- In C++, I must somehow manage the implementation objects. There are many ways to do this; keeping a reference counter or even using the Singleton pattern are possibilities. It is nice, however, not to have to consider this effort. This illustrates another advantage of automatic garbage collection.

---

7. Compound design patterns used to be called composite design patterns, but are now called compound design patterns to avoid confusion with the composite pattern.

8. For more information, refer to Riehle, D., "Composite Design Patterns," In, *Proceedings of the 1997 Conference on Object-Oriented Programming Systems, Languages and Applications* (OOPSLA '97), New York: ACM Press, 1997, pp. 218–228. Also refer to "Composite Design Patterns (They Aren't What You Think)," *C++ Report*, June 1998.

While the solution I developed with the Bridge pattern is far superior to the original solution, it is not perfect. One way of measuring the quality of a design is to see how well it handles variation. Handling a new implementation is very easy with a Bridge pattern in place. The programmer simply needs to define a new concrete implementation class and implement it. Nothing else changes.

The Bridge pattern solution is good, but not always perfect

However, things may not go so smoothly if I get a new concrete example of the abstraction. I may get a new kind of **Shape** that can be implemented with the implementations already in the design. However, I may also get a new kind of **Shape** that requires a new drawing function. For example, I may have to implement an ellipse. The current **Drawing** class does not have the proper method to do ellipses. In this case, I have to modify the implementations. However, even if this occurs, I at least have a well-defined process for making these changes (that is, modify the interface of the **Drawing** class or interface, and modify each **Drawing** derivative accordingly)—this localizes the impact of the change and lowers the risk of an unwanted side effect.

Bottom line: Patterns do not always give perfect solutions. However, because patterns represent the collective experience of many designers over the years, they are often better than the solutions you or I might come up with on our own.

In the real world, I do not always start out with multiple implementations. Sometimes, I know that new ones are *possible*, but they show up unexpectedly. One approach is to prepare for multiple implementations by always using abstractions. You get a very generic application.

Follow one rule, one place to help with refactoring

But I do not recommend this approach. It leads to an unnecessary increase in the number of classes you have. It is important to write code in such a way that when multiple implementations do occur (which they often will), it is not difficult to modify the code to incorporate the Bridge pattern. Modifying code to improve its structure without adding function is called *refactoring*. As defined by Martin Fowler, "Refactoring is the process of changing a software system in such a way that it does not alter the external behavior of the code yet improves its internal structure."[9]

In designing code, I was always attending to the possibility of refactoring by following the one rule, one place mandate. The `drawLine` method was a good example of this. Although the place the code was actually implemented varied, moving it around was fairly easy.

Refactoring.

Refactoring is commonly used in object-oriented design. However, it is not strictly an OO thing . . . It is modifying code to improve its structure without adding function.

A useful way to look at the bridge pattern

While deriving the pattern, I took the two variations present (shapes and drawing programs) and encapsulated each in their own abstract class. That is, the variations of shapes are encapsulated in the **Shape** class, the variations of drawing programs are encapsulated in the **Drawing** class.

Stepping back and looking at these two polymorphic structures, I should ask myself, "What do these abstract classes represent?" For the shapes, it is pretty evident that the class represents different kinds of shapes. The **Drawing** abstract class represents how I will implement the **Shape**s. Thus, even in the case where I described how new requirements for the **Drawing** class may arise (say, if I need to implement ellipses) there is a clear relationship between the classes.

---

9. Fowler, M., *Refactoring: Improving the Design of Existing Code*, Reading, Mass.: Addison-Wesley, 2000, p. xvi.

Summary

In learning the Bridge pattern, I looked at a problem where there were two variations in the problem domain—shapes and drawing programs. In the problem domain, each of these varied. The challenge came in trying to implement a solution based on all of the special cases that existed. The initial solution, which naively used inheritance too much, resulted in a redundant design that had tight coupling and low cohesion, and was thus difficult to maintain.

In this chapter

You learned the Bridge pattern by following the basic strategies for dealing with variation:

- Find what varies and encapsulate it.
- Favor composition over inheritance.

Finding what varies is always a good step in learning about the problem domain. In the drawing program example, I had one set of variations using another set of variations. This indicates that the Bridge pattern will probably be useful.

In general, you should identify which patterns to use by matching them with the characteristics and behaviors in the problem domain. By understanding the *whys* and *whats* of the patterns in your repertoire, you can be more effective in picking the ones that will help you. You can select patterns to use before deciding how the pattern's implementation will be done.

By using the Bridge pattern, the design and implementation are more robust and better able to handle changes in the future.

While I focused on the pattern during the chapter, it is worth pointing out several object-oriented principles that are used in the Bridge pattern.

Summary of object-oriented principles used in the Bridge pattern

Concept	Discussion
Objects are responsible for themselves	I had different kinds of **Shapes**, but all drew themselves (via the *draw* method). The **Drawing** classes were responsible for drawing elements of objects.
Abstract class	I used abstract classes to represent the concepts. I actually had rectangles and circles in the problem domain. The concept "**Shape**" is something that lives strictly in our head, a device to bind the two concepts together; therefore, I represent it in the **Shape** class as an *abstract class*. **Shape** will never get instantiated because it never exists in the problem domain (only **Rectangle**s and **Circle**s do). The same thing is true with drawing programs.
Encapsulation via an abstract class	I have two examples of encapsulation through the use of an abstract class in this problem. • A client dealing with the Bridge pattern will have only a derivation of **Shape** visible to it. However, the client will not know what type of **Shape** it has (it will be just a **Shape** to the client). Thus, I have encapsulated this information. The advantage of this is if a new type of **Shape** is needed in the future, it does not affect the client object. • The **Drawing** class hides the different drawing derivations from the **Shape**s. In practice, the abstraction may know which implementation it uses because it might instantiate it. See page 155 of the Gang of Four book for an explanation as to why this might be a good thing to do. However, even when that occurs, this knowledge of implementations is limited to the abstraction's constructor and is easily changed.
One rule, one place	The abstract class often has the methods that actually use the implementation objects. The derivations of the abstract class call these methods. This allows for easier modification if needed, and allows for a good starting point even before implementing the entire pattern.

Supplement: C++ Code Examples

Example 9-4   C++ Code Fragments: Rectangles Only

```cpp
void Rectangle::draw () {
   drawLine(_x1,_y1,_x2,_y1);
   drawLine(_x2,_y1,_x2,_y2);
   drawLine(_x2,_y2,_x1,_y2);
   drawLine(_x1,_y2,_x1,_y1);
}

void V1Rectangle::drawLine
   (double x1, double y1,
    double x2, double y2) {
   DP1.draw_a_line(x1,y1,x2,y2);
}

void V2Rectangle::drawLine
   (double x1, double y1,
    double x2, double y2) {
   DP2.drawline(x1,x2,y1,y2);
}
```

Example 9-5   C++ Code Fragments:
Rectangles and Circles without Bridge

```cpp
class Shape {
  public: void draw ()=0;
}
class Rectangle : Shape {
  public:
    void draw();
  protected:
    void drawLine(
        double x1,y1, x2,y2)=0;
}
void Rectangle::draw () {
  drawLine(_x1,_y1,_x2,_y1);
  drawLine(_x2,_y1,_x2,_y2);
  drawLine(_x2,_y2,_x1,_y2);
  drawLine(_x1,_y2,_x1,_y1);
}
```

(continued)

Example 9-5 C++ Code Fragments:
Rectangles and Circles without Bridge *(continued)*

```cpp
// V1Rectangle and V2Rectangle both derive from
// Rectangle header files not shown
void V1Rectangle::drawLine (
  double x1,y1, x2,y2) {
  DP1.draw_a_line(x1,y1,x2,y2);
}
void V2Rectangle::drawLine (
   double x1,y1, x2,y2) {
  DP2.drawline(x1,x2,y1,y2);
   }
}

class Circle : Shape {
  public:
    void draw() ;
  protected:
    void drawCircle(
      double x, y, z) ;
}
void Circle::draw () {
  drawCircle();

}

// V1Circle and V2Circle both derive from Circle
// header files not shown
void V1Circle::drawCircle (
  DP1.draw_a_circle(x, y, r);
}

void V2Circle::drawCircle (
  DP2.drawcircle(x, y, r);
}
```

Example 9-6   C++ Code Fragments:
The Bridge Implemented

```
void main (String argv[]) {
  Shape *s1;
  Shape *s2;
  Drawing *dp1, *dp2;

  dp1= new V1Drawing;
  s1=new Rectangle(dp,1,1,2,2);

  dp2= new V2Drawing;
  s2= new Circle(dp,2,2,4);

  s1->draw();
  s2->draw();

  delete s1; delete s2;
  delete dp1; delete dp2;
}

// NOTE: Memory management not tested.
// Includes not shown.

class Shape {
  public: draw()=0;
  private: Drawing *_dp;
}
Shape::Shape (Drawing *dp) {
  _dp= dp;
}
void Shape::drawLine(
  double x1, double y1,
  double x2, double y2)
    _dp->drawLine(x1,y1,x2,y2);
}

Rectangle::Rectangle (Drawing *dp,
  double x1, y1, x2, y2) :
  Shape( dp) {
  _x1= x1; _x2= x2;
  _y1= y1; _y2= y2;
}
```

(continued)

Example 9-6 C++ Code Fragments:
The Bridge Implemented (continued)

```cpp
void Rectangle::draw () {
  drawLine(_x1,_y1,_x2,_y1);
  drawLine(_x2,_y1,_x2,_y2);
  drawLine(_x2,_y2,_x1,_y2);
  drawLine(_x1,_y2,_x1,_y1);
}
class Circle {
  public: Circle (
      Drawing *dp,
      double x, double y, double r);
};

Circle::Circle (
    Drawing *dp,
    double x, double y,
    double r) : Shape(dp) {
    _x= x;
    _y= y;
    _r= r;
}

Circle::draw () {
    drawCircle( _x, _y, _r);
}

class Drawing {
  public: virtual void drawLine (
      double x1, double y1,
      double x2, double y2)=0;
};

class V1Drawing :
  public Drawing {
    public: void drawLine (
        double x1, double y1,
        double x2, double y2);
      void drawCircle(
        double x, double y, double r);
};

void V1Drawing::drawLine (
  double x1, double y1,
  double x2, double y2) {
  DP1.draw_a_line(x1,y1,x2,y2);
}
```

(continued)

Example 9-6   C++ Code Fragments:
The Bridge Implemented *(continued)*

```cpp
void V1Drawing::drawCircle (
   double x1, double y, double r) {
     DP1.draw_a_circle (x,y,r);
}
class V2Drawing : public
   Drawing {
   public:
     void drawLine (
       double x1, double y1,
       double x2, double y2);
     void drawCircle(
       double x, double y, double r);
};
void V2Drawing::drawLine (
  double x1, double y1,
  double x2, double y2) {
    DP2.drawline(x1,x2,y1,y2);
}

void V2Drawing::drawCircle (
  double x, double y, double r) {
    DP2.drawcircle(x, y, r);
}

// We have been given the implementations for
// DP1 and DP2

class DP1 {
  public:
    static void draw_a_line (
      double x1, double y1,
      double x2, double y2);
    static void draw_a_circle (
      double x, double y, double r);
};

class DP2 {
  public:
    static void drawline (
      double x1, double x2,
      double y1, double y2);
    static void drawcircle (
      double x, double y, double r);
};
```

CHAPTER 10

The Abstract Factory Pattern

Overview

I will continue our study of patterns with the Abstract Factory pattern, which is used to create families of objects.

In this chapter

In this chapter,

- I derive the pattern by working through an example.

- I present the key features of the Abstract Factory pattern.

- I relate the Abstract Factory pattern to the CAD/CAM problem.

Introducing the Abstract Factory Pattern

According to the Gang of Four, the intent of the Abstract Factory pattern is to "provide an interface for creating families of related or dependent objects without specifying their concrete classes."[1]

Intent: coordinate the instantiation of objects

Sometimes, several objects need to be instantiated in a coordinated fashion. For example, when dealing with user interfaces, the system might need to use one set of objects to work on one operating system and another set of objects to work on a different operating system. The Abstract Factory pattern ensures that the system always gets the correct objects for the situation.

---

1. Gamma, E., Helm, R., Johnson, R., Vlissides, J., *Design Patterns: Elements of Reusable Object-Oriented Software*, Reading, Mass.: Addison-Wesley, 1995, p. 87.

Learning the Abstract Factory Pattern: An Example

A motivating example: select device drivers according to the machine capacity

Suppose I have been given the task of designing a computer system to display and print shapes from a database. The type of resolution to use to display and print the shapes depends on the computer that the system is currently running on: the speed of its CPU and the amount of memory that it has available. My system must be careful about how much demand it is placing on the computer.

The challenge is that my system must control the drivers that it is using: low-resolution drivers in a less-capable machine and high-resolution drivers in a high-capacity machine, as shown in Table 10-1.

Table 10-1   Different Drivers for Different Machines

For driver...	In a low-capacity machine, use...	In a high-capacity machine, use...
Display	LRDD Low-resolution display driver	HRDD High-resolution display driver
Print	LRPD Low-resolution print driver	HRPD High-resolution print driver

Define families based on a unifying concept

In this example, the families of drivers are mutually exclusive, but this is not usually the case. Sometimes, different families will contain objects from the same classes. For example, a mid-range machine might use a low-resolution display driver (LRDD) and a high-resolution print driver (HRPD).

The families to use are based on the problem domain: which sets of objects are required for a given case? In this case, the unifying concept focuses on the demands that the objects put on the system:

- *A low-resolution family*—LRDD and LRPD, those drivers that put low demands on the system

- *A high-resolution family*—HRDD and HRPD, those drivers that put high demands on the system

My first attempt might be to use a switch to control the selection of driver, as shown in Example 10-1.

Alternative 1: use a switch to select the driver

Example 10-1 Java Code Fragments:
A Switch to Control Which Driver to Use

```java
// JAVA CODE FRAGMENT

class ApControl {
  .  .  .
  void doDraw () {
    .  .  .
    switch (RESOLUTION) {
      case LOW:
        // use lrdd
      case HIGH:
        // use hrdd
    }
  }
  void doPrint () {
    .  .  .
    switch (RESOLUTION) {
    case LOW:
        // use lrpd
      case HIGH:
        // use hrpd
    }
  }
}
```

While this does work, it presents problems. The rules for determining which driver to use are intermixed with the actual use of the driver. There are problems both with coupling and with cohesion:

. . . but there are problems with coupling and cohesion

- *Tight coupling*—If I change the rule on the resolution (say, I need to add a MIDDLE value), I must change the code in two places that are otherwise not related.

- *Low cohesion*—I am giving `doDraw` and `doPrint` two unrelated assignments: they must both create a shape and must also worry about which driver to use.

Tight coupling and low cohesion may not be a problem right now. However, they usually increase maintenance costs. Also, in the real world, I would likely have many more places affected than just the two shown here.

Switches may indicate a need for abstraction.

Often, a switch indicates (1) the need for polymorphic behavior, or (2) the presence of misplaced responsibilities. Consider instead a more general solution such as abstraction or giving the responsibility to other objects.

Alternative 2: use inheritance

Another alternative would be to use inheritance. I could have two different **ApControl**s: one that uses low-resolution drivers and one that uses high-resolution drivers. Both would be derived from the same abstract class, so common code could be maintained. I show this in Figure 10-1.

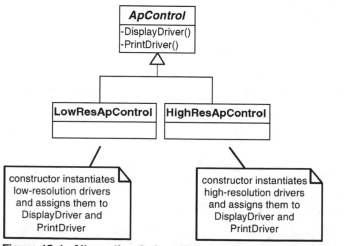

Figure 10-1 Alternative 2—handling variation with inheritance.

While inheritance could work in this simple case, it has so many dis-advantages that I would rather stay with the switches. For example:

. . . but this also has problems

- *Combinatorial explosion*—For each different family and each new family I get in the future, I must create a new concrete class (that is, a new version of **ApControl**).

- *Unclear meaning*—The resultant classes do not help clarify what is going on. I have specialized each class to a particular special case. If I want my code to be easy to maintain in the future, I need to strive to make it as clear as possible what is going on. Then, I do not have to spend a lot of time trying to relearn what that section of code is trying to do.

- *Need to favor composition*—Finally, it violates the basic rule to "favor composition over inheritance."

In my experience, I have found that switches often indicate an opportunity for abstraction. In this example, LRDD and HRDD are both display drivers and LRPD and HRPD are both print drivers. The abstractions would therefore be *display drivers* and *print drivers*. Figure 10-2 shows this conceptually. I say "conceptually" because **LRDD** and **HRDD** do not really derive from the same abstract class.

Alternative 3: replace switches with abstraction

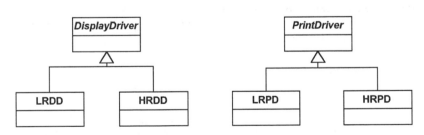

Figure 10-2 Drivers and their abstractions.

Note: At this point, I do not have to be concerned that they derive from different classes because I know I can use the Adapter pattern to adapt the drivers, making it appear they belong to the appropriate abstract class.

The code is simpler to understand

Defining the objects this way would allow for **ApControl** to use a **DisplayDriver** and a **PrintDriver** without using switches. **ApControl** is much simpler to understand because it does not have to worry about the type of drivers it has. In other words, **ApControl** would use a **DisplayDriver** object or a **PrintDriver** object without having to worry about the driver's resolution.

See Figure 10-3 and the code in Example 10-2.

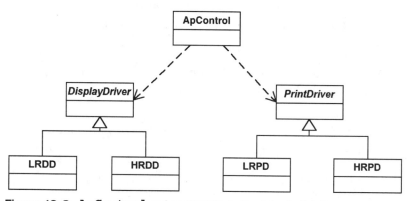

Figure 10-3   **ApControl** using drivers in the ideal situation.

Example 10-2   Java Code Fragments:
Using Polymorphism to Solve the Problem

```
// JAVA CODE FRAGMENT

class ApControl {
   .  .  .
  void doDraw () {
     .  .  .
    myDisplayDriver.draw();
  }
  void doPrint () {
     .  .  .
    myPrintDriver.print();
  }
}
```

One question remains: How do I create the appropriate objects? *Factory objects*

I could have **ApControl** do it, but this can cause maintenance problems in the future. If I have to work with a new set of objects, I will have to change **ApControl**. Instead, if I use a "factory" object to instantiate the objects I need, I will have prepared myself for new families of objects.

In this example, I will use a factory object to control the creation of the appropriate family of drivers. The **ApControl** object will use another object—the factory object—to get the appropriate type of display driver and the appropriate type of print driver for the current computer being used. The interaction would look something like the one shown in Figure 10-4.

From **ApControl**'s point of view, things are now pretty simple. It *The factory is* lets **ResFactory** worry about keeping track of which drivers to *responsible . . .* use. Although I am still faced with writing code to do this track- and *cohesive* ing, I have decomposed the problem according to responsibility. **ApControl** has the responsibility for knowing how to work with the appropriate objects. **ResFactory** has the responsibility for deciding which objects are appropriate. I can use different factory objects or even just one object (that might use switches). In any case, it is better than what I had before.

This creates cohesion: all that **ResFactory** does is create the appropriate drivers; all **ApControl** does is use them.

There are ways to avoid the use of switches in **ResFactory** itself. *. . . and it encapsu-* This would allow me to make future changes without affecting any *lates variation in a* existing factory objects. I can encapsulate a variation in a class by *class* defining an abstract class that represents the factory concept. In the case of **ResFactory**, I have two different behaviors (methods):

- Give me the display driver I should use.
- Give me the print driver I should use.

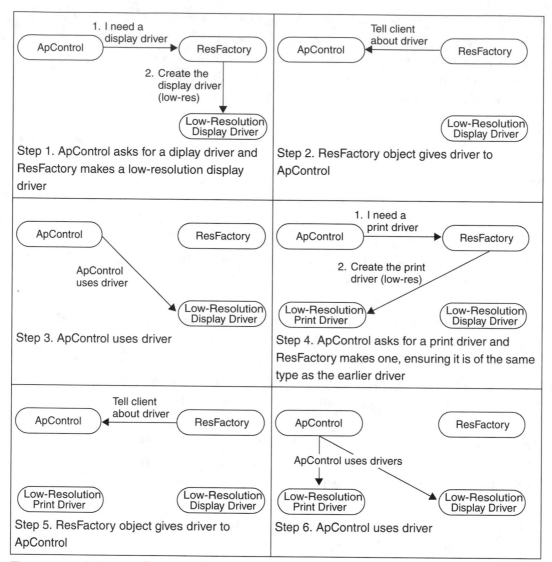

Figure 10-4 `ApControl` **gets its drivers from a factory object.**

`ResFactory` can be instantiated from one of two concrete classes and derived from an abstract class that has these public methods, as shown in Figure 10-5.

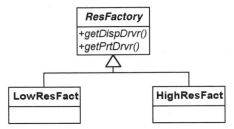

Figure 10-5   The ResFactory encapsulates the variations.

Strategies for bridging analysis and design.

Below are three key strategies involved in the Abstract Factory.

Strategy	Shown in the Design
Find what varies and encapsulate it.	The choice of which driver object to use was varying. So, I encapsulated it in `ResFactory`.
Favor composition over inheritance.	Put this variation in a separate object—`ResFactory`—and have `ApControl` use it as opposed to having two different `ApControl` objects.
Design to interfaces, not to implementations.	`ApControl` knows how to ask `ResFactory` to instantiate drivers—it does not know (or care) how `ResFactory` is actually doing it.

Learning the Abstract Factory Pattern: Implementing It

Example 10-3 shows how to implement the Abstract Factory objects for this design.

Implementation of the design

Example 10-3   Java Code Fragments: Implementation of ResFactory

```java
abstract class ResFactory {
  abstract public DisplayDriver getDispDrvr();
  abstract public PrintDriver getPrtDrvr();
}

class LowResFact extends ResFactory {
  public DisplayDriver getDispDrvr() {
    return new LRDD();
  }
  public PrintDriver getPrtDrvr() {
    return new LRPD();
  }
}

class HighResFact extends ResFactory {
  public DisplayDriver getDispDrvr() {
    return new HRDD();
  }
  public PrintDriver getPrtDrvr() {
    return new HRPD();
  }
}
```

Putting it together: the Abstract Factory

To finish the solution, I have the **ApControl** talk with the appropriate factory object (either **LowResFact** or **HighResFact**); this is shown in Figure 10-6. Note that **ResFactory** is abstract, and that this hiding of **ResFactory**'s implementation is what makes the pattern work. Hence, the name Abstract Factory for the pattern.

How this works

ApControl is given either a **LowResFact** object or a **HighResFact** object. It asks this object for the appropriate drivers when it needs them. The factory object instantiates the particular driver (low or high resolution) that it knows about. **ApControl** does not need to worry about whether a low-resolution or a high-resolution driver is returned since it uses both in the same manner.

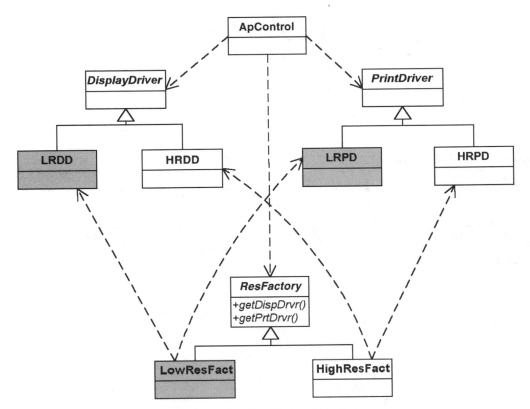

Figure 10-6   Intermediate solution using the Abstract Factory.

I have ignored one issue: LRDD and HRDD may not have been derived from the same abstract class (as may be true of LRPD and HRPD). Knowing the Adapter pattern, this does not present much of a problem. I can simply use the structure I have in Figure 10-6, but adapt the drivers as shown in Figure 10-7.

The LRDD/HRDD and LRPD/HRPD pairs do not necessarily derive from the same classes

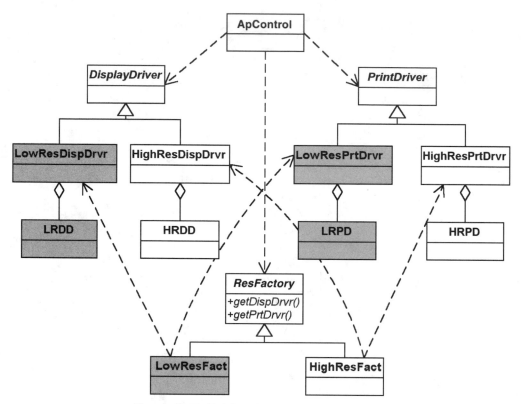

Figure 10-7 Solving the problem with the Abstract Factory and Adapter.

How this works

The implementation of this design is essentially the same as the one before it. The only difference is that now the factory objects instantiate objects from classes I have created that adapt the objects I started with. This is an important modeling method. By combining the Adapter pattern with the Abstract Factory pattern in this way, I can treat these conceptually similar objects as if they were siblings even if they are not. This enables the Abstract Factory to be used in more situations.

In this pattern,

The roles of the objects in the Abstract Factory

- The client object just knows who to ask for the objects it needs and how to use them.

- The Abstract Factory class specifies which objects can be instantiated by defining a method for each of these different types of objects. Typically, an Abstract Factory object will have a method for each type of object that must be instantiated.

- The concrete factories specify which objects are to be instantiated.

Field Notes: The Abstract Factory Pattern

Deciding which factory object is needed is really the same as determining which family of objects to use. For example, in the preceding driver problem, I had one family for low-resolution drivers and another family for high-resolution drivers. How do I know which set I want? In a case like this, it is most likely that a configuration file will tell me. I can then write a few lines of code that instantiate the proper factory object based on this configuration information.

How to get the right factory object

I can also use an Abstract Factory so I can use a subsystem for different applications. In this case, the factory object will be passed to the subsystem, telling the subsystem which objects it is to use. In this case, it is usually known by the main system which family of objects the subsystem will need. Before the subsystem is called, the correct factory object would be instantiated.

The Abstract Factory Pattern: Key Features

Intent	You want to have families or sets of objects for particular clients (or cases).
Problem	Families of related objects need to be instantiated.
Solution	Coordinates the creation of families of objects. Gives a way to take the rules of how to perform the instantiation out of the client object that is using these created objects.
Participants and Collaborators	The **AbstractFactory** defines the interface for how to create each member of the family of objects required. Typically, each family is created by having its own unique **ConcreteFactory**.
Consequences	The pattern isolates the rules of which objects to use from the logic of how to use these objects.
Implementation	Define an abstract class that specifies which objects are to be made. Then implement one concrete class for each family. Tables or files can also be used to accomplish the same thing.
GoF Reference	Pages 87–96.

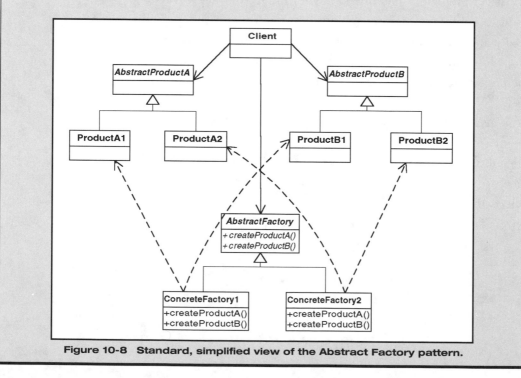

Figure 10-8   Standard, simplified view of the Abstract Factory pattern.

Figure 10-8 shows a **Client** using objects derived from two different server classes (**AbstractProductA** and **AbstractProductB**).
It is a design that simplifies, hides implementations, and makes a
system more maintainable.

*How Abstract
Factory works and
what its benefits are*

- The client object does not know which particular concrete
  implementations of the server objects it has because the factory
  object has the responsibility to create them.

- The client object does not even know which particular factory it
  uses since it only knows that it has an Abstract Factory object. It
  has a **ConcreteFactory1** or a **ConcreteFactory2** object, but
  it doesn't know which one.

I have hidden (encapsulated) from the **Client** the choice about
which server objects are being used. This will make it easier in the
future to make changes in the algorithm for making this choice
because the **Client** is unaffected.

The Abstract Factory pattern affords us a new kind of decomposition—decomposition by responsibility. Using it decomposes our
problem into

- Who is using our particular objects (**ApControl**)

- Who is deciding upon which particular objects to use
  (**AbstractFactory**)

Using the Abstract Factory is indicated when the problem domain
has different families of objects present and each family is used
under different circumstances.

*Abstract Factory
applies when there
are families of objects*

You may define families according to any number of reasons.
Examples include:

- Different operating systems (when writing cross-platform applications)

- Different performance guidelines

- Different versions of applications

- Different traits for users of the application

Once you have identified the families and the members for each family, you must decide how you are going to implement each case (that is, each family). In my example, I did this by defining an abstract class that specified which family member types could be instantiated. For each family, I then derived a class from this abstract class that would instantiate these family members.

A variation of the Abstract Factory pattern: configuration files

Sometimes you will have families of objects but do not want to control their instantiation with a different derived class for each family. Perhaps you want something more dynamic.

Examples might be

- You want to have a configuration file that specifies which objects to use. You can use a switch based on the information in the configuration file that instantiates the correct object.

- Each family can have a record in a database that contains information about which objects it is to use. Each column (field) in the database indicates which specific class type to use for each make method in the Abstract Factory.

A further variation: using the Class class in Java

If you are working in Java, you can take the configuration file concept one step further. Have the information in the field names represent the class name to use. It does not need to be the full class name as long as you have a set convention. For example, you could have a set prefix or suffix to add to the name in the file. Using Java's Class class you can instantiate the correct object based on these names.[2]

---

2. For a good description of Java's Class class see Eckel, B., *Thinking in Java*, Upper Saddle River, N.J.: Prentice Hall, 2000.

In real-world projects, members in different families do not always have a common parent. For example, in the earlier driver example, it is likely that the LRDD and HRDD driver classes are not derived from the same class. In cases like this, it is necessary to adapt them so an Abstract Factory pattern can work.

Adapters and the Abstract Factory

Relating the Abstract Factory Pattern to the CAD/CAM Problem

In the CAD/CAM problem, the system will have to deal with many sets of features, depending upon which CAD/CAM version it is working with. In the V1 system, all of the features will be implemented for V1. Similarly, in the V2 system, all of the features will be implemented for V2.

The families that I will use for the Abstract Factory pattern will be V1 Features and V2 Features.

Summary

The Abstract Factory is used when you must coordinate the creation of families of objects. It gives a way to take the rules regarding how to perform the instantiation out of the client object that is using these created objects.

In this chapter

- First, identify the rules for instantiation and define an abstract class with an interface that has a method for each object that needs to be instantiated.

- Then, implement concrete classes from this class for each family.

- The client object uses this factory object to create the server objects that it needs.

Supplement: C++ Code Examples

Example 10-4   C++ Code Fragments:
A Switch to Control Which Driver to Use

```cpp
// C++ CODE FRAGMENT

// class ApControl
   .   .   .
void ApControl::doDraw () {
   .   .   .
  switch (RESOLUTION) {
    case LOW:
      // use lrdd
    case HIGH:
      // use hrdd
  }
}
void ApControl::doPrint () {
   .   .   .
  switch (RESOLUTION) {
    case LOW:
      // use lrpd
    case HIGH:
      // use hrpd
  }
}
```

Example 10-5   C++ Code Fragments:
Using Polymorphism to Solve the Problem

```cpp
// C++ CODE FRAGMENT

// class ApControl
   .   .   .
void ApControl::doDraw () {
   .   .   .
  myDisplayDriver->draw();
}
void ApControl::doPrint () {
   .   .   .
  myPrintDriver->print();
}
```

Example 10-6 C++ Code Fragments: Implementation of ResFactory

```cpp
class ResFactory {
  public:
    virtual DisplayDriver *getDispDrvr()=0;
    virtual PrintDriver *getPrtDrvr()=0;
}

class LowResFact : public ResFactory {
  public:
    DisplayDriver *getDispDrvr();
    PrintDriver *getPrtDrvr();
}

DisplayDriver *LowResFact::getDispDrvr() {
  return new LRDD;
}

PrintDriver *LowResFact::getPrtDrvr() {
  return new LRPD;
}

class HighResFact : public ResFactory {
  public:
    DisplayDriver *getDispDrvr();
    PrintDriver *getPrtDrvr();
}

DisplayDriver *HighResFact::getDispDrvr() {
  return new HRDD;
}

PrintDriver *HighResFact::getPrtDrvr() {
  return new HRPD;
}
```

PART IV

Putting It All Together: Thinking in Patterns

Part Overview

In this part, I propose an approach to designing object-oriented systems based on patterns. I have proven this approach in my own
design practice. I apply this approach to the CAD/CAM problem
that we have been examining since Chapter 3, "A Problem That
Cries Out for Flexible Code."

This approach first tries to understand the context in which objects
show up.

In this part

Chapter	Discusses These Topics
11	• A discussion of Christopher Alexander's ideas and how experts use these ideas to design.
12	• Application of this approach to solve the CAD/CAM problem first presented in Chapter 3. • A comparison of this solution with the solution I developed in Chapter 4.
13	• A summary of what I have discussed about object-orientation and design patterns. • The concepts here are what I call *pattern-oriented design*.

CHAPTER 11

How Do Experts Design?

Overview

When trying to design, how do you start? Do you first get the details and see how they are put together? Or do you look from the big picture and break it down. Or is there another way?

In this chapter

Christopher Alexander's approach is to focus on the high-level relationships—in a sense, working from the top down. Before making any design decision, he feels it is essential to understand the context of the problem we are solving. He uses patterns to define these relationships. However, more than just presenting a collection of patterns, he offers us an entire approach to design. The area about which he is writing is architecture, designing places where people live and work, but his principles apply to software design as well.

In this chapter,

- I discuss Alexander's approach to design.
- I describe how to apply this in the software arena.

Building by Adding Distinctions

Now that you have a handle on some of the design patterns, it is time to see how they can work together. For Alexander, it is not enough to simply describe individual patterns. He uses them to develop a new paradigm for design.

The Timeless Way of Building: a book about architecture

. . . came to shape me as a designer

His book, *The Timeless Way of Building*, is both about patterns and how they work together. This is a beautiful book. It is one of my favorite books both on a personal level and on a professional level. It has helped me appreciate things in my life, to understand the environment in which I live, and also to achieve better software design.

How can this be? How can a book about designing buildings and towns have such a profound influence on designing software? I believe it is because it describes a paradigm that Alexander says a designer should work from. *Any* designer. It is this paradigm of design that I find most interesting.

I wish that I could say I had immediately adopted Alexander's insights the first time I read his book; however, that was not the case. My initial reaction to this book was, "This is very interesting. It makes sense." And then I went back to the traditional design methods that I had been using for so long.

But sometimes the old sayings turn out to be true. As in, "Luck is when opportunity meets with preparedness." Or, "Chance favors the prepared mind." I got "lucky" and that has made all the difference.

Within a few weeks of reading *The Timeless Way of Building*, I was faced with an opportunity. I was on a design project and my standard approaches weren't working. I had designs, but they weren't good enough. All of my tried and true design methods were failing me. I was very frustrated. Fortunately, I was wise enough to try a new way—Alexander's way—and was delighted with the results.

In the next chapter, I will describe what I did. But first, let's look at what Alexander offers us.

Design is often thought of as a process of synthesis, a process of putting together things, a process of combination. According to this view, a whole is created by putting together parts. The parts come first: and the form of the whole comes second.[1]

It is natural to design from parts to the whole, starting with the concrete things that I know.

When I first read this, I thought, "Yes. That is pretty much how I look at things. I figure out what I need and then put it together." That is, I identify my classes and then see how they work together. After assembling the pieces, I may step back to see that they fit in the big picture. But even when I switch my focus from local to global, I am still thinking about the pieces throughout the process.

As an object-oriented developer, these *pieces* are objects and classes. I identified them. I defined behavior and interfaces. But I started with pieces and typically stayed focused on them.

Think about the original CAD/CAM solution in Chapter 4, "A Standard Object-Oriented Solution." I started out thinking about the different classes I needed: slots, holes, cutouts, and so on. Knowing that I needed to relate these to a V1 system and a V2 system, I thought I needed a set of these classes that worked with V1 and another set of these classes that worked with V2. Finally, after coming up with these classes, I saw how they tied together.

But it is impossible to form anything which has the character of nature by adding preformed parts.[2]

---

1. Alexander, C., Ishikawa, S., Silverstein, M., *The Timeless Way of Building*, New York: Oxford University Press, 1979, p. 368.
2. ibid, p. 368.

Alexander's thesis is that building from the pieces is not a good way to design.

Even though Alexander is talking about architecture, many software design practitioners whom I respect said that his insights were valid for us as well. I had to open my mind to this new way of thinking. And when I did so, I heard Alexander say that "good software design cannot be achieved simply by adding together preformed parts" (i.e., parts defined before seeing how they would fit together).

Building by pieces will not get us elegance

When parts are modular and made before the whole, by definition then, they are identical, and it is impossible for every part to be unique, according to its position in the whole. Even more important, it simply is not possible for any combination of modular parts to contain the number of patterns which must be present simultaneously in a place which is alive.[3]

Alexander's talk about modularity was confusing to me at first. Then I realized that if we start out with modules before we have the big picture, the modules would be the same, since there would be no reason to for them to be different.

This seems to be the goal of reuse. Don't we want to use exactly the same modules again and again? Yes. But we also want maximum flexibility and robustness. Simply creating modules does not guarantee this.

Once I started to learn how to use design patterns—as Alexander teaches—I learned how to create reusable—and flexible—classes to a greater extent than I had been able to do before. I became a better designer.

---

3. ibid, pp. 368–369.

It is only possible to make a place which is alive by a process in which each part is modified by its position in the whole.[4]

Good design requires keeping the big picture in mind

When you read *alive*, think *robust and flexible systems*.

Earlier, Alexander said that parts need to be unique so that they can take advantage of their particular situation. Now, he takes this deeper. It is in coping with and fitting into the surroundings that gives a place its character. Think of examples in architecture:

- *A Swiss village*—Your mind's eye brings up a village of closely nestled cottages, each looking quite similar to the one next to it, but each one different in its own way. The differences are not arbitrary, but reflect the financial means of the builder and owner as well as the need of the building to blend in with its immediate surroundings. The effect is a very nice, comfortable image.

- *An American suburb*—All of the houses are pretty much cookie-cutter designs. Attention is rarely paid to the natural surroundings of the house. Covenants and standards attempt to enforce this homogeneity. The effect is a depersonalization of the houses and is not at all pleasing.

Applying this to software design might seem a bit too "conceptual" at this point. For now, it is enough to understand that the goal is to design pieces—classes, objects—within the context in which they must live in order to create robust and flexible systems.

In short, each part is given its specific form by its existence in the context of the larger whole.

The design process involves complexification

This is a differentiating process. It views design as a sequence of acts of *complexification*; structure is injected

---

4. ibid, p. 369.

into the whole by operating on the whole and crinkling it, not by adding little parts to one another. In the process of differentiation, the whole gives birth to its parts: The form of the whole, and its parts, come into being simultaneously. The image of the differentiating process is the growth of an embryo.[5]

"Complexification." What in the world does that mean? Isn't the goal to make things simpler, not more complex?

What Alexander is describing is a way to think about design that starts by looking at the problem in its simplest terms and then adds additional features (distinctions), making the design more complex as we go because we are adding more information.

This is a very natural process. We do it all the time. For example, suppose you need to arrange a room for a lecture with an audience of 40 people. As you describe your requirements to someone, you might say something like, "I'll need a room 30 feet by 30 feet" (starting simple). Then, "I'd like the chairs arranged theater style: 4 rows of 8" (adding information, you have made the description of the room more complex). And then, "I need a lectern at the front of the room" (even more complex).

How do we do this? What is the process of design?

The unfolding of a design in the mind of its creator, under the influence of language, is just the same.

Each pattern is an operator that differentiates space: that is, it creates distinctions where no distinction was before. And in the language the operations are arranged in sequence: so that, as they are done, one after another, gradually a complete thing is born, general in the sense

5. ibid, p. 370.

that it shared its patterns with other comparable things; specific in the sense that it is unique, according to its circumstances.

The language is a sequence of these operators, in which each one further differentiates the image, which is the product of the previous differentiations.[6]

Alexander asserts that design should start with a simple statement of the problem, then make it more detailed (complex) by injecting information into the statement. This information takes the form of a pattern. To Alexander, a pattern defines relationships between the entities in his problem domain.

For example, consider the Courtyard pattern discussed in Chapter 5, "An Introduction to Design Patterns." The pattern must describe the entities that are involved in a courtyard and how they relate. Entities such as

- The open spaces of the courtyard
- The crossing paths
- The views outward
- And even the people who are going to use the courtyard

Thinking in terms of how these entities need to relate to each other gives us a considerable amount of information with which to design the courtyard. We refine the design of the courtyard by thinking about the other patterns that would exist in the context of the courtyard pattern, such as porches or verandas facing the courtyard.

---

6. ibid, pp. 372–373.

What makes this analytical method so powerful is that it does not have to rely on my experience or my intuition or my creativity. Alexander's thesis is that these patterns exist independent of any person. A space is alive because it follows a natural process, not simply because the designer was a genius. Since the quality of a design is dependent upon following this natural process, it should not be surprising that quality solutions for similar problems appear very much alike.

Based on this, he gives us the rules a good designer would follow.

- *One at a time*—Patterns should be applied one at a time in sequence.

- *Context first*—Apply those patterns first that create the context for the other patterns.

Patterns define relationships.

The patterns that Alexander describes define relationships between the entities in the problem domain. These patterns are not as important as the relationships but give us a way to talk about them.

The steps to follow   Alexander's approach also applies to software design. Perhaps not literally but certainly philosophically. What would Alexander say to software designers?

Alexander's Steps	Discussion
Identify patterns	Identify the patterns that are present in your problem. Think about your problem in terms of the patterns that are present. Remember, the purpose of the pattern is to define relationships among entities.
Start with context patterns	Identify the patterns that create the context for the other patterns. These should be your starting point.
Then, work inward from the context	Look at the remaining patterns and at any other patterns that you might have uncovered. From this set, pick the patterns that define the context for the patterns that would remain. Repeat.
Refine the design	As you refine, always consider the context implied by the patterns.
Implement	The implementation incorporates the details dictated by the patterns.

Using Alexander in software design: a personal observation.

The first time I used Alexander's approach, I took his words too literally. His concepts—rooted in architecture—do not usually translate directly to software design (or other kinds of design). In some ways, I was lucky in my early experiences in using design patterns in that the problems I solved had the patterns follow pretty well-defined orders of context. However, this also worked against me in that I naively assumed that this method would work in general (it does not).

This was compounded by the fact that many key designers in the software community were espousing the development of "pattern languages"—looking for formal ways to apply Alexander to software. I interpreted this to mean that we were close to being able to apply Alexander's approach directly in software design (I no longer believe this to be true). Since Alexander said patterns in architecture had predetermined orders of context, I assumed patterns in software also had this predetermined order. That is, one type of pattern would always create the context for another type. I began to evangelize about Alexander's approach—as I understood it—while teaching others. A few months and a few projects later, I began to see the problems. There were cases where a preset order of contexts did not work.

Having been trained as a mathematician, I only needed one counterexample to disprove my theory. This started me questioning everything about my approach—something I usually did, but had forgotten in my excitement.

Since that early stage, I now look at the *principles* upon which Alexander's work is based. While they manifest themselves differently in architecture and in software development, these principles do apply to software design. I see it in improved designs. I see it in more rapid and robust analysis. I experience it every time I have to maintain my software.

Summary

In this chapter

Design is normally thought of as a process of synthesis, a process of putting things together. In software, a common approach is to look immediately for objects and classes and components and then think about how they should fit together.

In *The Timeless Way of Building*, Christopher Alexander described a better approach, one that is based on patterns:

1. Start out with a conceptual understanding of the whole in order to understand what needs to be accomplished.

2. Identify the patterns that are present in the whole.

3. Start with those patterns that create the context for the others.

4. Apply these patterns.

5. Repeat with the remaining patterns, as well as with any new patterns that were discovered along the way.

6. Finally, refine the design and implement within the context created by applying these patterns one at a time.

As a software developer, you may not be able to apply Alexander's pattern language approach directly. However, designing by adding concepts within the context of previously presented concepts is surely something that all of us can do. Keep this in mind as you learn new patterns later in this book. Many patterns create robust software because they define contexts within which the classes that implement them can work.

CHAPTER 12

Solving the CAD/CAM Problem with Patterns

Overview

In this chapter, I apply design patterns to solve the CAD/CAM problem presented in Chapter 3, "A Problem That Cries Out for Flexible Code."

In this chapter

In this chapter,

- I walk through the methods needed to solve the earlier CAD/CAM problem.

- I take you through the initial design phase. The details of implementation are left to you.

- I compare the new solution with the previous solution.

Review of the CAD/CAM Problem

In Chapter 3, I described the requirements for the CAD/CAM problem, a real-world problem that first got me on the road to using design patterns.

The requirements

The problem domain is in computer systems to support a large engineering organization, specifically, to support their CAD/CAM system.

The basic requirement is to create a computer program that can read a CAD/CAM dataset and extract the features that an existing expert system needs to be able to do intelligent design. This system is supposed to shield the expert system from the CAD/CAM system. The complication is that the CAD/CAM system was in the midst of

changes. Potentially, there could be multiple versions of the CAD/
CAM system that the expert system would have to interface with.

After initial interviews, I developed the high-level system architecture shown in Figure 12-1 and the following set of requirements for
the system:

Requirement	Description
Read a CAD/CAM model and extract features	• My system must be able to analyze and extract CAD/CAM descriptions of pieces of sheet metal. • The expert system then determines how the sheet metal should be made and generates the required instructions so that a robot can make it.
Be able to deal with many kinds of parts	• Initially, I am concerned with sheet metal parts. • Each sheet metal part can have multiple kinds of features, including slots, holes, cutouts, specials, and irregulars. It is unlikely that there will be other features in the future.
Handle multiple versions of the CAD/CAM system	• From Figure 12-1, you can infer that I need the ability to plug-and-play different CAD/CAM systems without having to change the expert system.

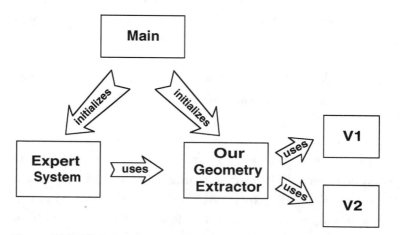

Figure 12-1 High-level view of the solution.

Thinking in Patterns

You have learned several patterns and have seen Alexander's philosophy of design: start with the big picture and add details. To accomplish this on a software project, I use the following steps:

The steps to thinking in patterns

1. Find the patterns I have in my problem domain. This is the set of patterns to be analyzed.

2. For the set of patterns to be analyzed, do the following:

   a. Pick the pattern that provides the most context for the other patterns.

   b. Apply this pattern to my highest conceptual design.

   c. Identify any additional patterns that might have come up. Add them to the set of patterns to be analyzed.

   d. Repeat for the sets of patterns that have not yet been analyzed.

3. Add detail as needed to the design. Expand the method and class definitions.

Admittedly this works only when you can understand the entire problem domain in terms of patterns. Unfortunately, this does not happen all the time. Design patterns give you the way to get started and then you have to fill in the rest by identifying relationships amongst the concepts in the problem domain. The method for doing this uses commonality/variability analysis and is outside the scope of this book. However, you can get more information about CVA on this book's Web site at *http://www.netobjectives.com/dpexplained*.

Thinking in Patterns: Step 1

In the previous chapters, I identified four patterns in the CAD/CAM problem. They are:

1. Identify the patterns

- Abstract Factory
- Adapter
- Bridge
- Facade

No other patterns stand out at this point, but I am open to some additional ones showing up.

Thinking in Patterns: Step 2a

Work through the patterns by context

I will work through the patterns, selecting them based on how each pattern creates the context for the other patterns.

2a. See which one creates the context for the others

When determining which patterns create the context for others in my problem domain, I apply an easy technique: I look through all possible pairings of the patterns, taken two at a time. In this case, there are six possible pairings, as shown in Figure 12-2.

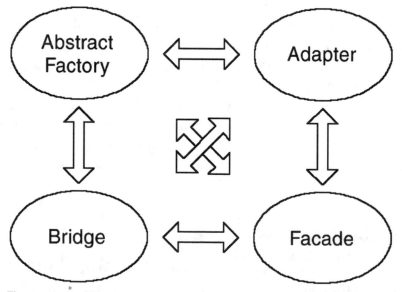

Figure 12-2 Different possible relationships between the patterns.

If you have several other patterns, it may look like this process could get very involved. That turns out not to be the case. With a little experience, many of the patterns can easily be eliminated up front from contention for the primary pattern. Usually, you have to deal with only a handful or so.

This doesn't take very long

In this case, there are few enough combinations that we can look at all of the possibilities.

What exactly do we mean when we say one pattern creates the context for another? One definition of *context* is the interrelated conditions in which something exists or occurs—an environment, a setting.

We look for what creates context

In the courtyard example in Chapter 11, "How Do Experts Design?" Alexander said that a porch exists in the context of the courtyard. The courtyard defines the environment or the settings in which the porch exists.

A pattern in a system often relates to other patterns in the system by providing a context for these other patterns. In your analysis, it is always valuable to look for whether and how a pattern relates to the other patterns, to look for the contexts that the pattern creates or provides for the other patterns as well as those contexts in which the pattern itself exists. You may not be able to find these every time. But, by looking, you will create higher-quality solutions.

Looking for context is an essential tool to add to your bag of analysis and design tools.

A rule to use when considering context.

During one of my projects, I was reflecting on my design approaches. I noticed something that I did consistently, almost unconsciously: I never worried about how I was going to instantiate my objects until I knew what I wanted my objects to be. My chief concern was with relationships between objects as if they already existed. I assumed that I would be able to construct the objects that fit in these relationships when the time comes to do so.

The reason I do this is that I need to minimize the number of things that I have to keep in my head during a design. Usually I can do so with a minimal amount of risk when I delay thinking about how to instantiate objects that meet my requirements. Worrying too early is counterproductive; it is better not to worry about instantiating objects until I know what it is that I need to instantiate. I will let tomorrow take care of itself—at least when it comes to instantiation!

Perhaps this seems sensible to you. I had never heard it stated as a rule and I wanted to check it out before adopting it as universal. I trust my intuition as a designer, but I am certainly not foolproof. So, I have conferred with several other experienced developers on this subject; without exception, they also follow this rule. That gives me confidence to offer it to you:

> *Rule: Consider what you need to have in your system before you concern yourself with how to create it.*

This fits Alexander's context rule: When you have a design pattern that involves creating objects, the objects set the context for the pattern.

When I am considering which pattern creates context for the others, I begin with Abstract Factory. The Abstract Factory's context is determined by the objects it needs to instantiate, as shown by the following:

Start with (and reject) Abstract Factory

- There will be a set of *make* methods, the implementation of each having a *return new xxx* in it.

- At this time, I do not know what *xxx* will be.

- *xxx* will be determined by the objects I am using.

- The objects that I will need to use are defined by other patterns.

Since I cannot even define the Abstract Factory until I know the classes the other patterns will define, it is not the seniormost pattern (the pattern that creates the context for the other patterns). Therefore, I reject it for now as the pattern to start working on.

In fact, the Abstract Factory will be the *last* pattern I do (unless another creational pattern shows up during my initial design, in which case, both creational patterns will vie for being last).

Seniormost patterns constrain the other patterns.

Seniormost is my term for the one or two patterns that establish a context for the other patterns in my system. This is the pattern that constrains what the other patterns can do. Other terms you could use are *outermost patterns* or *context-setting patterns*.

There are three pairs of patterns left to consider:

Three pairs left

- Adapter–Bridge

- Bridge–Facade

- Facade–Adapter

As someone new to patterns, I may not see any pattern that is obviously dependent on another pattern, nor any pattern that sets the context for all others.

When there is not an obvious choice, I have to work through the combination of patterns systematically looking for the following:

- Does one pattern define how the other pattern behaves?

- Do two patterns mutually influence each other?

Is there a relationship between the patterns?

The Adapter pattern is about modifying the interface of a class into another interface that the client is expecting. In this case, the interface that needs adapting is the **OOGFeature**. The Bridge pattern is about separating multiple concrete examples of an abstraction from their implementation. In this case, the abstraction is **Feature** and the implementations are the V1 and V2 systems. It sounds like the Bridge will need the Adapter to modify **OOGFeature**'s interface, that is, the Bridge will use the Adapter.

Clearly there is some relationship between Bridge and Adapter.

Are the patterns interrelated?

Can I define one of the patterns without another, or is one of the patterns needed by another?

Looking at the patterns tells us what to do.

- I can talk about the Bridge pattern as separating the **Feature**s from the V1 and V2 systems without actually knowing how I will use the V1 and V2 systems.

- However, I cannot talk about using an Adapter pattern to modify the V2 system's interface without knowing what it will be modified into. Without the Bridge pattern, this interface doesn't exist. The Adapter pattern exists to modify the V2 system's interface to the implementation interface the Bridge pattern defines.

Thus, the Bridge pattern creates the context for the Adapter pattern. I can eliminate the Adapter pattern as a candidate for seniormost pattern.

The relationship between *context* and *used by*.

Often, it seems that when one pattern uses another pattern, the pattern that is used is within the context of the pattern doing the using. There are likely exceptions to this rule, but it seems to hold most of the time.

Now I only have to compare Bridge–Facade and Facade–Adapter.

One down, two to go

I will look at the Bridge and Facade relationship first because if the Bridge turns out to be the primary pattern there as well, I do not need to consider the Adapter–Facade relationship (remember, I am only trying to identify the seniormost pattern at this point).

It should be readily apparent that the same logic that applied to Bridge and Adapter also applies to Bridge and Facade:

The Bridge–Facade relationship

- I will be using the Facade pattern to simplify the V1 system's interface.

- But what will be using the new interface I create? One of the implementations of the Bridge pattern.

Therefore, the Bridge pattern creates the context for the Facade. The Bridge is the seniormost pattern.

The Bridge is the winner

According to Alexander, I am supposed to start with the whole. Going back to the beginning, I find that I do not yet have the context for the Bridge.

Thinking in Patterns: Step 2b

The problem stated
as a whole

So, I retrace the design steps until I come to the context in which the Bridge pattern shows up. I want to build a system that translates CAD/CAM models into an NC set to give to a machine so that the part described by the model can be built (see Figure 12-3).

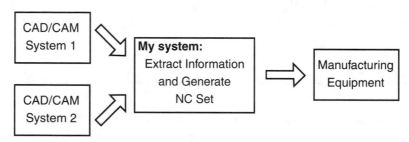

Figure 12-3 High-level view of system.

The expanded design

Of course, I had expanded this design by noting that I could use object-oriented design techniques to have the expert system use a **Model** class to get its information. **Model** would have two versions, one for each of the CAD/CAM systems. This is shown in Figure 12-4.

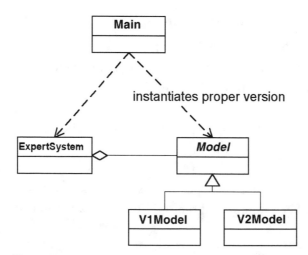

Figure 12-4 The classes to generate the NC set.

Remember, I am not concerned about the design of the expert system. While interesting (and, in many ways more challenging), that design had already been worked out. My focus is on the design of the **Model**. I know that the **Model** consists of **Feature**s, as shown in Figure 12-5.[1]

Expanding the design

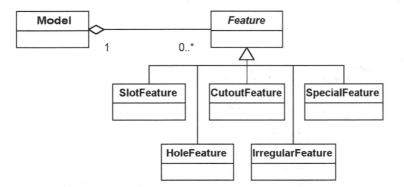

Figure 12-5 The Model design.

Now, I am ready for the Bridge pattern. It is apparent that I have multiple **Feature**s (the abstraction) with multiple CAD/CAM systems (the implementations). These are the objects that set the context for the Bridge pattern.

Ready for the Bridge

The Bridge pattern relates the **Feature**s to the different CAD/CAM system implementations. The **Feature** class is the **Abstraction** in the Bridge pattern while the V1 and V2 systems are the **Implementations**. But what about the **Model**? Is there a Bridge pattern present here as well? Not really. I can build the **Model** using inheritance because the only thing about the **Model** that varies is the implementation that is being used. In this case, I could make derivations of the **Model** for each CAD/CAM system as in Figure 12-6. If I tried using a Bridge pattern for the **Model**, I'd get the design shown in Figure 12-7.

How do we handle the Model?

---

1. The differences between **V1Model** and **V2Model** present little difficulty. Therefore, I will only discuss **Model** in general.

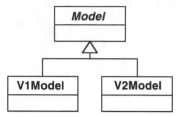

Figure 12-6 Using inheritance to handle the two model types.

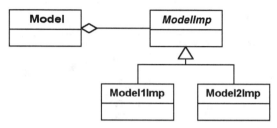

Figure 12-7 Using the Bridge pattern to handle the two model types.

Note that I do not really have a Bridge pattern in Figure 12-7 because **Model** is not varying except for the implementation. In the **Feature**, I have different types of **Feature**s that have different types of implementations—a Bridge pattern does exist here.

Start with the canonical form

I start implementing the Bridge pattern by using **Feature** as the abstraction and using V1 and V2 as the basis for the implementations. To translate the problem into the Bridge pattern, I start with the standard example of the Bridge pattern and then substitute classes into it. Figure 12-8 shows the standardized, simplified form (sometimes called the *canonical* form).

. . . and map classes into it

In the problem, **Feature** maps to **Abstraction**. There are five different kinds of features: slot, hole, cutout, irregular, and special. The implementations are the V1 and V2 systems; I choose to name the classes responsible for these implementations **V1Imp** and **V2Imp**, respectively.

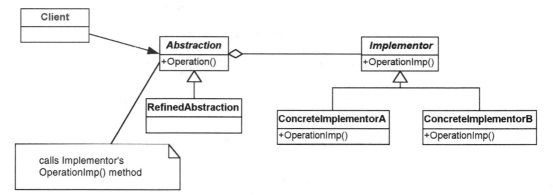

Figure 12-8   The canonical Bridge pattern.

Substituting the classes into the canonical Bridge pattern gives Figure 12-9.

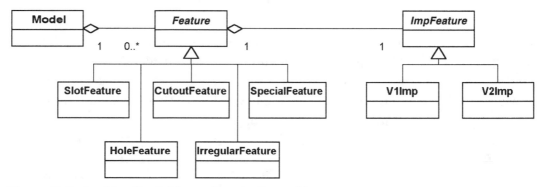

Figure 12-9   Applying the Bridge pattern to the problem.

In Figure 12-9, the **Feature**s are being implemented by an **ImpFeature**, which is either a **V1Imp** or a **V2Imp**. In this design, **ImpFeature** would have to have an interface that allowed for **Feature** to get whatever information it needed to give **Model** the information it requested. Thus, **ImpFeature** would have an interface including methods such as

- *getX* to get the X position of **Feature**

- *getY* to get the Y position of **Feature**

- *getLength* to get the length of **Feature**

It would also have methods used by only some **Feature**s:

- *getEdgeType* to get the type of edge of **Feature**

Note: Only features that need this information should call this method. Later, I will talk about how to use this contextual information to help debug the code.

Thinking in Patterns: Step 2c

Not done yet

Maybe I cannot see how to finish the implementation yet, and that is okay. I still have other patterns to apply.

Identifying any additional patterns

Looking at Figure 12-9, I should ask myself if any other patterns show up that I had not previously identified. I do not see any additional patterns. There is only the challenge of hooking the V1 and V2 CAD/CAM systems into the design. That is what the Facade and Adapter patterns will do for me.

Thinking in Patterns: Step 2d (Facade)

Do the remaining patterns create a context for each other?

Next, I need to verify if any of the remaining patterns create a context for each other. In this case, Facade and Adapter now clearly relate to different pieces of the design and are independent of each other. Therefore, I can apply them in whatever order I choose. I will arbitrarily pick the Facade to apply next, which results in Figure 12-10.

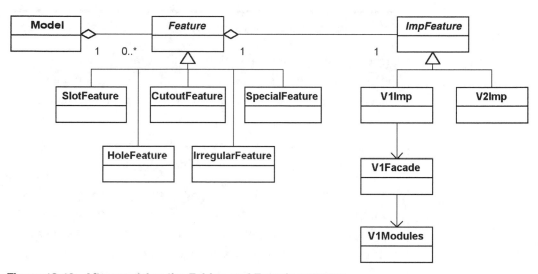

Figure 12-10   After applying the Bridge and Facade patterns.

Applying the Facade pattern means that I insert a facade between the V1 modules and the **V1Imp** object that is going to use them. **V1Facade** has simplified methods that relate to what **V1Imp** needs to do. Each method in **V1Facade** will look like a series of function calls on the V1 system.

The Facade

The kind of information that I need in order to call these functions will determine how **V1Imp** is implemented. For example, when using V1, I need to tell it which model to use and what the **Feature**'s ID is. All **V1Imp** objects that use the **V1Facade** will therefore need to know this information. Since this is implementation-specific information, it will need to know it itself, rather than getting it from the calling **Feature**. Thus, in a V1 system, each **Feature** will need its own **V1Imp** object (to remember system-specific information about the feature). I will go over this in more detail once the general architecture is completed.

Taking advantage of nongeneralities to debug code.

Earlier in this chapter, I mentioned that some of the methods of the implementation should only be called by certain **Feature** objects. I can take advantage of knowing what should be calling what to put checks in the code. I do not need to do this, and I may need to remove these checks if the rules change. Nevertheless, it can be useful the first time in.

For example, in the CAD/CAM solution, there are **Feature**s containing an implementation object. One of the implementation methods is *getEdgeType*. This only makes sense if a **Feature** is a slot or a cutout. Other **Feature**s do not have edge types. If I have implemented things properly, the *getEdgeType* method will never get called except by slots and cutouts. I can check that this happens by using an assert in the *getEdgeType* method that verifies that the calling **Feature** is of the appropriate type.

Thinking in Patterns: Step 2d (Adapter)

Pick Adapter next   Having applied Facade, I can now apply Adapter. This results in Figure 12-11.

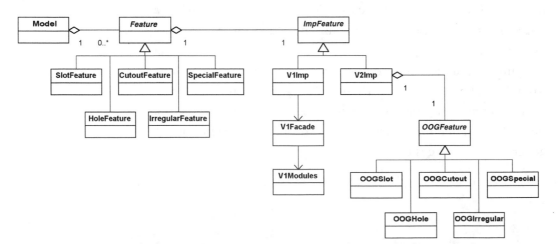

Figure 12-11 After applying the Bridge, Facade, and Adapter.

Thinking in Patterns: Step 2d (Abstract Factory)

All that is left is the Abstract Factory. As it turns out, this pattern is not needed. The rationale for using an Abstract Factory was to ensure all of the implementation objects were of type **V1** if I had a V1 system or of type **V2** if I had a V2 system. However, the **Model** object itself will know this. There is no point implementing a pattern if some other object can easily encapsulate the rules of creation. I left the Abstract Factory in the set of patterns because while I was first solving this problem I did think the Abstract Factory was present. It also illustrates how thinking that a pattern is present when it is not is not necessarily counterproductive.

Finally, do Abstract Factory

Thinking in Patterns: Step 3

The details of the design may still take some work. However, I would continue with the design by following Alexander's mandate of designing by context. For example, when I see how I need to implement a **SlotFeature** class or the **V1Imp** class, I should remember how the patterns involved are used. In this case, I note that in the Bridge pattern, the methods involving the abstractions are independent of implementation. This means that the **Abstraction** class (**Feature**) and all of its derivations (**Slot-Feature**, **HoleFeature**, and so forth) contain no implementation information. Implementation information is left to the **Implementation** classes.

Finishing the rest

This means the **Feature** derivations will have methods such as *getLocation* and *getLength*, while the **Implementation**s will contain a way to access this required information. A **V1Imp** object, for example, would need to know the ID of the **Feature** in the V1 system. Since each **Feature** has a unique ID, this means there will be one **Implementation** object for each **Feature** object. The methods in the **V1Imp** object will use this ID to ask the **V1Facade** for information about the object.

Assigning responsibilities

A comparable solution will exist for the V2 implementations. In this case, the `V2Imp` objects will contain a reference to the `OOGFeature` in question.

Comparison with the Previous Solution

Comparing solutions

Compare this new solution, shown in Figure 12-11, with the earlier solution, which is shown again in Figure 12-12.

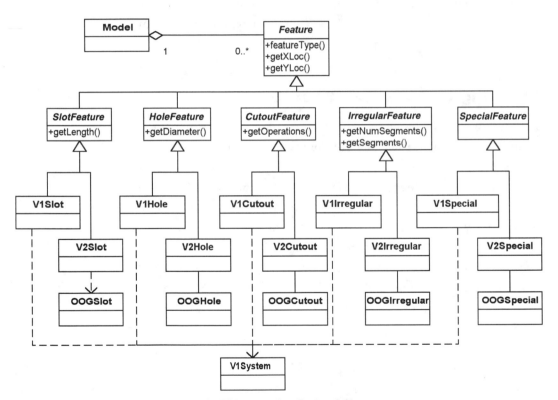

Figure 12-12   This was the first solution.

A different way to compare solutions

Another way to compare two solutions is to *read* them. In other words, the diagrams visually show inheritance (the *is-a* relationship) and composition (the *has-a* relationship). Read these diagrams using those words where the relationships are present.

In the original solution, I had a model that contains **Feature**s. **Feature**s are either slot features, hole features, cutout features, irregular features, or special features. Slot features are either V1 slots or V2 slots. V1 slots use the V1 system while the V2 slots use the **OOGSlot**. Hole features are either V1 hole features or V2 hole features. V1 hole features use the V1 system while the V2 hole features use the **OOGHole**. Getting tired of this already, aren't you?

Now read the latest solution. I have a model that contains **Feature**s. **Feature**s are either slot features, hole features, cutout features, irregular features, or special features. All features contain an implementation which is either a V1 implementation or a V2 implementation. V1 implementations use a V1 Facade to access the V1 system while V2 implementations adapt an **OOGFeature**. That's it. It sounds much better than just a portion of the other solution.

Summary

In this chapter, I showed how the standard way of doing designs can often lock us into systems that are hard to maintain. Often, it can be difficult to see the forest for the trees because I become overly focused on the details of the system—the classes.

In this chapter

Christopher Alexander gives us a better way. By using patterns in the problem domain, I can look at the problem in a different way. I start with the big picture and add distinctions as I go. Each pattern gives me more information than what I had before I used it.

By selecting the pattern that creates the biggest picture—the context for the system—and then inserting the next significant pattern, I developed an application architecture that I could not have seen by looking at the classes alone. Thus, I begin to learn to design by context instead of by putting together pieces that were identified locally.

Like the two carpenters in Chapter 5, "An Introduction to Design Patterns," who were trying to decide between a dovetail joint and a miter joint, it is the context that should shape the design. In design decisions, we often get bogged down by the details and forget about the larger context of the system. The details cast a cloud around the bigger picture by focusing us on small, local decisions. Patterns give you the language to rise above the details and bring the context into the discussion in practical ways. This makes it more likely that you will see the forces present in the problem domain. Patterns help us apply what other designers before us have learned about what does and does not work. In so doing, they help to create systems that are robust, maintainable, and alive.

CHAPTER 13

The Principles and Strategies of Design Patterns

Overview

Previously, I described how design patterns can be used at both the local and global levels. At local levels, patterns tell us how to solve particular problems within the context of the patterns. At global levels, patterns create a map of how the components of the application interrelate with one another. One way to study design patterns is to learn how to use them more effectively at both the local and global levels. They will give you tools to get a better handle on your problem.

In this chapter

Another way to study design patterns is learn their mechanisms and the principles and strategies that underlie them. Learning these will improve your abilities as an analyst and designer. You will know what to do even in situations when a design pattern has not yet been developed, because you will already have the building blocks needed to solve the problem.

In this chapter,

- I describe the open-closed principle, which underlies many design patterns.

- I discuss the principle of designing from context, which was an initial objective of Alexander's patterns.

- I discuss the principle of containing variation.

The Open-Closed Principle

Extend software capabilities without changing it

Software clearly needs to be extensible. However, making changes to software runs the risk of introducing problems. This dilemma led Bertrand Meyer to propose the *open-closed principle*.[1] To paraphrase this principle, the modules, methods, and classes should be open for extension, while closed for modification.[2] In other words, we must design our software so that we can extend the capabilities of our software without changing it.

As contradictory as this may sound at first, you have already seen examples of it. In the Bridge pattern, for instance, it is quite possible to add new implementations (that is, to extend the software) without changing any of the existing classes.

The Principle of Designing from Context

Patterns are microcosms of Alexander's philosophy

Alexander tells us to design from context, to create the big picture before designing the details in which our pieces appear. Most design patterns follow this approach, some to a greater extent than others. Of the four patterns I have described so far, the Bridge pattern is the best example of this.

Refer to the Bridge pattern diagram in Chapter 9, "The Bridge Pattern," (see Figure 9-13). When deciding how to design the **Implementation** classes, think about their context: the way that the classes derived from the **Abstraction** class will use them.

For example, if I were writing a system that needed to draw shapes on different types of hardware and that therefore required different implementations, I would use a Bridge pattern. The Bridge tells me that the shapes will use my implementations (that is, the drawing

---

1. Meyer, B., *Object-Oriented Software Construction*, Upper Saddle River, N.J.: Prentice Hall, 1997, p. 57.
2. See this book's Web site for a link to "The Open-Closed Principle," an excellent article by Robert C. Martin. Go to *http://www.netobjectives.com/dpexplained*.

programs I will write) through a common interface. Designing from context, as Alexander would have, means that I should first look at the requirements of my shapes—that is, what am I going to have to draw? These shapes will determine the required behaviors for my implementations. For example, the implementations (the drawing programs) may have to draw lines, circles, and so forth.

By using commonality/variability analysis in conjunction with the context within which my classes occur, I can simultaneously see both the cases I must handle now and possible future cases. I can then decide how generalized I want to make the implementations based on the cost of extra generalization. This often leads to a more general implementation than I would have thought of otherwise, but with only marginally higher cost.

Advantages to designing from context

For example, when looking at my needs to draw shapes, I might readily identify lines and circles as requirements. If I ask myself, "What shapes do I not support with lines and circles," I might notice that I would not be able to implement ellipses. Now I have a choice:

- Implement a way to draw ellipses in addition to the lines and circles.

- Realize that ellipses are a generalized case of circles and implement them instead of circles.

- Don't implement ellipses if the cost is greater than the perceived gain.

The prior example illustrates another important concept in design: just because an opportunity exists doesn't mean it has to be pursued. My experience with design patterns is that they give me insights into my problem domains. However, I don't always (nor even usually) act on these insights by writing for situations that have not yet arisen. However, by helping me design from context,

Identifying opportunities doesn't mean having to follow them

the patterns themselves allow me to anticipate possible variation because I have divided my system into well-behaved classes, thereby making changes easier to accommodate. Design patterns help me see where variations may occur, not so much which particular variations will occur. The well-defined interface I use to contain my current variations often contains the impacts of new requirements just as well.

The context of the
Abstract Factory

The Abstract Factory is another good example of designing by context. I may understand early on that a factory object of some sort will be used to coordinate the instantiation of families (or sets) of objects. However, there are many different ways to implement it as follows.

Implementation . . .	Comments . . .
Using derived classes	The classic Abstract Factory implementation requires me to implement a derivation for each set that I need. This is a little cumbersome but has the advantage of allowing me to add new classes without changing any of my existing classes.
Using a single object with switches	If I am willing to change the Abstract Factory class as needed, I can simply have one object that contains all of the rules. While this doesn't follow the open-closed principle, it does contain all of my rules in one place and is not hard to maintain.
Using a configuration file with switches	This is more flexible than the prior case, but still requires modifying the code at times.
Using a configuration file with RTTI (runtime-type-identification)	RTTI includes a way of instantiating objects based on the name of the object placed in a string. Implementations of this sort have great flexibility in that new classes and new combinations can be added without having to change any code.

With all of these choices, how do you decide which one to use to implement the Abstract Factory? Decide from the context in which it appears. Each of the four cases just shown has advantages over the others, depending upon factors such as

How to decide?

From the context

- The likelihood of future variation

- The importance of not modifying our current system

- Who controls the sets to be created (us or another development group)

- The language in use

- The availability of a database or configuration file

This list is not complete, nor even is the list of implementation possibilities. What should be evident to you, however, is that trying to decide how to implement an Abstract Factory without understanding how it will be used (that is, without understanding its context) is a fool's errand.

How to make design decisions.

When trying to decide between alternative implementations, many developers ask the question, "Which of these implementations is better?" This is not the best question to ask. The problem is that often one implementation is not inherently better than another. A better set of questions to ask is, for each alternative, "Under what circumstances would this alternative be better than the other alternative?" Then ask, "Which of these circumstance is most like my problem domain?" It is a small matter of stopping and stepping back. Using this approach tends to keep me more aware of the variation and scalability issues in my problem domain.

The context of the Adapter

The Adapter pattern illustrates design from context because it almost always shows up within a context. By definition, an Adapter is used to convert an existing interface into another interface. The obvious question is, "How do I know what to convert the existing interface to?" You typically don't until the context is presented (that is, the class to which you are adapting).

I have already shown that Adapters can be used to adapt a class to fit the role of a pattern that is present. This was the case in my CAD/CAM problem, where I had an existing implementation that needed to be adapted into my Bridge-driven implementation.

The context of the Facade

The Facade pattern is very similar to the Adapter pattern in terms of context. Typically, it is defined in the context of other patterns or classes. That is, I must wait until I can see who wants to use the Facade in order to design its interface.

A word of warning

Early on in my use of patterns I tended to think I could always find which patterns created context for others. In Alexander's *A Pattern Language*, he is able to do just that with patterns in architecture. Since many people are talking about pattern languages for software, I wondered, "Why can't I?" It seems pretty clear that Adapters and Facades would always be defined in the context of something else. Right?

Wrong.

One great advantage of being a software developer who also teaches is that I have the opportunity to get involved in many more projects than I could possibly be involved in as a developer only. Early in my teachings of design patterns I thought Adapters and Facades would always come after other noncreational patterns in the order of defining context. In fact, they usually do. However, some systems have the requirement of building to a particular interface. In this case, it is a Facade or an Adapter (just one of many in the system, of course) that may be the seniormost pattern.

The Principle of Encapsulating Variation

Several people have remarked about a certain similarity in all of the designs they have seen me create: my inheritance hierarchies rarely go more than two levels of classes deep. Those that do typically fit into a design pattern structure that requires two levels as a base for the derived classes (the Decorator pattern, discussed in Chapter 15, is an example that uses three levels).

A note on my designs

The reason for this is that one of my design goals is never to have a class contain two things that are varying that are somehow coupled to each other. The patterns I have described so far do illustrate different ways of encapsulating variation effectively.

The Bridge pattern is an excellent example of encapsulated variation. The implementations present in the Bridge pattern are all different but are accessed through a common interface. New implementations can be accommodated by implementing them within this interface.

Encapsulating variation in the Bridge pattern

The Abstract Factory encapsulates the variation of which sets or families of objects can be instantiated. There are many different ways of implementing this pattern. It is useful to note that even if one implementation is initially chosen and then it is determined another way would have been better, the implementation can be changed without affecting any other part of the system (since the interface for the factory does not change, only the way it is implemented). Thus, the notion of the Abstract Factory itself (implementing to an interface) hides all of the variations of how to create the objects.

Encapsulating variation in the Abstract Factory

The Adapter pattern is a tool to be used to take disparate objects and give them a common interface. This is often needed now that I am designing to interfaces as called for in many patterns.

Using the Adapter pattern to help encapsulate variation

Encapsulating variation in the Facade pattern

The Facade typically does not encapsulate variation. However, I have seen many cases where a Facade was used to work with a particular subsystem. Then, when another subsystem came along, a Facade for the new subsystem was built with the same interface. This new class was a combination Facade and Adapter in that the primary motivation was simplification, but now had the added constraint of being the same as the one used before so none of the client objects would need to change. Using a Facade this way hides variations in the subsystems being used.

Not just about encapsulating variation

Patterns are not just about encapsulating variation, however. They also identify relationships between variations. I will show more about this in the next section of this book. Referring to the Bridge pattern again, note that the pattern not only defines and encapsulates the variations in the abstraction and implementation, but also defines the relationship between the two sets of variations.

Summary

In this chapter

In this chapter, I have shown how patterns illustrate two powerful design strategies:

- Design from context
- Encapsulate variations in classes

These strategies allow us to defer decisions until we can see the ramifications of these decisions. Looking at the context from which we are designing gives us better designs.

By encapsulating variation, I can accommodate many future variations that may arise but would not be accommodated when I do not try to make my designs more general-purpose. This is critical for those projects that do not have all of the resources you would like to have (in other words, all projects). By encapsulating variation appropriately, I can implement only those features I need without sacrificing future quality. Trying to figure out and accommodate all possible variations typically does not lead to better systems but often leads to no system at all. This is called paralysis by analysis.

PART V

Handling Variations with Design Patterns

Part Overview

In this part, I work through another case study. In this case study, I will consider the requirements for the problem one at a time, rather than specifying every requirement up front. I will describe a system that is currently working when a new requirement comes in that forces me to find the best way to modify the code. I will use this process to present a few new design patterns—one for each new requirement.

In this part

Chapter	Discusses These Topics
14	The **Strategy pattern**: How to handle varying algorithms and business rules.
15	The **Decorator pattern**: How to dynamically add behavior before or after an object's current behavior.
16	The **Singleton pattern** and the **Double-Checked Locking pattern**: How to ensure not more than one instance of a class is ever instantiated, even in a multithreaded environment.
17	The **Observer pattern**: How to let one part of a system know when an event takes place in another.
18	The **Template Method pattern**: What to do when you have different cases that use essentially the same procedure, but their steps must be implemented in slightly different ways.
19	The **Factory Method pattern**: How to defer instantiation of particular objects to derived classes.
20	The **Analysis Matrix**: How to track multiple variations that are present in your problem domain and map them into patterns.

When a new requirement is introduced to the problem, I will look at the different alternatives I could use, such as:

- Using switches in the code

- Specialization with inheritance

- Encapsulating what varies and containing it or using a reference to it

By looking at these alternatives, I show that there are similarities among many of the patterns: often, different patterns will approach handling variation and new requirements in a similar fashion.

CHAPTER 14

The Strategy Pattern

Overview

This chapter introduces a new case study, which comes from the area of *e-tailing* (electronic retailing over the Internet). It also begins a solution using the Strategy pattern. The solution to this case study will continue to evolve through Chapter 20, "The Analysis Matrix."

In this chapter

In this chapter,

- I describe an approach to handling new requirements.

- I introduce the new case study.

- I describe the Strategy pattern and show how it handles a new requirement in the case study.

- I describe the key features of the Strategy pattern.

An Approach to Handling New Requirements

Many times in life and many times in software applications, you have to make choices about the general approach to performing a task or solving a problem. Most of us have learned that taking the easiest route in the short run can lead to serious complications in the long run. For example, none of us would ignore oil changes for our car beyond a certain point. True, I may not change the oil every 3,000 miles, but I also do not wait until 30,000 miles before changing the oil (if I did so, there would be no need to change the oil any more: the car would not work!). Or consider desktop filing—the technique many of us have of using the tops of our desks as a filing cabinet. It works well in the short run, but in the long run, it

Disaster often comes in the long run from suboptimal decisions in the short run

becomes tough to find things as the piles grow. Disaster often comes in the long run from suboptimal decisions made in the short run.

This is true in software as well: we focus on immediate concerns and ignore the longer term

Unfortunately, when it comes to software development, many people have not learned these lessons yet. Many projects are only concerned with handling immediate, pressing needs, without concern for future maintenance. There are several reasons projects tend to ignore long-term issues like ease of maintenance or ability to change. Common excuses include

- "We really can't figure out how the new requirements are going to change."

- "If we try to see how things will change, we'll stay in analysis forever."

- "If we try to write our software so we can add new functionality to it, we'll stay in design forever."

- "We don't have the time or budget to do so."

The choices seem to be

- Overanalyze or overdesign—I like to call this "paralysis by analysis," or

- Just jump in, write the code without concern for long-term issues, and then get on another project before this short-sightedness causes too many problems. I like to call this "abandon (by) ship (date)!"

Since management is under pressure to deliver and not to maintain, maybe these results are not surprising. However, with a moment's reflection, it becomes apparent that there is an underlying belief system that prevents many software developers from seeing other alternatives—the belief that designing for change is more costly than designing without considering change.

But this is not necessarily the case. Indeed, the opposite is often true: When you step back to consider how your system may change over time, a better design usually becomes apparent to you—in virtually the same amount of time that would be required to do a "standard" get-it-done-now design.

The approach I use in the following case study considers how systems may change. However, it is important to note that I will be anticipating that changes will occur and look to see *where* they will occur. I will not be trying to anticipate the exact nature of the change. This approach is based on the principles described in the Gang of Four book:

Designing for change

- *"Program to an interface, not an implementation."*[1]

- *"Favor object composition over class inheritance."*[2]

- *"Consider what should be variable in your design.* This approach is the opposite of focusing on the cause of redesign. Instead of considering what might force a change to a design, consider what you want to be able to change without redesign. The focus here is on encapsulating the concept that varies, a theme of many design patterns."*[3]

What I suggest is that when faced with modifying code to handle a new requirement, you should at least consider following these strategies. If following these strategies will not cost significantly more to design and implement, then use them. You can expect a long-term benefit from doing so, with only a modest short-term cost (if any).

---

1. Gamma, E., Helm, R., Johnson, R., Vlissides, J., *Design Patterns: Elements of Reusable Object-Oriented Software*, Reading, Mass.: Addison-Wesley, 1995, p. 18.
2. ibid, p. 20.
3. ibid, p. 29.

I am not proposing to follow these strategies blindly, however. I can test the value of an alternative design by examining how well it conforms to the good principles of object-oriented design. This is essentially the same approach I used in deriving the Bridge pattern in Chapter 9, "The Bridge Pattern." In that chapter, I measured the quality of alternative designs by seeing which one followed object-oriented principles the best.

Initial Requirements of the Case Study

A motivating example: an e-tail system

Suppose I am writing an e-tail system that supports sales in the United States. The general architecture has a controller object that handles sales requests. It identifies when a sales order is being requested and hands the request off to a **SalesOrder** object to process the order.

The system looks something like Figure 14-1.

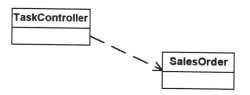

Figure 14-1   Sales order architecture for an e-tail system.

Some features of the system

The functions of **SalesOrder** include

- Allow for filling out the order with a GUI.

- Handle tax calculations.

- Process the order. Print a sales receipt.

Some of these functions are likely to be implemented with the help of other objects. For example, **SalesOrder** would not necessarily print itself; rather, it serves as a holder for information about sales orders. A particular **SalesOrder** object could call a **SalesTicket** object that prints the **SalesOrder**.

Handling New Requirements

After writing this application, suppose I receive a new requirement to change the way I have to handle taxes. Now, I have to be able to handle taxes on orders from customers outside the United States. At a minimum, I will need to add new rules for computing these taxes.

New requirement for taxation rules

How can I handle these new rules? I could attempt to reuse the existing **SalesOrder** object, processing this new situation like a new kind of sales order, only with a different set of taxation rules. For example, for Canadian sales, I could derive a new class called **CanadianSalesOrder** from **SalesOrder** that would override the tax rules. I show this solution in Figure 14-2.

*One approach: reuse the **SalesOrder** object*

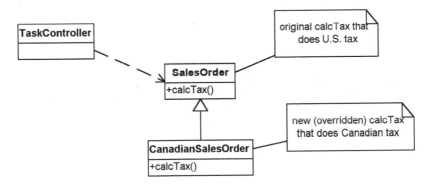

Figure 14-2 Sales order architecture for an e-commerce system.

Now, design patterns repeatedly demonstrate a fundamental rule of design patterns: "Favor object composition over class inheritance."[4] The solution in Figure 14-2 does just the opposite! In other words, I

. . . but this violates a fundamental rule of design patterns

---

4. ibid, p. 20.

have handled the variation in tax rules by using inheritance to derive a new class with the new rule.

Take a different approach

How could I approach this differently? Following the rules I stated earlier: attempt to "consider what should be variable in your design" . . . and "encapsulate the concept that varies."[5]

Following this two-step approach, I should do the following:

1. Find what varies and encapsulate it in a class of its own.

2. Contain this class in another class.

Step 1: Find what varies and encapsulate it

In this example, I have already identified that the tax rules are varying. To encapsulate them would mean creating an abstract class that defines how to accomplish taxation conceptually, and then derive concrete classes for each of the variations. In other words, I could create a **CalcTax** object that defines the interface to accomplish this task. I could then derive the specific versions needed. I show this in Figure 14-3.

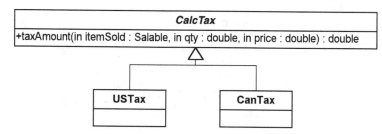

Figure 14-3 Encapsulating tax rules.

---

5. ibid, p. 29.

Continuing on, I now use composition instead of inheritance. This means, instead of making different versions of sales orders (using inheritance), I will contain the variation with composition. That is, I will have one **SalesOrder** class and have it contain the **CalcTax** class to handle the variations. I show this in Figure 14-4.

Step 2: Favor composition

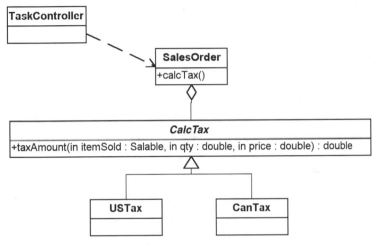

Figure 14-4   Favoring composition over inheritance.

UML Diagrams

In the UML, it is possible to define parameters in the methods. This is done by showing a parameter and its type in the parenthesis of the method.

Thus, in Figure 14-4, the *taxAmount* method has three parameters:

- *itemSold* of type **Salable**

- *qty* of type **double**

- *price* of type **double**

All of these are inputs denoted by the "in." The *taxAmount* method also returns a **double**.

How this works

I have defined a fairly generic interface for the **CalcTax** object. Presumably, I would have a **Saleable** class that defines saleable items (and how they are taxed). The **SalesOrder** object would give that to the **CalcTax** object, along with the quantity and price. This would be all the information the **CalcTax** object would need.

Improves cohesion, aids flexibility

Another advantage of this approach is that cohesion has improved. Sales tax is handled in its own class. Another advantage is that as I get new tax requirements, I simply need to derive a new class from **CalcTax** that implements them.

Easier to shift responsibilities

Finally, it becomes easier to shift responsibilities. For example, in the inheritance-based approach, I *had* to have the **TaskController** decide which type of **SalesOrder** to use. With the new structure, I can have either the **TaskController** do it or the **SalesOrder** do it. To have the **SalesOrder** do it, I would have some configuration object that would let it know which tax object to use (probably the same one the **TaskController** was using). I show this in Figure 14-5.

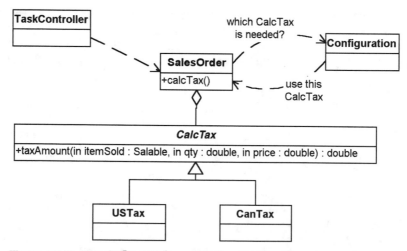

Figure 14-5 The SalesOrder object using Configuration to tell it which CalcTax to use.

This approach allows the business rule to vary independently from the `SalesOrder` object that uses it. Note how this works well for current variations I have as well as any future ones that might come along. Essentially, this use of encapsulating an algorithm in an abstract class (`CalcTax`) and using one of them at a time interchangeably is the Strategy pattern.

The Strategy pattern

The Strategy Pattern

According to the Gang of Four, the Strategy pattern's intent is to

The intent, according to the Gang of Four

> Define a family of algorithms, encapsulate each one, and make them interchangeable. Strategy lets the algorithm vary independently from the clients that use it.[6]

The Strategy pattern is based on a few principles:

The motivations of the Strategy pattern

- Objects have responsibilities.

- Different, specific implementations of these responsibilities are manifested through the use of polymorphism.

- There is a need to manage several different implementations of what is, conceptually, the same algorithm.

- It is a good design practice to separate behaviors that occur in the problem domain from each other—that is, to decouple them. This allows me to change the class responsible for one behavior without adversely affecting another.

---

6. ibid, p. 315.

The Strategy Pattern: Key Features

Intent	Allows you to use different business rules or algorithms depending upon the context in which they occur.
Problem	The selection of an algorithm that needs to be applied depends upon the client making the request or the data being acted upon. If you simply have a rule in place that does not change, you do not need a Strategy pattern.
Solution	Separates the selection of algorithm from the implementation of the algorithm. Allows for the selection to be made based upon context.

Participants and Collaborators

- The `Strategy` specifies how the different algorithms are used.
- The `ConcreteStrategies` implement these different algorithms.
- The `Context` uses the specific `ConcreteStrategy` with a reference of type `Strategy`. The `Strategy` and `Context` interact to implement the chosen algorithm (sometimes the `Strategy` must query the `Context`). The `Context` forwards requests from its `Client` to the `Strategy`.

Consequences

- The Strategy pattern defines a family of algorithms.
- Switches and/or conditionals can be eliminated.
- You must invoke all algorithms in the same way (they must all have the same interface). The interaction between the `ConcreteStrategies` and the `Context` may require the addition of *getState* type methods to the `Context`.

Implementation

Have the class that uses the algorithm (the `Context`) contain an abstract class (the `Stragegy`) that has an abstract method specifying how to call the algorithm. Each derived class implements the algorithm as needed. *Note:* this method wouldn't be abstract if you wanted to have some default behavior.

Note: In the prototypical Strategy pattern, the responsibility for selecting the particular implementation to use is done by the `Client` object and is given to the context of the `Strategy` pattern.

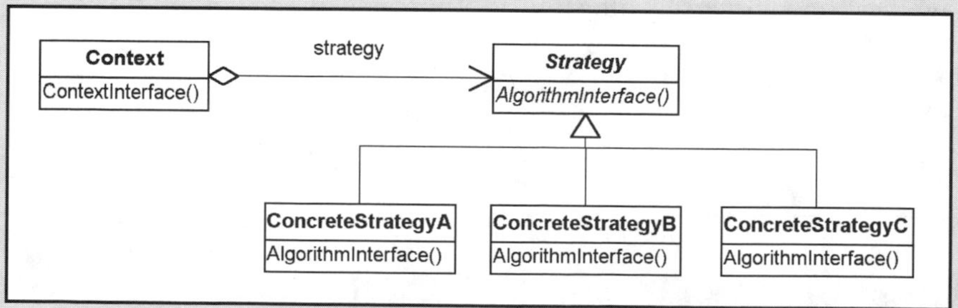

Figure 14-6   Standard, simplified view of the Strategy pattern.

Field Notes: Using the Strategy Pattern

I had been using the e-tail example in my pattern classes when someone asked, "Are you aware that in the UK people over a certain age don't get taxed on food?" I wasn't aware of this and the interface for the **CalcTax** object did not handle this case. I could handle this in at least one of three ways:

The limits proves the pattern

1. Pass the age of the **Customer** into the **CalcTax** object and use it if needed.

2. Be more general by passing in the **Customer** object itself and querying it if needed.

3. Be more general still by passing a reference to the **SalesOrder** object (that is, **this**) and letting the **CalcTax** object query it.

While it is true I have to modify the **SalesOrder** and **CalcTax** classes to handle this case, it is clear how to do this. I am not likely to introduce a problem because of this.

Technically, the Strategy pattern is about encapsulating algorithms. However, in practice, I have found that it can be used for encapsulating virtually any kind of rule. In general, when I am doing analysis and I hear about applying different business rules at different times, I consider the possibility of a Strategy pattern handling this variation for me.

Encapsulating business rules

The Strategy pattern requires that the algorithms (business rules) being encapsulated now lie outside of the class that is using them (the **Context**). This means that the information needed by the strategies must either be passed in or obtained in some other manner.

Coupling between context and strategies

The only serious drawback I have found with the Strategy pattern is the number of additional classes I have to create. While well worth the cost, there are a few things I have done to minimize this when I have control of all of the strategies. In this situation, if I am using

Ways of eliminating class explosions with the Strategy pattern

C++, I might have the abstract strategy header file contain all of the header files for the concrete strategies. I also have the abstract strategy cpp file contain the code for the concrete strategies. If I am using Java, I use inner classes in the abstract strategy class to contain all of the concrete strategies. I do not do this if I do not have control over all of the strategies; that is, if other programmers need to implement their own algorithms.

Summary

In this chapter

The Strategy pattern is a way to define a family of algorithms. Conceptually, all of these algorithms do the same things. They just have different implementations.

I showed an example that used a family of tax calculation algorithms. In an international e-tail system, there might be different tax algorithms to use for different countries. Strategy would allow me to encapsulate these rules in one abstract class and have a family of concrete derivations.

By deriving all the different ways of performing the algorithm from an abstract class, the main module (**SalesOrder** in the example above) does not need to worry about which of many possibilities is actually in use. This allows for new variations but also creates the need to manage these variations—a challenge I will discuss in Chapter 20, "The Analysis Matrix."

CHAPTER 15

The Decorator Pattern

Overview

This chapter continues the e-tailing case study introduced in Chapter 14, "The Strategy Pattern."

In this chapter

In this chapter,

- I describe a new requirement for the case study: Add header and footer information to the printed sales ticket.

- I show how the Decorator pattern handles the requirement flexibly.

- I discuss how the Decorator pattern can be used to handle input/output (especially Java I/O).

- I describe the key features of the Decorator pattern.

- I describe some of my experience using the Decorator pattern in practice.

A Little More Detail

Figure 14-2 showed the basic structure of the case study. Figure 15-1 shows this structure in more detail. Here, I show that the **SalesOrder** object uses a **SalesTicket** object to print a sales ticket.

Expanding the diagram

As you saw in Chapter 14, **SalesOrder** uses a **CalcTax** object to calculate the tax on the order. To implement the printing function, **SalesOrder** calls the **SalesTicket** object, requesting that it print the ticket. This is a fine, reasonably modular design.

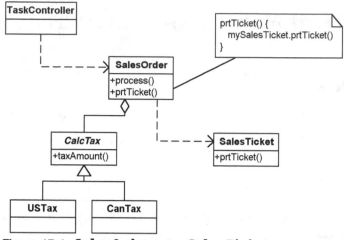

Figure 15-1 SalesOrder using SalesTicket.

New requirement:
add a header

In the process of writing the application, suppose I get a new requirement to add header information to the **SalesTicket**.

One approach:
use switches in
SalesTicket

How can I handle this new requirement? If I am writing the system to be used by just one company, it may be easiest simply to add the control of headers and footers in the **SalesTicket** class. This is shown in Figure 15-2.

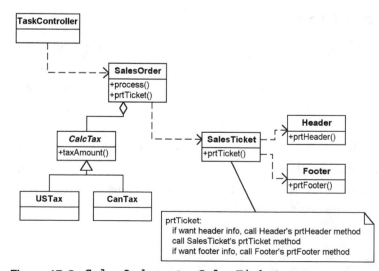

Figure 15-2 SalesOrder using SalesTicket with different options.

In this solution, I have put the control in **SalesTicket**, with flags saying whether it is to print the headers or the footers.

The approach is not flexible

This works quite well if I do not have to deal with a lot of options or if the sales orders using these headers do not change.

If I have to deal with many different types of headers and footers, printing only one each time, then I might consider using one Strategy pattern for the header and another Strategy pattern for the footer.

What happens if I have to print more than one header and/or footer at a time? Or what if the order of the headers and/or footers needs to change? The number of combinations can quickly overwhelm.

In situations like this, the Decorator pattern can be very useful. Instead of controlling added functionality by having a control method, the Decorator pattern says to control it by chaining together the functions desired in the correct order needed. The Decorator pattern separates the dynamic building of this chain of functionality from the client that uses it, in this case, the **SalesOrder**.

The Decorator pattern helps

The Decorator Pattern

According to Gang of Four, the Decorator pattern's intent is to

The intent, according to the Gang of Four

> Attach additional responsibilities to an object dynamically. Decorators provide a flexible alternative to subclassing for extending functionality.[1]

The Decorator pattern works by allowing me to create a chain of objects that starts with the *decorator* objects—the objects responsible for the new function—and ends with the original object. Figure 15-3 illustrates this.

How it works

---

1. Gamma, E., Helm, R., Johnson, R., Vlissides, J., *Design Patterns: Elements of Reusable Object-Oriented Software*, Reading, Mass.: Addison-Wesley, 1995, p. 315.

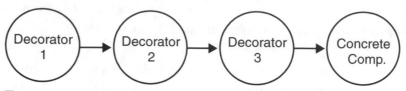

Figure 15-3   The Decorator chain.

The Decorator pattern is a chain of objects

The class diagram of the Decorator pattern in Figure 15-4 implies the chain of objects shown in Figure 15-3. Each chain starts with a **Component** (a **ConcreteComponent** or a **Decorator**). Each **Decorator** is followed either by another **Decorator** or by the original **ConcreteComponent**. A **ConcreteComponent** always ends the chain.

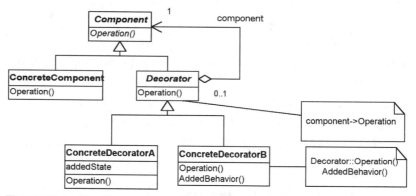

Figure 15-4   The Decorator pattern class diagram.

For example, in Figure 15-4, **ConcreteDecoratorB** performs its Operation and then calls the Operation method in **Decorator**. This calls **ConcreteDecoratorB**'s trailing **Component**'s Operation.

Applying the Decorator Pattern to the Case Study

In this case

In the case study, the **SalesTicket** is the **ConcreteComponent**. The concrete decorators are the headers and footers. Figure 15-5 shows the application of the Decorator pattern to the case study.

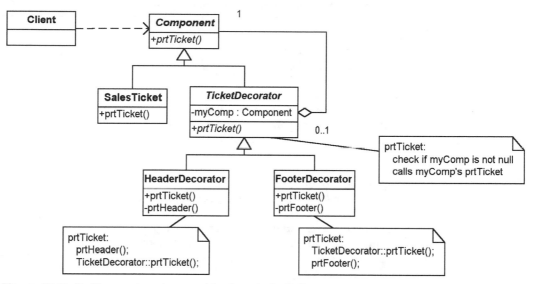

Figure 15-5 Setting up headers and footers to look like a report.

Figure 15-6 shows the application of Decorator to one header and one footer.

The pattern instantiated

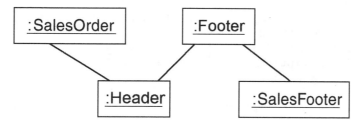

Figure 15-6 An example Decorator object diagram.

Each Decorator object wraps its new function around its trailing object. Each Decorator performs its added function either before its decorated function (for headers) or after it (for footers). The easiest way to see how it works is to look at code for a specific example and walk through it. See Example 15-1.

How it works: Decorators wrap their trailing object

Example 15-1 Java Code Fragment: Decorator

```java
class SalesTicket extends Component {
  public void prtTicket () {
    // sales ticket printing code here
  }
}
abstract class Decorator extends Component {
  private Component myComp;
  public Decorator (Component myC) {
    myComp= myC;
  }
  public void prtTicket () {
    if (myComp != null) myComp.prtTicket();
} }
class Header1 extends Decorator {
  public Header1 (Component myC) { super( myC); }
  public void prtTicket () {
    // place printing header 1 code here
    super.prtTicket();
} }
class Header2 extends Decorator {
  public Header2 (Component myC) { super( myC); }
  public void prtTicket () {
    // place printing header 2 code here
    super.prtTicket();
} }
class Footer1 extends Decorator {
  public Footer1 (Component myC) { super( myC); }
  public void prtTicket () {
    super.prtTicket();
    // place printing footer 1 code here
} }
class Footer2 extends Decorator {
  public Footer2 (Component myC) { super( myC); }
  public void prtTicket () {
    super.prtTicket();
    // place printing footer 2 code here
} }

class SalesOrder {
  void prtTicket () {
```

(continued)

Example 15-1 Java Code Fragment: Decorator *(continued)*

```
      Component myST;
      // Get chain of Decorators and SalesTicket built by
      // another object that knows the rules to use.
      // This may be done in constructor instead of
      // each time this is called.
      myST= Configuration.getSalesTicket()

      // Print Ticket with headers and footers as needed
      myST.prtTicket();
   }
}
```

If I want the sales ticket to look like:

What happens in the code

> HEADER 1
> SALES TICKET
> FOOTER 1

Then *Configuration.getSalesTicket* returns

```
return( new Header1( new Footer1( new SalesTicket()));
```

This creates a **Header1** object trailed by a **Footer1** object trailed by a **SalesTicket** object.

If I want the sales ticket to look like:

> HEADER 1
> HEADER 2
> SALES TICKET
> FOOTER 1

Then *Configuration.getSalesTicket* returns

```
return( new Header1( new Header2 (new Footer1(
                new SalesTicket())));
```

This creates a **Header1** object trailed by a **Header2** object trailed by a **Footer1** object trailed by a **SalesTicket** object.

Decomposing by responsibilities

The Decorator pattern helps to decompose the problem into two parts:

- How to implement the objects that give the new functionality
- How to organize the objects for each special case

This allows me to separate implementing the **Decorator**s from the object that determines how they are used. This increases cohesion because each of the **Decorator**s is only concerned with the function it adds—not in how it is added to the chain.

Another Example: Input/Output

Stream I/O

A common use for the Decorator pattern is in stream I/O. Let's look at stream I/O a little before seeing how the pattern can be used here. I will limit the discussion to input since output works in an analogous way (if you see how it works in one direction, it should be clear how it works in the other direction). For any particular stream input, there is exactly one source, but there can be any number (including zero) of actions to perform on the input stream. For example, I can read from

- A file
- A socket and then decrypt the incoming stream
- A file and then decompress the incoming data
- A string
- A file, decompress the input, and then decrypt it

Depending upon how the data were sent (or stored) any combination of behaviors is possible. Think of it this way: Any source can be decorated with any combination of behaviors. Some of the possibilities available for stream input are shown in Table 15-1.

Developers in object-oriented languages can take advantage of this by having source and behavior objects derive from a common abstract class. Each behavior object can be given its source or prior behavior in its constructor. A chain of actions is then built as the objects themselves are instantiated (each is given a reference to its trailing object). The sources derive from `ConcreteComponent` (see Figure 15-4), while the behaviors are decorators. Note that `ConcreteComponent` is now a misnomer because it is now abstract.

Languages reflect this

Table 15-1   Kinds of Sources and Behaviors

Sources	Behaviors
String	Buffered input
File	Run checksum
Socket (TCP/IP)	Unzip
Serial port	Decrypt (any number of ways)
Parallel port	Selection filters (any number of ways)
Keyboard	

For example, to get the behavior "read from a file, decompress the input, and then decrypt it," do the following:

1. Build the decorator chain by doing the following:

   a. Instantiate a file object.

   b. Pass a reference to it to the constructor of a decompression object.

   c. Pass a reference to that to the constructor of a decryption object.

2. Read, decompress, and decrypt the data—all transparently to the client object that is using it. The client merely knows it has some sort of input stream object.

If this client needs to get its input from a different source, the chain is created by instantiating a different source object using the same behavior objects.

Understanding "The Complete Stream Zoo."[*]

Java is notorious for a confusing array of stream inputs and associated classes. It is much easier to understand these classes in the context of the Decorator pattern. The classes directly derived from `java.io.InputStream` (`ByteArrayInputStream`, `FileInputStream`, `FilterInputStream`, `InputStream`, `ObjectInputStream`, `SequenceInputStream`, and `StringBufferInputStream`) all play the role of the decorated object. All of the decorators derive from the `FilterInputStream` (either directly or indirectly).

Keeping the Decorator pattern in mind explains why the Java language requires chaining these objects together when they are instantiated—this gives programmers the ability to pick any number of combinations from the different behaviors available.

[*] Horstmann, C., *Core Java—Volume 1—Fundamentals,* Palo Alto, CA: Pearson Education, 1999, p. 627.

Field Notes: Using the Decorator Pattern

Instantiating the chains

The power of the Decorator pattern requires that the instantiation of the chains of objects be completely decoupled from the `Client` objects that use it. This is most typically accomplished through the use of factory objects that instantiate the chains based upon some configuration information.

The Decorator Pattern: Key Features

Intent	Attach additional responsibilities to an object dynamically.
Problem	The object that you want to use does the basic functions you require. However, you may need to add some additional functionality to the object, occurring before or after the object's base functionality. Note that the Java foundation classes use the Decorator pattern extensively for I/O handling.
Solution	Allows for extending the functionality of an object without resorting to subclassing.
Participants and Collaborators	The `ConcreteComponent` is the class having function added to it by the `Decorators`. Sometimes classes derived from `ConcreteComponent` are used to provide the core functionality, in which case `Concrete-Component` is no longer concrete, but rather abstract. The `Component` defines the interface for all of these classes to use.
Consequences	Functionality that is to be added resides in small objects. The advantage is the ability to dynamically add this function before or after the functionality in the `ConcreteComponent`. *Note:* While a decorator may add its functionality before or after that which it decorates, the chain of instantiation always ends with the `ConcreteComponent`.
Implementation	Create an abstract class that represents both the original class and the new functions to be added to the class. In the decorators, place the new function calls before or after the trailing calls to get the correct order.
GoF Reference	Pages 175–184.

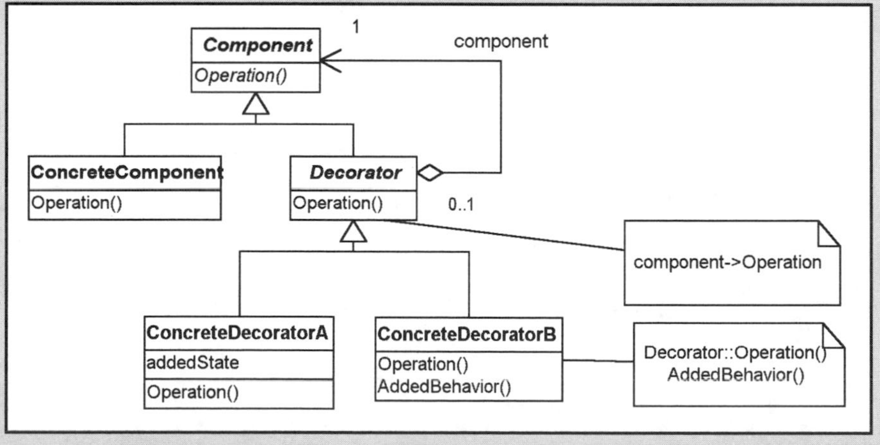

Figure 15-7 Standard, simplified view of the Decorator pattern.

Decorators in testing

I have used the Decorator to wrap precondition and postcondition tests on an object to be tested with nice results. During test, the first object in the chain can do an extensive test of preconditions prior to calling its trailing object. Immediately after the trailing object call, the same object calls an extensive test of postconditions. If I have different tests I want to run at different times, I can keep each test in a different Decorator and then chain them together according to the battery of tests I want to run.

Summary

In this chapter

The Decorator pattern is a way to add additional function(s) to an existing function dynamically. In practice, it requires building a chain of objects that give the desired behaviors. The first object in this chain is called by a **Client** that had nothing to do with the building of it. By keeping the creation of the chain independent from its use, the **Client** object is not affected by new requirements to add functionality.

Supplement: C++ Code Examples

Example 15-2   C++ Code Fragments

```
class SalesTicket : public Component {
  public:
    void prtTicket();
}
SalesTicket::prtTicket() {
  // sales ticket printing code here
}
class Decorator : public Component {
  public:
    virtual void prtTicket();
    Decorator( Component *myC);
  private:
    Component *myComp;
}
```

(continued)

Example 15-2   C++ Code Fragments *(continued)*

```cpp
Decorator::Decorator( Component *myC) {
  myComp= myC;
}
void Decorator::prtTicket() {
  myComp->prtTicket();
}
class Header1 : public Decorator {
  public:
    Header1( Component *myC);
    void prtTicket();
}
Header1::Header1 (Component *myC) : Decorator(myC) { }
void Header1::prtTicket () {
  // place printing header 1 code here
  Decorator::prtTicket();
}
class Header2 : public Decorator {
  public:
    Header2( Component *myC);
    void prtTicket();
}
Header2::Header2 (Component *myC) : Decorator(myC) { }
void Header2::prtTicket () {
  // place printing header 2 code here
  Decorator::prtTicket();
}
class Footer1 : public Decorator {
  public:
    Footer1( Component *myC);
    void prtTicket();
}
Footer1::Footer1 (Component *myC) : Decorator(myC) { }
void Footer1::prtTicket () {
  Decorator::prtTicket();
  // place printing footer 1 code here
}
class Footer2 : public Decorator {
  public:
    Footer2( Component *myC);
    void prtTicket();
}
```

(continued)

Example 15-2   C++ Code Fragments *(continued)*

```
Footer2::Footer2 (Component *myC) : Decorator(myC) { }
void Footer2::prtTicket () {
  Decorator::prtTicket();
  // place printing footer 2 code here
}

void SalesOrder::prtTicket () {

  Component *myST;
  // Get chain of Decorators and SalesTicket built by
  // another object that knows the rules to use.
  // This may be done in constructor instead of
  // each time this is called.
  myST= Configuration.getSalesTicket()

  // Print Ticket with headers and footers as needed
  myST->prtTicket();
}
```

CHAPTER 16

The Singleton Pattern and the Double-Checked Locking Pattern

Overview

This chapter continues the e-tailing case study discussed in Chapter 14, "The Strategy Pattern" and Chapter 15, "The Decorator Pattern."

In this chapter

In this chapter,

- I introduce the Singleton pattern.

- I describe the key features of the Singleton pattern.

- I introduce a variant to the Singleton called the Double-Checked Locking pattern.

- I describe some of my experiences using the Singleton pattern in practice.

The Singleton pattern and the Double-Checked Locking pattern are very simple and very common. Both are used to ensure that only one object of a particular class is instantiated. The distinction between the patterns is that the Singleton pattern is used in single-threaded applications while the Double-Checked Locking pattern is used in multithreaded applications.[1]

---

1. If you do not know what a multithreaded application is, don't worry; you need only concern yourself with the Singleton pattern at this time.

Introducing the Singleton Pattern

The intent, according to the Gang of Four

According to the Gang of Four, the Singleton's intent is to

> Ensure a class only has one instance, and provide a global point of access to it.[2]

How the Singleton pattern works

The Singleton pattern works by having a special method that is used to instantiate the desired object.

- When this method is called, it checks to see if the object has already been instantiated. If it has, the method simply returns a reference to the object. If not, the method instantiates it and returns a reference to the new instance.

- To ensure that this is the only way to instantiate an object of this type, I define the constructor of this class to be protected or private.

Applying the Singleton Pattern to the Case Study

A motivating example: instantiate tax calculation strategies only once and only when needed

In Chapter 14, I encapsulated the rules about taxes within strategy objects. I have to derive a **CalcTax** class for each possible tax calculation rule. This means that I need to use the same objects over and over again, just alternating between their uses.

For performance reasons, I might not want to keep instantiating them and throwing them away again and again. And, while I could instantiate all of the possible strategies at the start, this could

---

2. Gamma, E., Helm, R., Johnson, R., Vlissides, J., *Design Patterns: Elements of Reusable Object-Oriented Software*, Reading, Mass.: Addison-Wesley, 1995, p. 127.

become inefficient if the number of strategies grew large. (Remember, I may have many other strategies throughout my application.) Instead, it would be best to instantiate them as needed, but only do the instantiation once.

The problem is that I do not want to create a separate object to keep track of what I have already instantiated. Rather, I would like the objects themselves (that is, the strategies) be responsible for handling their own single instantiation.

This is the purpose of the Singleton pattern. It allows me to instantiate an object only once, without requiring the client objects to be concerned with whether it already exists or not.

Singleton makes objects responsible for themselves

The Singleton could be implemented in code as shown in Example 16-1. In this example, I create a method (*getInstance*) that will instantiate at most one **USTax** object. The Singleton protects against someone else instantiating the **USTax** object directly by making the constructor private, which means that no other object can access it.

Example 16-1 Java Code Fragment: Singleton Pattern

```
class USTax {
  private static USTax instance;
  private USTax():
  public static USTax getInstance() {
    if (instance== null)
      instance= new USTax();
    return instance;
  }
}
```

The Singleton Pattern: Key Features

Intent	You want to have only *one* of an object but there is no global object that controls the instantiation of this object.
Problem	Several different client objects need to refer to the same thing and you want to ensure that you do not have more than one of them.
Solution	Guarantees one instance.
Participants and Collaborators	**Client**s create an instance of the **Singleton** solely through the *getInstance* method.
Consequences	**Client**s need not concern themselves whether an instance of the **Singleton** exists. This can be controlled from within the **Singleton**.
Implementation	• Add a private static member of the class that refers to the desired object (initially, it is NULL). • Add a public static method that instantiates this class if this member is NULL (and sets this member's value) and then returns the value of this member. • Set the constructor's status to protected or private so that no one can directly instantiate this class and bypass the static constructor mechanism.
GoF Reference	Pages 127–134.

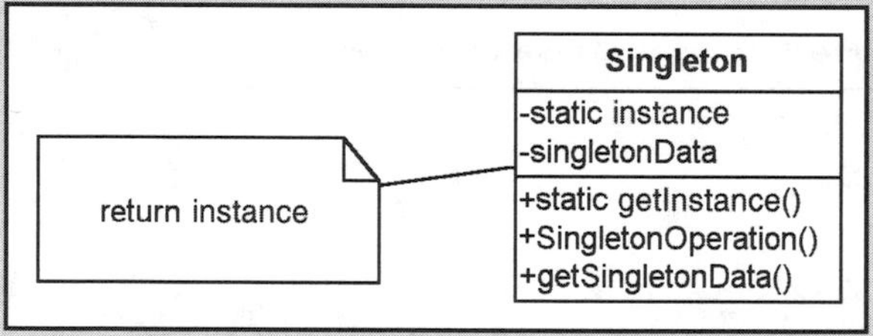

Figure 16-1 Standard, simplified view of the Singleton pattern.

A Variant: The Double-Checked Locking Pattern

Only for multithreaded applications

This pattern *only* applies to multithreaded applications. If you are not involved with multithreaded applications you might want to skip this section. This section assumes that you have a basic understanding of multithreaded issues, including synchronization.

A problem with the Singleton pattern may arise in multithreaded applications.

In a multithreaded mode, Singleton does not always work properly

Suppose two calls to *getInstance()* are made at exactly the same time. This can be very bad. Consider what can happen in this case:

1. The first thread checks to see if the instance exists. It does not, so it goes into the part of the code that will create the first instance.

2. However, before it has done that, suppose a second thread also looks to see if the instance member is NULL. Since the first thread hasn't created anything yet, the instance is still equal to NULL, so the second thread also goes into the code that will create an object.

3. Both threads now perform a *new* on the Singleton object, thereby creating two objects.

Is this a problem? It may or may not be.

None, small, bad, or worse

- If the Singleton is absolutely stateless, this may not be a problem.

- In Java, the problem will simply be that we are taking up an extra bit of memory.

- In C++, the program may create a memory leak, since it will only delete one of the objects when I have created two of them.

- If the Singleton object has some state, subtle errors can creep in. For example,

  - If the object creates a connection, there will actually be two connections (one for each object).

  - If a counter is used, there will be two counters.

It may be very difficult to find these problems. First of all, the dual creation is very intermittent—it usually won't happen. Second, it may not be obvious why the counts are off, as only one client object will contain one of the Singleton objects while all of the other client objects will refer to the other Singleton.

Synchronizing the creation of the Singleton object

At first, it appears that all I need to do is synchronize the test for whether the Singleton object has been created. The only problem is that this synchronization may end up being a severe bottleneck, because all of the threads will have to wait for the check on whether the object already exists.

Perhaps instead, I could put some synchronization code in after the if (instance== null) test. This will not work either. Since it would be possible that both calls could meet the NULL test and then attempt to synchronize, I could still end up making two Singleton objects, making them one at a time.

A simple solution: double-checked locking

The solution is to do a "synch" after the test for NULL and then check again to make sure the instance member has not yet been created. I show this in Example 16-2. This is called *double-checked locking*.[3] The intent is to optimize away unnecessary locking. This synchronization check happens at most one time, so it will not be a bottleneck.

The features of double-checked locking are as follows:

- Unnecessary locking is avoided by wrapping the call to *new* with another conditional test.

- Support for multithreaded environments.

---

3. Martin, R., Riehle, D., Buschmann, F., *Pattern Language of Program Design*, Reading, Mass.: Addison-Wesley, 1998, p. 363.

Example 16-2   Java Code Fragment: Instantiation Only

```
class USTax extends CalcTax {
    private static USTax instance;
    private USTax() {  }

    private synchronized static void doSync() {
        if (instance == null)instance = new USTax();
    }

    public static USTax getInstance() {
        if (instance == null)doSync();
        return instance;
    }
}
```

Field Notes: Using the Singleton and Double-Checked Locking Patterns

If you know you are going to need an object and no performance issue requires you to defer instantiation of the object until it's needed, it is usually simpler to have a static member contain a reference to the object.

Only use when needed

In multithreaded applications, Singletons typically have to be thread safe (because the single object may be shared by multiple objects). This means having no data members but using only variables whose scope is no larger than a method.

Typically stateless

Note: the Double-Checked Locking pattern has errors. See http://www.netobjectives.com/dpexplained/ dpe_olc_sup_pat.htm#DCL for up to date information.

Summary

The Singleton and Double-Checked Locking patterns are common patterns to use when you want to ensure that there is only one instance of an object. The Singleton is used in single-threaded applications while the Double-Checked Locking pattern is used in multithreaded applications.

In this chapter

Supplement: C++ Code Examples

Example 16-3   C++ Code Fragment: Singleton Pattern

```cpp
Class USTax {
  public:
    static USTax* getInstance();
  private:
    USTax();
    static USTax* instance;
}
USTax* USTax::instance= 0;

USTax* USTax::getInstance () {
  if (instance== 0) {
    instance= new USTax;
  }
return instance;
}
```

Example 16-4   C++ Code Fragment: Double-Checked Locking Pattern

```cpp
class USTax : public CalcTax {
  public:
    static USTax* getInstance();
  private:
    USTax();
    static USTax* instance;
};
USTax* USTax::instance= 0;

USTax* USTax::getInstance () {
  if (instance== 0) {
    // do sync here
    if (instance== 0) {
        instance= new USTax;
    }
  }
  return instance;
}
```

CHAPTER 17

The Observer Pattern

Overview

This chapter continues the e-tailing case study discussed in Chapters 14–16.

In this chapter

In this chapter,

- I introduce the categorization scheme of patterns.

- I introduce the Observer pattern by discussing additional requirements for the case study.

- I apply the Observer pattern to the case study.

- I describe the Observer pattern.

- I describe the key features of the Observer pattern.

- I describe some of my experiences using the Observer pattern in practice.

Categories of Patterns

There are many patterns to keep track of. To help sort this out, the Gang of Four has grouped patterns into three general categories, as shown in Table 17-1.[1]

The GoF has three categories

---

1. Gamma, E., Helm, R., Johnson, R., Vlissides, J., *Design Patterns: Elements of Reusable Object-Oriented Software*, Reading, Mass.: Addison-Wesley, 1995, p. 10.

Table 17-1   Categories of Patterns

Category	Purpose	Examples in This Book	Use For
Structural	Bring together existing objects	• Facade (Chapter 6) • Adapter (Chapter 7)	Handling interfaces
		• Bridge (Chapter 9) • Decorator (Chapter 15)	Relating implementations to abstractions
Behavioral	Give a way to manifest flexible (varying) behavior	• Strategy (Chapter 14)	Containing variation
Creational	Create or instantiate objects	• Abstract Factory (Chapter 10) • Singleton (Chapter 16) • Double-Checked Locking (Chapter 16) • Factory Method (Chapter 19)	Instantiating objects

A note on the classification of the Bridge and Decorator patterns

When I first started studying design patterns, I was surprised to see the Bridge and Decorator patterns were structural patterns rather than behavioral patterns. After all, they seemed to be used to implement different behaviors. At the time, I simply did not understand the GoF's classification system. Structural patterns are for tying together existing function. In the Bridge pattern, we typically start with abstractions and implementations and then bind them together with the bridge. In the Decorator pattern, we have an original functional class, and want to decorate it with additional functions.

My "fourth" category: decoupling

I have found it valuable to think of a fourth category of patterns, one whose primary purpose is to decouple objects from each other. One motivation for these is to allow for scalability or increased flexibility. I call this category of patterns *decoupling patterns*. Since most of the patterns in the decoupling category belong to the Gang of Four's behavioral category, I could almost call them a subset of the behavioral category. I chose to make a fourth category simply because my intent in this book is to reflect how I look at patterns, focusing on their motivations—in this case, decoupling.

I would not get too hung up on the whys and wherefores of the classifications. They are meant to give insights into what the patterns are doing.

This chapter discusses the Observer pattern, which is the best example of a decoupling pattern pattern there is. The Gang of Four classifies Observer as a Behavioral pattern.

Observer is a decoupling (behavioral) pattern

More Requirements for the Case Study

In the process of writing the application, suppose I get a new requirement to take the following actions whenever a new customer is entered into the system:

New requirement: take actions for new customers

- Send a welcome e-mail to the customer.
- Verify the customer's address with the post office.

Are these all of the requirements? Will things change in the future?

One approach

If I am reasonably certain that I know every requirement, then I could solve the problem by hard-coding the notification behavior into the **Customer** class, such as shown in Figure 17-1.

For example, using the same method that adds a new customer into the database, I will also make calls to the objects that generate welcome letters and verify post office addresses.

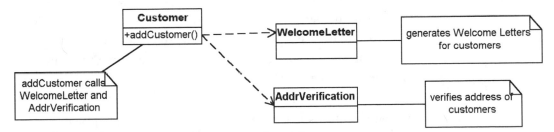

Figure 17-1 Hard-coding the behaviors.

These classes have the following responsibilities:

Class	Responsibility
Customer	When a customer is added, this object will make calls to the other objects to have the corresponding actions take place.
WelcomeLetter	Creates welcome letters for customers that let them know they were added to the system.
AddrVerification	This object will verify the address of any customer that asks it to.

The problem? Requirements always change

The hard-coding approach works fine—the first time. But requirements *always* change. I know that another requirement will come that will require another change to **Customer**'s behavior. For example, I might have to support different companies' welcome letters, which would require a different **Customer** object for each company. Surely, I can do better.

The Observer Pattern

The intent, according to the Gang of Four

According to the Gang of Four, the intent of the Observer pattern is to "Define a one-to-many dependency between objects so that when one object changes state, all its dependents are notified and updated automatically."[2]

What this means: Handling notification automatically

Often, I have a set of objects that need to be notified whenever an event occurs. I want this notification to occur automatically. However, I do not want to change the broadcasting object everytime there is a change to the set of objects listening to the broadcast. (That would be like having to change a radio transmitter every time a new car radio comes to town.) I want to decouple the notify-ors and the notify-ees.

---

2. Gamma, E., Helm, R., Johnson, R., Vlissides, J., *Design Patterns: Elements of Reusable Object-Oriented Software*, Reading, Mass.: Addison-Wesley, 1995, p. 293.

This pattern is a very common one. It also goes by the names *Dependents* and *Publish-Subscribe*,[3] and is analogous to the notify process in COM. It is implemented in Java with the **Observer** interface and the **Observable** class (more on these later). In rule-based, expert systems, they are often implemented with daemon rules.

A common pattern

Applying the Observer to the Case Study

My approach is to look in the problem for clues as to what is varying. Then, I attempt to encapsulate the variation. In the current case, I find:

Two things are varying

- **Different kinds of objects**—There is a list of objects that need to be notified of a change in state. These objects tend to belong to different classes.

- **Different interfaces**—Since they belong to different classes, they tend to have different interfaces.

First, I must identify all of the objects that want to be notified. I will call these the *observers* since they are waiting for an event to occur.

Step 1: Make the observers behave in the same way

I want all of the observers to have the same interface. If they do not have the same interface, then I would have to modify the *subject*—that is, the object that is triggering the event (for example, **Customer**), to handle each type of observer.

By having all of the observers be of the same type, the subject can easily notify all of them. To get all of the observers to *be* of the same type,

- In Java, I would probably implement this with an interface (either for flexibility or out of necessity).

---

3. ibid, p. 293.

- In C++, I would use single inheritance or multiple inheritance, as required.

Step 2: Have the observers register themselves

In most situations, I want the observers to be responsible for knowing what they are to watch for and I want the subject to be free from knowing which observers depend on it. To do this, I need to have a way for the observers to register themselves with the subject. Since all of the observers are of the same type, I must add two methods to the subject:

- `attach(Observer)`—adds the given **Observer** to its list of observers

- `detach(Observer)`—removes the given **Observer** from its list of observers

Step 3: Notify the observers when the event occurs

Now that the **Subject** has its **Observer**s registered, it is a simple matter for the **Subject** to notify the **Observer**s when the event occurs. To do this, each **Observer** implements a method called *update*. The **Subject** implements a *notify* method that goes through its list of **Observer**s and calls this *update* method for each of them. The *update* method should contains the code to handle the event.

Step 4: Get the information from the subject

But notifying each observer is not enough. An observer may need more information about the event beyond the simple fact that it has occurred. Therefore, I must also add method(s) to the subject that allow the observers to get whatever information they need. Figure 17-2 shows this solution.

How this works

In Figure 17-2, the classes relate to each other as follows:

1. The **Observer**s attach themselves to the **Customer** class when they are instantiated. If the **Observer**s need more information from the subject (**Customer**), the *update* method must be passed a reference to the calling object.

2. When a new **Customer** is added, the *notify* method calls these **Observer**s.

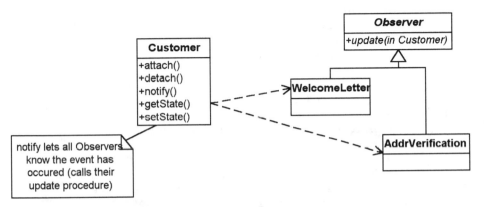

Figure 17-2 Implementing Customer with Observer.

Each **Observer** calls *getState* for information on the newly added **Customer** to see what it needs to do. *Note:* Typically, there would be several methods to get the needed information.

Note in this case, we use static methods for attach and detach because observers want to be notified for all new **Customer**s. When notified, they are passed the reference to the **Customer** created.

Example 17-1 shows some of the code required to implement this.

This approach allows me to add new **Observers** without affecting any existing classes. It also keeps everything loosely coupled. This organization works if I have kept all of the objects responsible for themselves.

Observer aids flexibility and keeps things decoupled

How well does this work if I get a new requirement? For example, what if I need to send a letter with coupons to customers located within 20 miles of one of the company's "brick and mortar" stores.

New requirement: send coupons, too

Example 17-1   Java Code Frament: Observer Implemented

```java
// Note: Do not actually use the name Observer
// as that is a Java class in java.util

class Customer {
  static private Vector myObs;
  static {
    myObs= new Vector();
  }
  public static void attach(Observer o){
    myObs.addElement(o);
  }
  public static void detach(Observer o){
    myObs.remove(o);
  }
  public String getState () {
    // have other methods that will give the
    // required information
  }

  public void notifyObs () {
    for (Enumeration e =
      myObs.elements();
      e.hasMoreElements() ;) {
        ((Observer) e).update(this);
    }
  }
}


abstract class Observer {
  public Observer () {
    Customer.attach( this);
  }
  abstract public void
    update(Customer myCust);
}

class AddrVerification extends Observer {
  public AddrVerification () {
    super();
  }
  public void update (
    Customer myCust) {
```

(continued)

Example 17-1   Java Code Frament: Observer Implemented *(continued)*

```
      // do Address verification stuff here
      // can get more information about customer
      // in question by using myCust
  }
}

class WelcomeLetter extends Observer {
  public WelcomeLetter () {
    super();
  }
  public void update (Customer myCust) {
    // do Welcome Letter stuff
    // here can get more
    // information about customer
    // in question by using myCust
  }
}
```

To accomplish this, I would simply add a new observer that sends the coupon. It only does this for new customers living within the specified distance. I could name this observer **BrickAndMortar** and make it an observer to the **Customer** class. Figure 17-3 shows this solution.

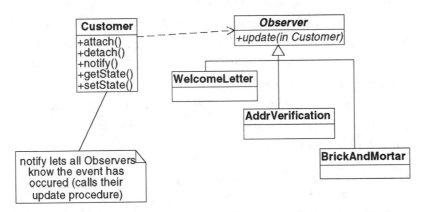

Figure 17-3 Adding the BrickAndMortar observer.

The **Observer** *in the real world*

Sometimes, a class that will become an **Observer** may already exist. In this case, I may not want to modify it. If so, I can easily adapt it with the Adapter pattern. Figure 17-4 shows an example of this.

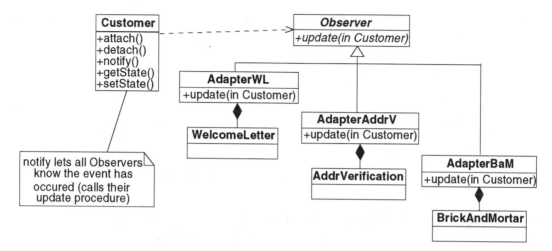

Figure 17-4   Implementing **Observer** **with** **Adapters.**

The Observable Class: A Note to Java developers.

The Observer pattern is so useful that Java contains an implementation of it in its packages. The **Observable** class and the **Observer** interface make up the pattern. The **Observable** class plays the role of the **Subject** in the Gang of Four's description of the pattern. Instead of the methods attach, detach, and notify, Java uses *addObserver*, *deleteObserver*, and *notifyObservers*, respectively (Java also uses *update*). Java also gives you a few more methods to make life easier.*

* See *http://java.sun.com/j2se/1.3/docs/api/index.html* for information on the Java API for **Observer** and **Observable**.

The Observer Pattern: Key Features

Intent	Define a one-to-many dependency between objects so that when one object changes state, all its dependents are notified and updated automatically.
Problem	You need to notify a varying list of objects that an event has occurred.
Solution	`Observers` delegate the responsibility for monitoring for an event to a central object: the `Subject`.
Participants and Collaborators	The `Subject` knows its `Observers` because the `Observers` register with it. The `Subject` must notify the `Observers` when the event in question occurs. The `Observers` are responsible both for registering with the `Subject` and for getting the information from the `Subject` when notified.
Consequences	`Subjects` may tell `Observers` about events they do not need to know if some `Observers` are interested in only a subset of events (see "Field Notes: Using the Observer Pattern" on page 274). Extra communication may be required if `Subjects` notify `Observers` which then go back and request additional information.
Implementation	• Have objects (`Observers`) that want to know when an event happens attach themselves to another object (`Subject`) that is watching for the event to occur or that triggers the event itself. • When the event occurs, the `Subject` tells the `Observers` that it has occurred. • The Adapter pattern is sometimes needed to be able to implement the `Observer` interface for all of the `Observer`-type objects.
GoF Reference	Pages 293–303.

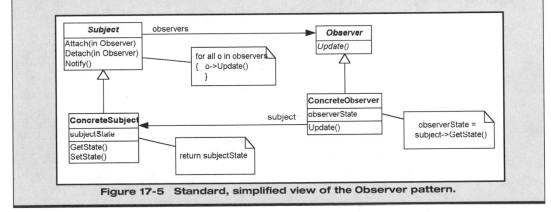

Figure 17-5 Standard, simplified view of the Observer pattern.

Field Notes: Using the Observer Pattern

Not for all dependencies

The Observer pattern is not meant to be used every time there is a dependency between objects. For example, in a ticket processing system a tax object handles taxes, it is clear that when items are added to the ticket the tax object must be notified so the tax can be recalculated. This is not a good place for an Observer pattern since this notification is known up front and others are not likely to be added. When the dependencies are fixed (or virtually so), adding an Observer pattern probably just adds complexity.

. . . but for changing or dynamic dependencies

If the list of objects that need to be notified of an event changes, or is somehow conditional, then the Observer pattern has greater value. These changes can occur either because the requirements are changing or because the list of objects that need to be notified are changing. The Observer pattern can also be useful if the system is run under different conditions or by different customers, each having a different list of required observers.

Whether to process an event

An observer may only need to handle certain cases of an event. The Brick and Mortar case was an example. In such situations, the observer must filter out extra notifications.

Extraneous notifications can be eliminated by shifting the responsibility for filtering out these notifications to the **Subject**. The best way to do this is for the **Subject** to use a Strategy pattern to test if notification should occur. Each observer gives the **Subject** the correct strategy to use when it registers.

How to process an event

Sometimes, **Subject**s will call the observers' *update* method, passing along information. This can save the need for callbacks from the observers to the **Subject**. However, it is often the case that different observers have different information requirements. In this case, a Strategy pattern can again be used. This time, the **Strategy** object is used for calling the observers' *update* procedure. Again, the observers must supply the **Subject** with the appropriate **Strategy** object to use.

Summary

In learning the Observer pattern, I looked at which object is best able to handle future variation. In the case of the Observer pattern, the object that is triggering the event—the **Subject**—cannot anticipate every object that might need to know about the event. To solve this, I create an **Observer** interface and require that all Observers be responsible for registering themselves with this **Subject**.

In this chapter

While I focused on the Observer pattern during the chapter, it is worth pointing out several object-oriented principles that are used in the Observer pattern.

Summary of object-oriented principles used

Concept	Discussion
Objects are responsible for themselves	There were different kinds of **Observer**s but all gathered the information they needed from the **Subject** and took the action appropriate for them on their own.
Abstract class	The **Observer** class represents the concept of objects that needed to be notified. It gave a common interface for the subject to notify the **Observer**s.
Polymorphic encapsulation	The subject did not know what kind of observer it was communicating with. Essentially, the **Observer** class encapsulated the particular **Observer**s present. This means that if I get new **Observer**s in the future, the **Subject** does not need to change.

Supplement: C++ Code Example

Example 17-2   C++ Code Fragment

```cpp
class Customer {

 public:
  static void attach(Observer *o);
  static void detach(Observer *o);
  String getState();
 private:
  Vector myObs;
  void notifyObs();
}

Customer::attach(Observer *o){
  myObs.addElement(o);
}
Customer::detach(Observer *o){
  myObs.remove(o);
}
Customer::getState () {
    // have other methods that will
    // give the required information
}

Customer::notifyObs () {
    for (Enumeration e =
      myObs.elements();
      e.hasMoreElements() ;) {
       ((Observer *) e)->
          update(this);
    }
  }
}

class Observer {
 public:
  Observer();
  void update(Customer *mycust)=0;
    // makes this abstract
}
```

(continued)

Example 17-2   C++ Code Fragment *(continued)*

```
Observer::Observer () {
    Customer.attach( this);
}
class AddrVerification : public Observer {
 public:
  AddrVerification();
  void update( Customer *myCust);
}

AddrVerification::AddrVerification () {
}
AddrVerification::update
   (Customer *myCust) {
    // do Address verification stuff here
    // can get more information about
    // customer in question by using myCust
}

class WelcomeLetter : public Observer {
 public:
  WelcomeLetter();
  void update( Customer *myCust);
}

WelcomeLetter::update( Customer *myCust) {
    // do Welcome Letter stuff here can get more
    // information about customer in question by
    // using myCust
}
```

CHAPTER 18

The Template Method Pattern

Overview

This chapter continues the e-tailing case study discussed thus far in Chapters 14–17.

In this chapter

In this chapter,

- I introduce the Template Method pattern by discussing additional requirements for the case study.

- I present the intent of the Template Method pattern.

- I describe the key features of the Template Method pattern.

- I describe some of my experiences using the Template Method pattern in practice.

More Requirements for the Case Study

In the process of writing the application, suppose I get a new requirement to support both Oracle and SQL Server databases. Both of these systems are based on SQL (Structured Query Language), the common standard that makes it easier to use databases. Yet, even though this is a common standard at the general level, there are still differences in the details. I know that in general, when executing queries on these databases, I will use the following steps:

New requirement: access multiple SQL database systems

1. Format the CONNECT command.

2. Send the database the CONNECT command.

3. Format the SELECT command.

4. Send the database the SELECT command.

5. Return the selected dataset.

. . . but the details differ

The specific implementations of the databases differ, however, requiring slightly different formatting procedures.

The Template Method Pattern

Standardizing on the steps

The Template Method is a pattern intended to help one abstract out a common process from different procedures. According to the Gang of Four, the intent of the Template method is to

> Define the skeleton of an algorithm in an operation, deferring some steps to subclasses. Redefine the steps in an algorithm without changing the algorithm's structure.[1]

In other words, although there are different methods for connecting and querying Oracle databases and SQL Server databases, they share the same conceptual process. The Template Method gives us a way to capture this common ground in an abstract class while encapsulating the differences in derived classes. The Template Method pattern is about controlling a sequence common to different processes.

Applying the Template Method to the Case Study

The details are varying

In this case study, the variations in database access occur in the particular implementations of the steps involved. Figure 18-1 illustrates this.

1.　Gamma, E., Helm, R., Johnson, R., Vlissides, J., *Design Patterns: Elements of Reusable Object-Oriented Software*, Reading, Mass.: Addison-Wesley, 1995, p. 325.

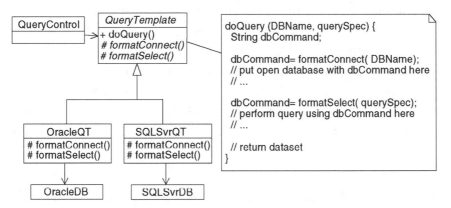

Figure 18-1   Using the Template Method pattern to perform a query.

I have created a method called *doQuery* that handles the query I need to perform. I pass in the name of the database and the query specification. The *doQuery* method follows the five general steps above, providing virtual methods for the steps (such as *format-Connect* and *formatSelect*) that must be implemented differently.

How this works: virtual methods for the steps that vary

The *doQuery* method is implemented as follows. As shown in Figure 18-1, it first needs to format the CONNECT command required to connect to the database. Although the abstract class (**QueryTemplate**) knows this format needs to take place, it doesn't know how to do this. The exact formatting code is supplied by the derived classes. This is true for formatting the SELECT command as well.

The Template Method manages to do this because the method call is made via a reference pointing to one of the derived classes. That is, although **QueryControl** has a reference of type **QueryTemplate**, it is actually referring to an **OracleQT** or an **SQLSvrQT** object. Thus, when the *doQuery* method is called on either of these objects, the methods resolved will first look for methods of the appropriate derived class. Let's say our **QueryControl** is referring to an **OracleQT** object. Since **OracleQT** does not override **Query-Template**, the **QueryTemplate**'s *doQuery* method is invoked. This starts executing until it calls the *formatConnect* method. Since the **OracleQT** object was requested to perform *doQuery*, the **OracleOT**'s *formatConnect* method is called. After this, control is returned to the **QueryTemplate**'s *doQuery* method. The code common to all queries is now executed until the next variation is needed—the *formatSelect* method. Again, this method is located in the object that **QueryControl** is referring to (**OracleQT** in this example).

When a new database is encountered, the Template Method provides us with a boilerplate (or template) to fill out. We create a new derived class and implement the specific steps required for the new database in it.

Field Notes: Using the Template Method Pattern

The Template Method is not coupled Strategies

Sometimes a class will use several different Strategy patterns. When I first looked at the class diagram for the Template Method, I thought, "Oh, the Template Method is simply a collection of Strategies that work together." This is dangerous (and usually incorrect) thinking. While it is not uncommon for several Strategies to appear to be connected to each other, designing for this can lead to inflexibility.

The Template Method is applicable when there are different, but conceptually similar processes. The variations for each process are coupled together because they are associated with a particular process. In the example I presented, when I need a format a CONNECT command for an Oracle database, if I need a format a QUERY command, it'll be for an Oracle database as well.

The Template Method Pattern: Key Features

Intent	Define the skeleton of an algorithm in an operation, deferring some steps to subclasses. Redefine the steps in an algorithm without changing the algorithm's structure.
Problem	There is a procedure or set of steps to follow that is consistent at one level of detail, but individual steps may have different implementations at a lower level of detail.
Solution	Allows for definition of substeps that vary while maintaining a consistent basic process.
Participants and Collaborators	The Template Method consists of an abstract class that defines the basic **TemplateMethod** (see figure below) classes that need to be overridden. Each concrete class derived from the abstract class implements a new method for the Template.
Consequences	Templates provide a good platform for code reuse. They also are helpful in ensuring the required steps are implemented. They bind the overridden steps together for each **Concrete** class, and so should only be used when these variations always and only occur together.
Implementation	Create an abstract class that implements a procedure using abstract methods. These abstract methods must be implemented in subclasses to perform each step of the procedure. If the steps vary independently, each step may be implemented with a Strategy pattern.
GoF Reference	Pages 325–330.

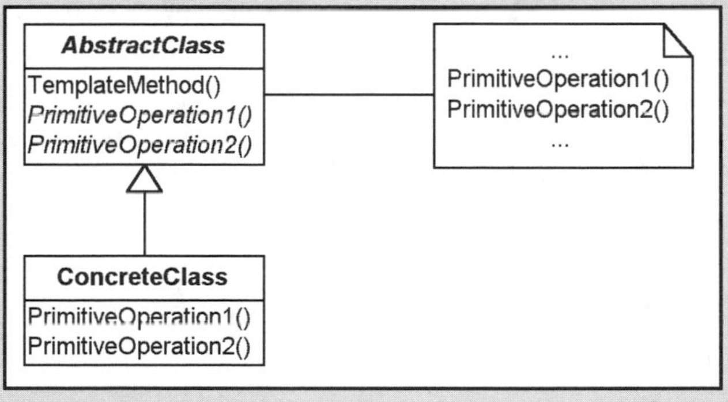

Figure 18-2 Standard, simplified view of the Template Method pattern.

Summary

In this chapter

Sometimes, I have a set of procedures that I must follow. The procedures are common at a high level, but implementing some of the steps can vary. For example, querying a SQL database is fairly routine at a high level, but some of the details—say, how to connect to the database—can vary based on details such as the platform.

The Template Method allows me to define the sequence of steps and then override those steps that need to change.

CHAPTER 19

The Factory Method Pattern

Overview

This chapter continues the e-tailing case study discussed thus far in Chapters 14–18.

In this chapter

In this chapter,

- I introduce the Factory Method pattern by discussing additional requirements for the case study.

- I present the intent of the Factory Method pattern.

- I describe the key features of the Factory Method pattern.

- I describe some of my experiences using the Factory Method pattern in practice.

More Requirements for the Case Study

In Chapter 18, "The Template Method Pattern," I ignored the issue of how to instantiate the database object required by my current context. I may not want to make the **Client** responsible for instantiating the database object. Instead, I might want to give that responsibility to the **QueryTemplate** class itself.

New requirement: responsibility for instantiating database objects

In Chapter 18, each derivation of the **QueryTemplate** was specialized for a particular database. Thus, I might want to make each derivation responsible for instantiating the database to which it corresponds. This would be true whether the **QueryTemplate** (and its derivations) was the only class using the database or not. Figure 19-1 shows this solution.

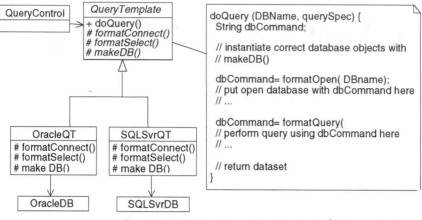

Figure 19-1 The Template Method (*doQuery*) using the Factory Method pattern (*makeDB*).

Template Method using Factory Method

In Figure 19-1, the *doQuery* method in the Template Method is using *makeDB* to instantiate the appropriate database object. **QueryTemplate** does not know which database object to instantiate; it only knows that one *must* be instantiated and provides an interface for its instantiation. The derived classes from **QueryTemplate** will be responsible for knowing which ones to instantiate. Therefore, at this level, I can defer the decisions on how to instantiate the database to a method in the derived class.

Since there is a method involved in making an object, this approach is called a *Factory Method*.

Public or protected methods?

Note that the *makeDB* methods are protected (as indicated by the # signs). In this case, only the **QueryTemplate** class and its derivations can access these methods. If I want objects other than **QueryTemplate** to be able to access these methods, then they should be public. This is another, quite common, way to use the Factory Method. In this case I still have a derived class making the decision as to which object to instantiate.

The Factory Method Pattern

The Factory Method is a pattern intended to help assign responsibility for creation. According to the Gang of Four, the intent of the Factory Method is to

Standardizing on the steps

> Define an interface for creating an object, but let subclasses decide which class to instantiate. Factory Method lets a class defer instantiation to subclasses.[1]

Field Notes: Using the Factory Method Pattern

In the classic implementation of the Abstract Factory, I had an abstract class define the methods to create a family of objects. I derived a class for each different family I could have. Each of the methods defined in the abstract class and then overridden in the derived classes were following the Factory Method pattern.

Abstract Factory can be implementeed as a family of Factory Methods

Sometimes it is useful to create a hierarchical class structure that is parallel to an existing class structure, with the new hierarchy containing some delegated responsibilities. In this case, it is important for each object in the original hierarchy to be able to instantiate the proper object in the parallel hierarchy. A Factory Method can be used for this purpose.

Useful to bind parallel class hierarchies

The Factory Method pattern is commonly used when defining frameworks. This is because frameworks exist at an abstract level. Usually, they do not know and should not be concerned about instantiating specific objects. They need to defer the decisions about specific objects to the users of the framework.

Factory Method is used in frameworks

---

1. Gamma, E., Helm, R., Johnson, R., Vlissides, J., *Design Patterns: Elements of Reusable Object-Oriented Software*, Reading, Mass.: Addison-Wesley, 1995, p. 325.

The Factory Method Pattern: Key Features

Intent	Define an interface for creating an object, but let subclasses decide which class to instantiate. Defer instantiation to subclasses.
Problem	A class needs to instantiate a derivation of another class, but doesn't know which one. Factory Method allows a derived class to make this decision.
Solution	A derived class makes the decision on which class to instantiate and how to instantiate it.
Participants and Collaborators	Product is the interface for the type of object that the Factory Method creates. Creator is the interface that defines the Factory Method.
Consequences	Clients will need to subclass the `Creator` class to make a particular `ConcreteProduct`.
Implementation	Use a method in the abstract class that is abstract (pure virtual in C++). The abstract class' code refers to this method when it needs to instantiate a contained object but does not know which particular object it needs.
GoF Reference	Pages 107–116.

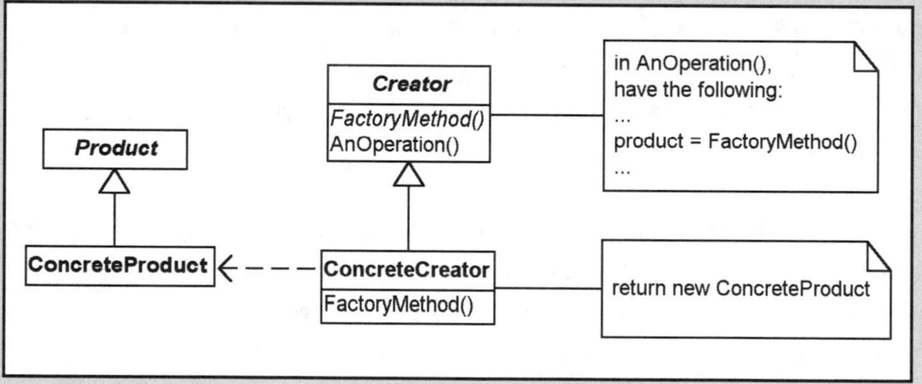

Figure 19-2 Standard, simplified view of the Factory Method pattern.

Summary

The Factory Method pattern is one of the straightforward patterns that you will use again and again. It is used in those cases where you want to defer the rules about instantiating an object to some derived class. In such cases, it is most natural to put the implementation of the method in the object that is responsible for that behavior.

In this chapter

CHAPTER 20

The Analysis Matrix

Overview

This chapter concludes the e-tailing case study discussed thus far in Chapters 14–19.

In this chapter

Now that I have discussed an entire set of individual patterns, it is time to step back to look at one of the biggest problems in software development: handling variation within the problem domain. Design patterns can help analysts identify and organize variations successfully.

In this chapter,

- I consider the problem of variation in the real world.

- I look at a portion of the e-tailing case study that represents significant problems of variation. In the process of solving this problem, I develop the Analysis Matrix, a simple variant on decision tables that I have found helpful to understand and coordinate variation in concepts. There is a parallel between this and the concepts of Christopher Alexander and Jim Coplien.

- I describe my use of the Analysis Matrix in the real world.

In the Real World: Variations

In the real world, problems are not tidy or well behaved. Except in the most trivial problems, there always seem to be exceptions and variations that are not well organized. They are the "gotchas" that rise up to wreck our finely crafted models.

More variation in the real world

For example, patients coming to a hospital typically go to the admitting office first. But when there is a life-threatening situation, the patient goes directly to the emergency room before having to go to admitting. These are the variations in the real world, the different special cases that our system has to deal with.

And this is what creates headaches for us analysts. Can patterns help us deal with variation more efficiently?

I have used an approach to make explicit the variations in the system and then use the analysis to identify the patterns I ought to use in my design. The steps in my approach are as follows:

1. Identify the most important features in one case and organize them in a matrix. Label each feature with the concept that the feature represents.

2. Proceed through the other cases, expanding the matrix as necessary. Handle each case independently of the others.

3. Expand the Analysis Matrix with new concepts.

4. Use the rows to identify rules.

5. Use the columns to identify specific cases.

6. Identify design patterns from this analysis.

7. Develop a high-level design.

Case Study in Variation: An International E-Tail System

E-tail: A case study in variation

Suppose an e-tail system must process sales orders in several different nations. Initially I have to handle just the United States and Canada. I look at my requirements and see several things that vary. I note these in Table 20-1.

Table 20-1   Different Cases Depending Upon Residence of Customer

Case	Procedure
U.S.A	• Calculate freight based on UPS charges. • Use U.S. postal rules for verifying addresses. • Calculate tax based on sales and/or services depending upon locale. • Handle money in U.S. $.
Canada	• Calculate freight based on main Canadian shipper. • Use Canadian postal rules for verifying addresses. • Calculate tax based on sales and/or services depending upon Canadian province taxing rules (using GST and PST). • Handle money in Canadian $.

The variations presented in this problem are not too complicated. Just by looking, it seems obvious how to deal with them. A simple problem, yes. But it illustrates a technique for dealing with variation that I have used many times. It is a simple technique but it seems to scale well for many real-world problems. I call this the *Analysis Matrix*.

. . . to illustrate the Analysis Matrix technique

At this stage, the objective is to find the *concepts* that are varying, to find points of commonality, and to uncover missing requirements. The concepts come from the specific requirements of each case. Design and implementation issues are handled in later stages.

Let's begin by looking at one case.

1. Identify the most important features in one case and organize them in a matrix

I look at each function that I must implement and label the concept it represents. Each function point will be put on its own line. I will put the concept it represents at the far left.

I will show this process step by step, starting with Table 20-2.

Table 20-2   Filling Out the Analysis Matrix: First Concept

	U.S. Sales
Calculate freight	Use UPS rates

Now, I continue with the next piece of information, "use U.S. postal rules for verifying addresses," by adding another row to hold that piece of information, as shown in Table 20-3.

Table 20-3   Filling Out the Analysis Matrix: Second Concept

	U.S. Sales
Calculate freight	Use UPS rates
Verify address	Use U.S. postal rules

I continue through all of the concepts in the first case, as shown in Table 20-4.

Table 20-4   Filling Out the Analysis Matrix: Complete First Case—U.S. Sales

	U.S. Sales
Calculate freight	Use UPS rates
Verify address	Use U.S. postal rules
Calculate tax	Use state and local taxes
Money	U.S. $

2. Proceed through the other cases, expanding the matrix as necessary

Now, I move to the next case and the other cases, one column per case, completing each cell with as much information as I have. The completed matrix for the next case is in Table 20-5.

Table 20-5   The Analysis Matrix for the Next Case—Canadian Sales

	U.S. Sales	Canadian Sales
Calculate freight	Use UPS rates	Use Canadian shipper
Verify address	Use U.S. postal rules	Use Canadian postal rules
Calculate tax	Use state and local taxes	Use GST and PST
Money	U.S. $	Canadian $

As I build the matrix, I discover gaps in the requirements. I will use this information to expand my analysis. These inconsistencies give clues about incomplete information from the customer. That is, in one case a customer might mention some specific requirement while another customer did not. For example, in getting requirements for the United States, no maximum weight may have been mentioned, while 31.5 kilograms might have been stated for Canada. By comparing the requirements I can fill in the holes by going back to my American contact and asking her specifically about weight limits (which, in fact, may not exist). *and look for incompleteness or inconsistencies as you go*

As time goes on we get new cases to handle (for example, we may expand into Germany). When you discover a new concept for one of the cases, add a new row even if it does not apply to any of the other cases. I illustrate this in Table 20-6. *3. Expand the Analysis Matrix with new concepts*

Table 20-6   Expanding the Analysis Matrix

	U.S. Sales	Canadian Sales	German Sales
Calculate freight	Use UPS rates	Use Canadian shipper	Use German shipper
Verify address	Use U.S. postal rules	Use Canadian postal rules	Use German postal rules
Calculate tax	Use state and local taxes	Use GST and PST	Use German VAT
Money	U.S. $	Canadian $	German DM
Dates	mm/dd/yyyy	mm/dd/yyyy	dd/mm/yyyy

A note about customers.

My experience with customers has taught me several things:

- They usually know their problem domain very well (most know it better than I ever will).

- In general, they do not express things on the conceptual level, as developers often do. Instead, they talk in specific cases.

- They often use the term *always* when they mean *usually*.

- They often use the term *never* when they mean *seldom*.

- They often say they have told me about all of the cases when in fact they have only told me what usually happens.

The bottom line is that I trust customers to tell me what happens when I ask specific questions but I do not trust their generalized answers. I try to interact with them at a very concrete level. Even those customers who sound like they think in a conceptual way often do not, but are trying to "help me out."

---

4. Use the rows to identify rules

Now that the concepts are revealed, what should I do with what I know? How do I begin to move toward implementation?

Look at the matrix in Table 20-6. The first row is labeled "Calculate freight," and includes "Use UPS rates," "Use Canadian shipper," and "Use German shipper." This row represents both

- A general rule to implement "Calculate freight rate"

- The specific set of rules that I must implement—that is, each shipper I may use in the different countries

In fact, each row represents specific ways of implementing a generalized concept. Two of the rows (money and dates) may be handled at the object level. For example, money can be handled with objects containing a currency object. Many computer languages support different date formats for different nationalities in their libraries. Table 20-7 shows the conceptual way of handling each row.

Table 20-7   Concrete Implementation Rules: Rows

	U.S. Sales	**Canadian Sales**	**German Sales**
Calculate freight	These are the concrete implementations for the ways to calculate freight rates.		
Verify address	These are the concrete implementations for the ways to verify addresses.		
Calculate tax	These are the concrete implementations for the ways to calculate tax due.		
Money	We can use Money objects that can contain Currency and Amount fields that convert currency automatically.		
Dates	We can use Date objects that can display as required for the country in which the customer lives.		

What do the columns represent? They are the specific implementations we will use for the case the column represents. This is illustrated in Table 20-8.

5. Use the columns to identify implementation

Table 20-8   Concrete Implementation Rules: Columns

	U.S. Sales	**Canadian Sales**	**German Sales**
Calculate freight	These implementations are used when we have a U.S. customer.	These implementations are used when we have a Canadian customer.	These implementations are used when we have a German customer.
Verify address			
Calculate tax			
Money			
Dates			

For example, the first column shows the concrete implementations to use to process a sales order in the United States.

6. Identify design patterns from this analysis: look at rows

How should I translate these insights into patterns? Look at Table 20-7 again. Each row represents the specific way to implement the concept stated in the leftmost column. For example,

- In the "Calculate freight" row, the "Use UPS rates," "Use Canadian shipper," entries really mean, "How should I calculate the freight?" The algorithm I am encapsulating is "freight rate calculation." My concrete rules will be "UPS rates," "Canadian rates," and "German rates."

- The next two rows are also organizations of different rules and their associated concrete implementations.

- The last two rows represent classes that may be consistent throughout the application, but which will behave differently depending upon the country involved.

Therefore, each of the first three rows can be thought of as a Strategy pattern. This is illustrated in Table 20-9. The objects in the first row can be implemented as a strategy pattern encapsulating the "Calculate freight" rule.

Table 20-9 Implementing with the Strategy Pattern

	U.S. Sales	Canadian Sales	German Sales
Calculate freight	The objects in this row can be implemented as a Strategy pattern encapsulating the "Calculate freight" rule.		
Verify address	The objects in this row can be implemented as a Strategy pattern encapsulating the "Verify address" rule.		
Calculate tax	The objects in this row can be implemented as a Strategy pattern encapsulating the "Calculate tax" rule.		
Money	We can use Money objects that can contain Currency and Amount fields that convert currency automatically.		
Dates	We can use Date objects that can display as required for the country in which the customer lives.		

In a similar vein, I can look at the columns. Each column describes which rules to use for each case. These entries represent the family of objects needed for that case. This sounds like the Abstract Factory pattern. This is shown in Table 20-10.

7. Identify design patterns from this analysis: look at columns

Table 20-10   Implementing with the Abstract Factory Pattern

	U.S. Sales	Canadian Sales	German Sales
Calculate freight			
Verify address	These objects can be coordinated with the use of the Abstract Factory pattern.	These objects can be coordinated with the use of the Abstract Factory pattern.	These objects can be coordinated with the use of the Abstract Factory pattern.
Calculate tax			
Money			
Dates			

Armed with the information that some of the rows represent a Strategy pattern and each column represents a family in an Abstract Factory pattern, I can develop a high-level application design as shown in Figure 20-1.

8. Develop a high-level design

Field Notes

In practice, almost any kind of pattern that involves polymorphism could be present in the Analysis Matrix. Of the patterns I've presented, this would include Bridge, Decorator, Template, and Observer. Other patterns I have used in an Analysis Matrix are Composite, Proxy, Chain of Responsibility, Command, Iterator, Mediator, and Visitor.

Other patterns present

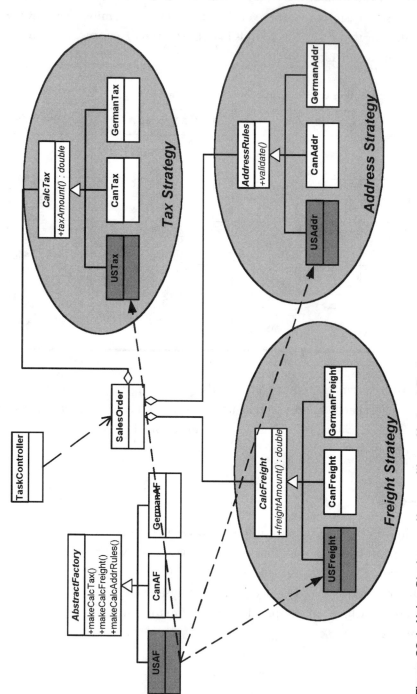

Figure 20-1   Using Strategy patterns with an Abstract Factory.

For example, if in our e-tail system I included requirements on printing sales tickets and found the following variations:

- U.S. sales tickets need headers

- Canadian sales tickets need headers and footers

- German sales tickets need two different footers

I would include this information in its own row, each entry relating to the format of sales tickets. I would implement this row's requirements with a Decorator pattern.

Although the Analysis Matrix rarely captures all aspects of a particular problem domain, I have found it useful for at least part of most problem domains. I find it most useful when I am given so many special cases that I can't get my head around the big picture.

Applicability of the Analysis Matrix

It is usually worse than this. Rarely are different cases of requirements stated to analysts or developers in any coordinated fashion. This does not significantly complicate the Analysis Matrix process, however. In these situations, I take a feature and look in the leftmost column and see what concept it is a variant of. If I find the concept, I put the feature in that row. Not being able to find such a concept indicates I must create a new row.

More useful as problems get bigger

In extreme situations, the Analysis Matrix may be the only way to get a handle on things. I once had a client that literally had dozens of special cases. Each case was a separately developed document control system. The problem was to integrate all of these document control systems together. So many special cases were present (there were also dozens of rows) that it was impossible to think about the entire problem all at once. The analysts did not have a good conceptual grasp of what was involved. They just talked about general rules and exception cases. By considering each case individually, I was able to abstract out the common data and behavior (which showed up in the leftmost columns) and then implement them with design patterns.

Summary

In this chapter

Variation in concepts can be one of the greatest challenges that an analyst can face. In this chapter, I presented a simple analysis tool that I have found helpful in making sense of such variation. I call this tool the Analysis Matrix, and it is based on the concepts of Christopher Alexander and Jim Coplien. I applied this tool to a sample problem to show how it might reveal the types of patterns that are inherent in the problem. While this tool is very useful in containing variation and helping me think about my problem domain, I do not pretend it captures all aspects of a design.

Part VI

Endings and Beginnings

Part Overview

In this part I continue with our new perspective on object-oriented design. In particular, I describe how design patterns use this perspective in their design and implementation. I close this section with recommendations for further reading.

In this part

Chapter	Discusses These Topics
21	Looks at the motivations and relationships of design patterns within the context of this new perspective on object-oriented design
22	Suggests books and other resources for future study

CHAPTER 21

Design Patterns Reviewed from the New Perspective of Object-Oriented Design

Overview

At the end of any book, it is always nice to step back and see what we have gained. In this book, I have tried to give you a better and perhaps new understanding of object-oriented principles by teaching you design patterns and understanding how design patterns explain the object-oriented paradigm.

In this chapter

In this chapter, I review the following:

- The new perspective of object-oriented principles, based on an understanding of design patterns

- How design patterns help us encapsulate implementations

- Commonality/Variability analysis and design patterns and how they help to understand abstract classes

- Decomposing a problem domain by the responsibilities involved

- Specifying relationships between objects

- Design patterns and contextual design

Finally, I offer some field notes from my own practice.

A Summary of Object-Oriented Principles

In the course of the discussion on design patterns, I have stated a number of the principles of the object-oriented paradigm. These principles can be summarized as follows:

Objects from the new perspective

- Objects are things with well-defined responsibilities.

- Objects are responsible for themselves.

- Encapsulation means any kind of hiding
  - Data-hiding
  - Class hiding (behind an abstract class or interface)
  - Implementation hiding

- Abstract out variations in behavior and data with commonality/variability analysis.

- Design to interfaces.

- Think of inheritance as a method of conceptualizing variation, not for making special cases of existing objects.

- Keep variations in a class decoupled from other variations in the class.

- Strive for loose coupling.

- Strive for high cohesion.

- Be absolutely meticulous in applying the once and only once rule.

How Design Patterns Encapsulate Implementations

Hiding variations in detail

Several of the design patterns I have presented have the characteristic that they shield implementation details from a **Client** object. For example, the Bridge pattern hides from the **Client** how the classes derived from the **Abstraction** are implemented. Additionally, the **Implementation** interface hides the family of implementations from the **Abstraction** and its derivations as well. In the Strategy pattern, the implementations of each **ConcreteStrategy** are hidden. This is true of most of the patterns described by the Gang of Four: they give ways to hide specific implementations.

The value of hiding the implementations is that the patterns allow for easily adding new implementations, since the client objects do not know how the current implementation works.

Commonality/Variability Analysis and Design Patterns

In Chapter 9, "The Bridge Pattern," I showed how the Bridge pattern can be derived using commonality/variability analysis. Many other patterns can be derived as well, including the Strategy, Iterator, Proxy, State, Visitor, Template Method, and Abstract Factory. What is more important, however, is how many patterns are implemented by using commonality/variability analysis. Looking for commonalities can help us discover that a pattern is present in our problem domain.

Commonality/ variability analysis

For example, in the Bridge pattern, I may start with several special cases:

- Draw a square with drawing program one.
- Draw a circle with drawing program two.
- Draw a rectangle with drawing program one.

Knowing the Bridge helps me see these as special cases of two commonalities:

- Drawing programs
- Shapes to draw

The Strategy pattern is similar in that when I see several different rules, I know to look for a commonality amongst the rules so I can encapsulate them.

But please keep learning patterns. Read the literature. Patterns provide the backdrop for discussions about lessons learned in analysis and design. They give a team of developers a common vocabulary for discussing a problem. They enable you to incorporate best-practice approaches into your code.

Decomposing a Problem Domain into Responsibilities

The next step in commonality/ variability analysis

Commonality/variability analysis identifies my conceptual view (the commonality) and my implementation view (each particular variation). If I consider just the commonalities and the objects that use them, I can think about the problems in a different way—a decomposition of responsibilities.

In the Bridge pattern, for example, the pattern says to look at my problem domain as being composed of two different types of entities (abstractions and implementations). I therefore do not need to be limited by just doing object-oriented decomposition (that is, decomposing my problem domain into objects), I can also try decomposing my problem domain into responsibilities, if that is easier for me to do. I can then define the objects that I require to implement these responsibilities (ending up with object decomposition).

This is just an extension of the rule I stated earlier that designers should not worry about how to instantiate objects until after they know all of the objects they need. That rule can be viewed as a decomposing the problem domain into two parts:

- Which objects are needed

- How these objects are instantiated

Specific patterns often give us assistance in thinking about how to decompose responsibilities. For example, the Decorator pattern gives me a way to combine objects flexibly if I decompose my problem domain into the main set of responsibilities I always use (the `ConcreteComponent`) and the variations I optionally have—my decorators. Strategies decompose my problem into an object that uses rules and the rules themselves.

Relationships Within a Pattern

I must admit, in my courses, I have some fun with a certain quote from Alexander. After I have been talking about how great patterns are for two-thirds of a day, I pick up Alexander's *Timeless Way of Building*, turn to the end, and say

Patterns aren't really the important thing

> This book is 549 pages long. On page 545, which, I think you will agree, is pretty close to the end, Alexander says, *"At this final stage, the patterns are no longer important:..."*[1]

I pause to say, "I wish he'd have told me this at the beginning and I could have saved myself some time!" Then I continue to quote from him: *"The patterns have taught you to be receptive to what is real."*[2]

I finish with, "If you read Alexander's book, you will know what is real—the relationships and forces described by the patterns."

The patterns give us a way to talk about these. However, it is not the patterns themselves that are important. This is true for software patterns as well.

A pattern describes the forces, motivations, and relationships about a particular problem in a particular context and provides us with an approach to addressing these issues. The Bridge pattern, for example, is about the relationship between the derived classes of an

Software patterns are multidimensional descriptions

---

1. Alexander, C., Ishikawa, S., Silverstein, M., *The Timeless Way of Building*, New York: Oxford University Press, 1979, p. 545.
2. ibid, p, 545.

abstraction and their possible implementations. A Strategy pattern is about the relationships between

- A class that uses one of a set of algorithms (the `Context`)

- The members of this set of algorithms (the strategies)

- The `Client`, which uses the context and specifies which of the algorithms to use

Patterns and Contextual Design

Patterns are micro-cosmic examples of contextual design

In the CAD/CAM problem earlier in this book, I showed how design patterns can be used by focusing on their context with each other. Design patterns working together can assist in the development of an application's architecture. It is also useful to distinguish how many of the patterns are microcosmic examples of design by context.

For example,

- The Bridge pattern tells me to define my `Implementation`s within the context of the derivations of my `Abstraction`.

- The Decorator pattern has me design my `Decorator`s within the context of my original component.

- The Abstract Factory has me define my families within the context of my overall problem so I can see which particular objects need to be implemented.

Designing to an interface is designing within a context

In fact, designing to interfaces and polymorphism in general is a kind of design by context. Look at Figure 21-1, which is a reprint of Figure 8-4. Notice how the abstract class' interface defines the context within which all of its derived classes must be implemented.

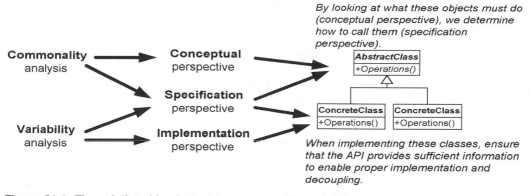

Figure 21-1 The relationships between commonality/variability analysis, perspectives, and abstract classes.

Field Notes

As you learn patterns, it is useful to look for the following forces and concepts:

Approaches to take

- *What implementations does this pattern hide?* Thereby allowing me to change them.

- *What commonalities are present in this pattern?* This helps me identify them.

- *What are the responsibilities of the objects in this pattern?* As it may be easier to do my decomposition by responsibility.

- *What are the relationships between these objects?* This will give me information about the forces present with these objects.

- *How may the pattern itself be a microcosmic example of designing by context?* This affords me a better understanding of why the pattern is good design.

Summary

In this chapter I summarized our new perspective on object-oriented design. I described how design patterns manifest this. I suggested that it is useful to look at patterns by seeing

In this chapter

- What they encapsulate

- How they use commonality/variability analysis

- How they decompose a problem domain into responsibilities

- How they specify relationships between objects

- How they illustrate contextual design

CHAPTER 22

Bibliography

This book has been an introduction. An introduction to design patterns, object orientation, and to a more powerful way to design computer systems. Hopefully, it has given you some tools to get started in this rich and rewarding way of thinking.

In this chapter

Where should you turn next in your study? I conclude this book with an annotated list of my current recommendations.

In this chapter,

- I give the address of the Web site companion for this book.
- I offer my recommendations for
  - Further reading in design patterns.
  - Java developers.
  - C++ developers.
  - COBOL programmers who want to learn object orientation.
  - Learning the powerful development methodology called XP (eXtreme Programming).
- I conclude with a list of the books that have been influential to me personally, in the belief that life is more than programming, and that more rounded individuals make better programmers.

Design Patterns Explained: The Web Site Companion

The Web site for this book is located at
http://www.netobjectives.com/dpexplained

The Web site

At this site you will find additional information on design patterns, including

- Code examples, frequently asked questions, discussions organized by chapters of this book

- Discussions on issues in refactoring

- A summary of design patterns in a nice reference format

- A description of the courses we offer on design patterns and other design-related topics

You will also find a form that you can use to send us your comments and questions about this book.

Electronic magazine   We also publish an e-zine on design patterns and general object-oriented design. To subscribe, send an e-mail with your name, company name, and address to *info@netobjectives.com* with the word "subscribe" in the subject line.

Recommended Reading on Design Patterns and Object Orientation

Object-oriented programming and the UML   I recommend the following books and references on object-oriented programming and the UML:

- Fowler, M., *Refactoring: Improving the Design of Existing Code*, Reading, Mass.: Addison-Wesley, 2000. *The most extensive treatment of refactoring available.*

- Fowler, M., Scott, K., *UML Distilled Second Edition: A Brief Guide to the Standard Object Modeling Language*, Reading, Mass.: Addison-Wesley, 2000. *This is by far my favorite source for learning the UML. It is both approachable to begin with and useful as a reference. I find myself referring to it again and again.*

- Meyer, B., *Object-Oriented Software Construction*, Upper Saddle River, N.J.: Prentice Hall, 1997. *An incredibly thorough book by one of the brilliant minds in our industry.*

The field of design patterns continues to evolve and deepen. One can study the field on a variety of levels and from many perspectives. I recommend the following books and references to help you on your journey:

Design patterns

- Alexander, C., Ishikawa, S., Silverstein, M., *The Timeless Way of Building*, New York: Oxford University Press, 1979. *Both a personal and professional favorite. It is both entertaining and insightful. If you read only one book from this list, have it be this one.*

- Alexander, C., Ishikawa, S., Silverstein, M., *A Pattern Language: Towns/Buildings/Construction*, New York: Oxford University Press, 1977.

- Alexander, C., Ishikawa, S., Silverstein, M., *Notes on Synthesis of Form*, New York: Oxford University Press, 1970.

- Coplien, J., *Multi-Paradigm Design for C++*, Reading, Mass.: Addison-Wesley, 1998. *Chapters 2–5 are a must read even for non-C++ developers. This book contains the best description of commonality/variability analysis anywhere. See our book's Web site for an on-line version of Jim's doctoral dissertation, which is equivalent to his book.*

- Gamma, E., Helm, R., Johnson, R., Vlissides, J., *Design Patterns: Elements of Reusable Object-Oriented Software*, Reading, Mass.: Addison-Wesley, 1995. *Still the best design patterns book available. A must for C++ developers.*

- Gardner, K., *Cognitive Patterns: Problem-Solving Frameworks for Object Technology*, New York: Cambridge University Press, 1998. *This approaches patterns from the perspective of cognitive science and artificial intelligence. Dr. Gardner was also heavily influenced by Alexander's work.*

- Schmidt, D., Stal, M., Rohnert, H., Busehmann, F., *Pattern-Oriented Software Architecture, Vol. 2*, New York: John Wiley, 2000. *The book to use for multithreaded and distributed environments.*

- Vlissides, J., *Pattern Hatching*, Reading, Mass.: Addison-Wesley, 1998. *This is a good advanced book on design patterns. Illustrates several ways that patterns work together. Both our book and the GoF book should be read before reading this one.*

Recommended Reading for Java Programmers

Learning Java

When it comes to learning Java, my favorite books are:

- Eckel, B., *Thinking in Java, 2nd Edition*, Upper Saddle River, N.J.: Prentice Hall, 2000. *One of the best Java books on the market. See http://www.eckelobjects.com/DownloadSites for a downloadable version of this book.*

- Horstmann, C., *Core Java 2—Volume 1—Fundamentals*, Palo Alto: Pearson Education, 1999. *Another good book for learning Java.*

Implementing design patterns in Java

Each language has its own set of issues when it comes to implementing design patterns. I recommend the following books and references when it comes to Java:

- Coad, P., *Java Design*, Upper Saddle River, N.J.: Prentice Hall, 2000. *If you are a Java developer, this book is a must read. It discusses most of the principles and strategies we have found useful in using design patterns even though it doesn't mention design patterns specifically.*

- Grand, M., *Patterns in Java, Vol. 1*, New York: John Wiley, 1998. *If you are a Java developer, you may find this book useful. It has its examples in Java and it uses the UML. However, the authors believe the discussions on forces and motivations in the GoF book are more useful than is presented in Grand's book. However, there is a lot of value by getting another set of examples, particularly when in the language of use (Java).*

- See *http://java.sun.com/j2se/1.3/docs/api/index.html* for information on the Java API for Observer and Observable.

There are special considerations when it comes to dealing with threads in Java. I recommend the following resources to help learn about this area:

Threads in Java

- Hollub, A., *Taming Java Threads*, Berkeley: APress, 2000.

- Hyde, P., *Java Thread Programming: The Authoritative Solution*, Indianapolis: SAMS, 1999.

- Lea, D., *Concurrent Programming in Java: Design Principles and Patterns, Second Edition*, Reading, Mass.: Addison-Wesley, 2000.

Recommended Reading for C++ Programmers

I have found the following essential for using C++ for UNIX:

C++ and UNIX

- Stevens, W., *Advanced Programming in the UNIX Environment*, Reading, Mass.: Addison-Wesley, 1992. *This is a **must** resource for anyone doing C++ development on UNIX.*

Recommended Reading for COBOL Programmers

I have found the following helpful for COBOL programmers who want to learn object-oriented design:

Learning OO

- Levey, R., *Reengineering Cobol with Objects*, New York: McGraw-Hill, 1995. *A useful book for COBOL programmers who are trying to learn object-oriented design.*

Recommended Reading on eXtreme Programming

Learning XP

When it comes to gaining proficiency in eXtreme Programming (XP), my two best recommendations are

- *http://www.netobjectives.com/xp*—Our own Web site on XP, including articles and courses on XP.

- Beck, K., *Extreme Programming Explained: Embrace Change*, Reading, Mass.: Addison-Wesley, 2000. *This is worthwhile reading for anyone involved in software development, even if you are not planning on using XP. I have selected 30 or so pages I consider essential reading and list them on our XP site.*

Net Objectives' process

We are in the process of defining our own software development process which we call Lightweight Pattern-Accelerated Software development (LPA). This is an integration of several methodologies, analysis techniques and design techniques. See *http://www.netobjectives.com/lpa* for more information.

Recommended Reading on General Programming

Being a better programmer

This book mirrors my philosophy of being introspective and always looking to see how I can improve myself and my work:

- Hunt, A., Thomas, D., *The Pragmatic Programmer: From Journeyman to Master*, Reading, Mass.: Addison-Wesley, 2000. *This is one of those lovely books that I read a few pages of each day. When I come across things I already do, I take the opportunity to acknowledge myself. When I find things I'm not doing, I take the opportunity to learn.*

Personal Favorites

It is my belief that the best designers are not those who live and breathe programming and nothing else. Rather, being able to think and to listen, having a more complete and deep personality, and knowing ideas are what make for great designers. You can connect better with other people. You can glean ideas from other disciplines (for example, as we did from architecture and from anthropology). You will create systems that better take into account human beings, for whom our systems exist anyway.

Beyond programming

Many of my students ask about what I like to read, what has shaped how I think and helped me in my journey. The following are my recommendations.

Alan recommends the following:

Alan's list

- Grieve, B., *The Blue Day Book: A Lesson in Cheering You Up*, Kansas City: Andrews McMeel Publishing, 2000. *This is a fun and delightful book. Read it whenever you are feeling down (it's short).*

- Hill, N., *Think and Grow Rich*, New York: Ballantine Books, 1960. *"Rich" doesn't only mean in money—it means in whatever form **you** want to be rich in. This book has had a profound impact on both my personal and business success.*

- Kundtz, D., *Stopping: How to Be Still When You Have to Keep Going*, Berkeley: Conari Press, 1998. *As a recovering workaholic, this book is a beautiful reminder of how to slow down and enjoy life, but still get things done.*

- Mandino, O., *The Greatest Salesman in the World*, New York: Bantam Press, 1968. *I read and "practiced" this book a few years ago. It has helped me live my life the way I've always wanted to. If you read it, I strongly suggest doing what the scrolls tell Hafid to do—not just read about it (you'll know what I mean when you read the book).*

- Pilzer, P., *Unlimited Wealth: The Theory and Practice of Economic Alchemy,* Crown Publishers, 1990. *This book presents both a new paradigm for resources and wealth, and how to take advantage of it. A must-read in the information age.*

- Remen, R., *My Grandfather's Blessings: Stories of Strength, Refuge, and Belonging,* New York: Riverhead Books, 2000. *A lovely book to reflect on one's blessings.*

Jim's list

Jim recommends the following:

- Buzan, T., and Buzan, B., *The Mind Map Book: How to Use Radiant Thinking to Maximize Your Brain's Untapped Potential,* New York: Dutton Books, 1994. *This has revolutionized how I teach, communicate, think, and take notes. An incredibly powerful technique. I use this daily.*

- Cahill, T., *How the Irish Saved Civilization,* New York: Doubleday, 1995. *If you have any Irish blood in you, this will make you proud. Cannibals turned to the greatest force for civilization and rescue Europe.*

- Dawson, C., *Religion and the Rise of Western Culture,* New York: Doubleday, 1950. *How religion shaped the development of Western civilization and kept at bay the "barbarianism that is always lurking just below the surface." Important insights into scientific thought.*

- Jensen, B., *Simplicity: The New Competitive Advantage in a World of More, Better, Faster,* Cambridge, Mass.: Perseus Books, 2000. *A revolution in thought and knowledge management. Designing systems that are simpler for people to use, taking humans into account in our processes and technologies.*

- Lingenfelter, S., *Transforming Culture,* Grand Rapids: Baker Book House, 1998. *A model for understanding cultures through social game theory.*

- Spradely, J. P., *The Ethnographic Interview*, New York: Harcourt Brace Jovanovich College Publishers, 1979. *A must-read for anyone who wants to become a better interviewer. The classic text used by all students of anthropology.*

- Wiig, K., *Knowledge Management Methods*, Dallas: Schema Press, 1995. *A virtual encyclopedia of techniques for helping organizations exploit their knowledge resources more effectively.*

Index

inform IT

www.informit.com

YOUR GUIDE TO IT REFERENCE

Articles

Keep your edge with thousands of free articles, in-depth features, interviews, and IT reference recommendations – all written by experts you know and trust.

Online Books

Answers in an instant from **InformIT Online Book's** 600+ fully searchable on line books. For a limited time, you can get your first 14 days **free**.

Catalog

Review online sample chapters, author biographies and customer rankings and choose exactly the right book from a selection of over 5,000 titles.

Register
Your Book

at www.awprofessional.com/register

You may be eligible to receive:

- Advance notice of forthcoming editions of the book
- Related book recommendations
- Chapter excerpts and supplements of forthcoming titles
- Information about special contests and promotions throughout the year
- Notices and reminders about author appearances, tradeshows, and online chats with special guests

Contact us

If you are interested in writing a book or reviewing manuscripts prior to publication, please write to us at:

Editorial Department
Addison-Wesley Professional
75 Arlington Street, Suite 300
Boston, MA 02116 USA
Email: AWPro@aw.com

Addison-Wesley

Visit us on the Web: http://www.awprofessional.com